PUNISHMENT

AND

SOCIAL STRUCTURE

PUNISHMENT
AND
SOCIAL STRUCTURE

By

GEORG RUSCHE *and* OTTO KIRCHHEIMER

With a Foreword by

THORSTEN SELLIN

NEW YORK / RUSSELL & RUSSELL

A PUBLICATION OF THE
INTERNATIONAL INSTITUTE OF SOCIAL RESEARCH

COPYRIGHT, 1939, 1967, BY COLUMBIA UNIVERSITY PRESS
REISSUED, 1968, BY RUSSELL & RUSSELL
A DIVISION OF ATHENEUM PUBLISHERS, INC.
BY ARRANGEMENT WITH COLUMBIA UNIVERSITY PRESS
L. C. CATALOG CARD NO: 68-15157
ISBN: 0-8462-1176-9
PRINTED IN THE UNITED STATES OF AMERICA
BY SENTRY PRESS, NEW YORK

FOREWORD

M OST liberal-minded penologists today claim that the aim of punishment is the protection of society. This point of view may be said to be a by-product of cultural change in general, but it is apparently conditioned to a considerable degree by the growth in recent decades of psychological, psychiatric, and sociological knowledge about the offender. Those who hold it are likely to think of punishment or rather penal treatment as something to be inflicted only after an unemotional, cool, and scientific approach of the problem. They think in terms of the means by which protection is to be achieved: research into the causation of crime in order to make possible the effective removal of criminogenic factors, the rehabilitation or the segregation—perhaps even the extermination—of offenders after a scientific appraisal of the chances of their reintegration into social life as useful members of the community. The end result—social protection—is often looked upon as an aim, different in kind from revenge or retribution, said to be characteristic of punishment in earlier days and surviving in some measure in the criminal law of our era.

There is something curiously lacking in the logic of such thinking. It is impossible to place "protection of society" and "revenge or retribution" into juxtaposition. Every social group, every organized political society imposes punishment upon those who violate its rules. These rules have developed because the society in question has created or adopted social values by which it sets some store and which it wants to defend against aggression. Such values come to be regarded as essential properties necessary for social survival or stability and any threat against them or any violation of the rules which guard them is looked upon as an injury to be prevented by punishment, the actual infliction of which becomes not merely evidence of the group's insistence on obedience but constitutes a defense re-action on the part of the group against violators. In other words the protection of society is the aim of all punishment or penal treatment no matter what form it may take.

We might go one step farther. The social values which are given the protection of the law, the rules which are enforced by the political power of the state because they are embodied in the criminal code, are those which are deemed desirable by those social groups within the state who have the power to make law. This fact is not so easy to discern when we confine our observations to democratic states, but in other forms of political organization it is obvious. The class distinctions in the criminal law—different penalties for masters and slaves, for nobles and commoners, for instance—furnish good illustrations. Fundamentally, then, the aim of all punishment is the protection of those social values which the dominant social group of a state regard as good for "society."

The multiplicity of theories of punishment and the confusion of thinking they have produced seems to be due to a confusion of ends with means. The *means* to secure the protection of "society" have varied greatly because the law-enforcing powers of different societies have chosen those means which they believed to be at a given time most likely to secure obedience to their law. These beliefs are in turn dependent on tradition, the level of knowledge, and the nature of social and economic institutions and conditions. The sanguinary punishments and tortures of old are no evidence of bloodthirstiness or sadism on the part of those who used them. They rather testify to the fact that those who designed them could conceive of no better, that is more efficient, way of securing protection for the social values which they treasured. The character of punishments, then, is inextricably associated with and dependent on the cultural values of the state that employs them.

One of the merits of the authors of the work here presented is that they have shown the close interrelationships between punishment and the culture which has produced them. They have furthermore made available a considerable amount of historical information not hitherto presented in English. Even those who may find in their interpretation too strict a confinement to one point of view will find in this book a stimulant of thought which all too few publications in this field of research provide.

THORSTEN SELLIN

PREFACE

THE INTERNATIONAL Institute of Social Research was established in Frankfurt am Main in 1923 as an affiliate of the University. In the spring of 1933 the Institute was closed by the German government. In 1934 the Institute transferred its main activities to New York City, where it is affiliated with Columbia University. The members of the Institute form a group of German émigré scholars working and teaching in the fields of philosophy, psychology, economics, sociology, and law. Their work is held together by a common purpose: to make the social sciences useful for an analysis of the main tendencies of present-day society.

The previous publications of the Institute are all in German and deal with such problems as Authority and Family, Transition from Feudal to Modern Thought, Economic and Social Structure of China, and Economic Planning. The Institute also has published since 1932 the *Zeitschrift für Sozialforschung*, with contributions in German, English, and French (F. Alcan, Paris, France; three issues a year). In this periodical the members of the Institute and other scholars deal with problems arising from their research and review the major publications in the social sciences.

The present book is the first of the new American series, which will be continued. The formulation of the problem and the method of analysis are closely bound up with the field of investigation which the Institute has chosen, namely, the interrelationship among various social spheres.

The Institute addressed itself to the interrelationship between punishment and the labor market when in 1931 Dr. Georg Rusche suggested that he be commissioned to write a manuscript dealing with that subject. His manuscript was delivered after the Institute had left Germany and, upon the advice of eminent American authorities, the Institute decided that a more comprehensive treatment of the subject was necessary. Since Dr. Rusche was not available for the reworking of his manuscript, the task was assigned to Dr. Kirchheimer, who has prepared this new work, retaining in essence the underlying concepts of Dr. Rusche's original draft in Chapters II to VIII; the remaining chapters represent Dr. Kirchheimer's own ideas.

The English version was prepared by Mr. M. I. Finkelstein of the College of the City of New York in close collaboration with Dr. Kirchheimer.

We owe a particular debt to Professor Sellin for his kindness. He read the original manuscript and has gone over the revised work as well. His general counsel and numerous suggestions have been invaluable.

We are grateful to the following for the privilege of reprinting copyrighted material: Alfred A. Knopf; Little, Brown and Company; Longmans, Green and Company; *Yale Law Journal;* and Victor Gollancz.

MAX HORKHEIMER, *Director*
COLUMBIA UNIVERSITY *International Institute*
IN THE CITY OF NEW YORK *of Social Research*
June, 1938

CONTENTS

CONTENTS

TABLES

PUNISHMENT

AND

SOCIAL STRUCTURE

I

INTRODUCTION

T HE relationship between crime and the social environment has been the subject of frequent investigation ever since the studies of Quetelet and von Mayr.[1] The basic social causation of the great mass of crimes against property and public order seems to be clearly established. It is of no moment in this connection whether we are dealing with variations in crime resulting from temporary economic changes, or with deep structural changes like the steady increase in fraud resulting from the growing pressure on the middle classes in a world moving from comparatively free competition to monopoly capitalism.

Although the sociology of crime has been receiving more and more attention, methods of punishment and their historical development have rarely been studied from a historical approach. Why are certain methods of punishment adopted or rejected in a given social situation? To what extent is the development of penal methods determined by the basic social relations? These questions are at least as important as the problem of the relationship between crime and the social environment. The neglect of the sociology of penal systems can probably be attributed primarily to the fact that the problem is generally approached from the standpoint of penal theory. None of the theories of punishment, neither the absolute nor the teleological, is able to explain the introduction of specific methods of punishment into the whole social process. Absolute theories fail from the very outset because they see in the relationship between guilt and atonement a problem of juristic imputation in which the individual appears as a free moral agent. Teleological theories, on the other hand, concentrating on real or hypostatized social needs, tend to consider hindrances to the achievement of their program as technical problems rather than historical.

Not only have penal theories made little direct contribution

but they have had a negative influence on the historical-socio-
logical analysis of penal methods. Insofar as the theories consider
punishment to be something eternal and immutable, they interfere with every historical investigation. Furthermore, even a
realization of the development of systems of punishment, insofar
as development can be seen from its reflection in the progress of
penal theory, does not of itself lead to a historical approach. As
soon as any given stage of development is hypostatized in a penal
theory, only a limited sphere remains in which to examine the
causal relationships between methods of punishment and the
organization of society. It might be argued that theorists in a
later epoch have the opportunity to subject the theories of earlier
periods to a critical historical analysis. But that is true only to a
very slight degree because the analysis is restricted by the social
needs of the later epoch, specifically by the need to defend the
ideological integrity of the institution of punishment, an institution as necessary in the present as it was in the past. Scholars
have frequently attempted to get around a critical historical
analysis of past periods by characterizing them as ages in which
the principle of revenge, not punishment, was dominant; such
an approach is still common enough. The criminal law of the
Enlightenment illustrates this position with particular clarity.
So long as the doctrine of retribution was dominated by the ra-
tionalism of the Enlightenment, there was as little opportunity
for a historical conception of penology as for natural law in
general. By and large it is correct to say that the notion of development in criminal law was foreign to the classical theorists.

Their successors worked under the influence of historicism,
a more favorable atmosphere for the development of a historical
approach. But they were generally in danger of writing a history
of the idea of punishment rather than of methods of punishment.
The historicism of this period was characterized by an effort to
view the development of criminal law and systems of punishment—like all law—as the unfolding of a specific idea.[2] It was
also common practice to limit oneself to a mere schema of the
succession of historical manifestations, a mass of data supposedly
bound together by the notion that they reveal progress.[3]

In order to provide a more fruitful approach to the sociology of penal systems, it is necessary to strip from the social institution of punishment its ideological veils and juristic appearance and to describe it in its real relationships. The bond, transparent or not, that is supposed to exist between crime and punishment prevents any insight into the independent significance of the history of penal systems. It must be broken. Punishment is neither a simple consequence of crime, nor the reverse side of crime, nor a mere means which is determined by the end to be achieved. Punishment must be understood as a social phenomenon freed from both its juristic concept and its social ends. We do not deny that punishment has specific ends, but we do deny that it can be understood from its ends alone. By way of analogy, it might be noted that no one would dream of developing the history of military institutions or of a specific army out of the immutable purpose of such institutions.

Punishment as such does not exist; only concrete systems of punishment and specific criminal practices exist. The object of our investigation, therefore, is punishment in its specific manifestations, the causes of its changes and developments, the grounds for the choice or rejection of specific penal methods in specific historical periods. The transformation in penal systems cannot be explained only from changing needs of the war against crime, although this struggle does play a part. Every system of production tends to discover punishments which correspond to its productive relationships. It is thus necessary to investigate the origin and fate of penal systems, the use or avoidance of specific punishments, and the intensity of penal practices as they are determined by social forces, above all by economic and then fiscal forces.

Such an interpretation does not mean that the goals of punishment should be ignored, but rather that they constitute a negative conditioning factor. So long as society believes that the prospect and infliction of punishment can frighten people away from crime, methods are selected which shall have a frightening effect on the potential criminal. If one accepts that premise, furthermore, there is validity in the doctrine that deterrent penalties are a necessary evil, a tax on a socially protected good.[4] If we consider the actual structure of modern society with all its differentiations, however, this principle means that to combat crime among the underprivileged social strata, the penalties must be of such a nature that the latter will fear a further decline in their mode of existence. It is obvious that this negative condition, this teleological side of the selection of penalties, will also find its concrete pattern in the transformations of the social structure.

When we return to the positive conditioning factors, we see that the mere statement that specific forms of punishment correspond to a given stage of economic development is a truism. It is self-evident that enslavement as a form of punishment is impossible without a slave economy, that prison labor is impossible without manufacture or industry, that monetary fines for all classes of society are impossible without a money economy. On the other hand, the disappearance of a given system of production makes its corresponding punishments inapplicable. Only a specific development of the productive forces permits the introduction or rejection of corresponding penalties. But before these potential methods can be introduced, society must be in a position to incorporate them as integrated parts of the whole social and economic system. Thus, if a slave economy finds the supply of slaves meager and the demand pressing, it cannot neglect penal slavery. In feudalism, on the other hand, not only could this form of punishment no longer be used but no other method was discovered for the proper use of the labor power of the convict. A return to the old methods, capital and corporal punishment, was therefore necessary, since the introduction of monetary fines for all classes was impossible on economic grounds. The house of correction reached a peak under mercantilism and gave great impetus to the development of the new mode of production. The economic importance of the house of correction then disappeared with the rise of the factory system. These problems form part of the subject matter of the present work. A particular aim is to show that the transition to modern industrial society, which demands the freedom of labor as a necessary condition for the productive employment of labor power, reduced the economic role of convict labor to a minimum.

Insofar as the basic economic needs of a commodity-producing society do not directly determine the creation and shaping of punishments, that is to say, insofar as convicts are not used to fill out the gaps in the labor market, the choice of methods is largely influenced by fiscal interests. Society struggles to keep to a minimum the *faux frais* which are tied up with the existence of crime and the need for criminal procedure. This is very clear in the penal practice of the feudal lords, which served them as a good source of income and involved punishments which cost nothing. That is not possible in modern society for obvious reasons. The fiscal approach has not disappeared, however, despite the fact that the rise of a state bureaucracy and the "budgeting of crime" have militated against it. We shall see that fiscal motives have shaped the typical punishment of modern society, the fine, both in its rise and in its form. With the decline of convict labor as an essential element in production and with the disappearance of the crudest forms of fiscalism in the nineteenth century, the social consciousness acquired a wider field of activity in developing punishments. Just how broad the field is, and what determines its limits, constitute a further problem of the present study.

II

SOCIAL CONDITIONS AND PENAL ADMINISTRATION IN THE LATER MIDDLE AGES

IN THE history of penal administration several epochs can be distinguished during which entirely different systems of punishment were prevalent. Penance and fines were the preferred methods of punishment in the early Middle Ages. They were gradually replaced during the later Middle Ages by a harsh system of corporal and capital punishment which, in its turn, gave way to imprisonment about the seventeenth century.

1. PENANCE AND FINES

The different penal systems and their variations are closely related to the phases of economic development. In the early Middle Ages there was not much room for a system of state punishment. The law of feud and penance was essentially a law regulating relations between equals in status and wealth.[1] It assumed the existence of sufficient land to meet the requirements of a continually increasing population without lowering their standard of living. Although the population of western and central Europe increased rapidly after 1200, the social conditions of the lower classes remained relatively favorable, particularly on the land. The colonization of eastern European territories by the Germans, with its constant demand for man power, enabled the agricultural population of other provinces to escape the pressure to which the landlords sometimes subjected them. The possibility of migrating to the new towns provided a similar opportunity of escape through the attainment of personal freedom. These developments induced the landlords to treat their serfs with more care.[2] The relations between the warrior-landlords and their serfs were of a traditional character, tantamount to a precisely determined legal relationship. These conditions tended to prevent social tension and to provide that cohesion which was characteristic of the period. Criminal law played an unimportant role as a means of preserving the social hierarchy. Tradition, a well-balanced system of social dependence, and the religious acknowledgment of the established order of things were sufficient and efficient safeguards. The main emphasis of criminal law lay on the maintenance of public order between equals in status and wealth. If, in the heat of the moment or in a state of intoxication, someone committed an offense against decency, accepted morality, or religion, or severely injured or killed his neighbor—violation of property rights did not count much in this society of landowners—a solemn gathering of free men would be held to pronounce judgment and make the culprit pay *Wergeld* or do penance so that the vengeance of the injured parties should not develop into blood feud and anarchy. An English proverb says: "Buy off the spear or bear it." [3] The chief deterrent to crime was fear of the private vengeance of the injured party. Crime was looked upon as an act of war. In the absence of a strong central power the public peace was endangered by the smallest quarrel between neighbors, as these quarrels automatically involved relatives and servants. The preservation of peace was, therefore, the primary preoccupation of criminal law. As a result of its method of private arbitration, it performed this task almost entirely by the imposition of fines.

Class distinctions were manifested by differences in the extent of penance. Penance was carefully graded according to the social status of the evildoer and of the wronged party. [4] Although this class differentiation affected only the degree of penance at first, it was at the same time one of the principal factors in the evolution of systems of corporal punishment. The inability of lower-class evildoers to pay fines in money led to the substitution of corporal punishment in their case. The penal system thus came to be more and more restricted to a minority of the population. [5] This development can be traced in every European country. A Sion statute of 1338 provided a fine of twenty livres in assault cases; if the offender could not pay he was to receive corporal punishment by being thrown into prison and fed on bread and water until the citizens interceded or the bishop pardoned him.[6] This statute not only illustrates the automatic character of the transformation of penance into corporal punishment, but it also shows that imprisonment was regarded as a form of corporal punishment at this time.

There were three main forces which militated against the private character of early medieval criminal law and which transformed it into an instrument of domination. One lay in the increasing prominence of the disciplinary function of the feudal lords against those who were in a state of economic subjection.[7] The only limit to the exercise of this disciplinary power was a jurisdictional claim by another lord. The second factor was the struggle of the central authorities to strengthen their influence by extending their judicial rights. It is immaterial for the decline of private criminal law whether the tendency toward centralization was fostered by royalty, as in England and France, or by the princes, as in Germany. The third and most significant factor was the fiscal interest, common to authorities of every type. The administration of criminal law, as we shall see later, proved to be a fruitful source of income rather than a financial burden until comparatively recent times. The payment of those who administered the law or empowered others to do so in their name was financed by the legal costs imposed upon those under trial. Far from involving expenditures, the administration of justice brought in a considerable revenue in the form of confiscations and fines imposed in addition to, or instead of, the penance due the damaged party. The remark of Holdsworth, that the king's rights to escheats and forfeitures and to the chattels of felons sometimes seemed to interest the judges almost as much as the due maintenance of law and order,[8] reveals the main consideration of the administrators of justice at the time. In Tuscany and upper Germany, in England and France,[9] the attempt to extract revenue from the administration of criminal justice was one of the principal factors in transforming criminal law from a mere arbitration between private interests, with the representative of public authority simply in the position of arbitrator, to a decisive part of the public law.

2. SOCIAL DEVELOPMENTS IN THE MIDDLE AGES

The conditions of the lower classes began to become less favorable in Italy in the fifteenth century, and then in Germany, Flanders, and France. The decline in population caused by the Black Death all over Europe in the middle of the fourteenth century, with the possible exception of France, had been overcome. The urban population, which was steadily being replenished from the land, increased with particular rapidity. The number of downtrodden, unemployed, and propertyless people rose everywhere.[10] Several concomitant causes were responsible for this change. One important factor seems to have been the exhaustion of the soil and decreasing yield. In earlier days, with a smaller population, it had frequently been possible to open up tracts of virgin land by draining marshes or burning down forests, so that previously cultivated lands could be left fallow for a very long period in order to give them an opportunity to regain their fertility. As the population increased, however, the newly won land became permanently occupied and the three-field system had to be introduced, whereby only a third of the land was allowed to lie fallow. The yield of the soil then began to decrease steadily in spite of the temporary rise in fertility from improved methods of cultivation.

At this stage, part of western Germany was turned into meadow land, while large estates in the east were devoted to the cultivation of grain which was then exported to the west by way of Danzig. This became possible when agriculture in the west could no longer meet the needs of the growing urban population and a demand arose for cheap imported grain. Originally, land in the east had little value. Because of the impossibility of marketing their products locally, landowners were glad to find small farmers who paid them a nominal rent for the right to till the soil. Now that markets were assured, however, agriculture became a paying proposition. Land became valuable and was closed to the newcomers.

The population of the plains began to increase rapidly, with alarming consequences.[11] The few remaining free spaces were quickly filled and the gradually increasing labor reserve made it possible for the landowners to depress the living standard of the peasants dependent upon them. Agrarian conditions in the east were radically altered. By the beginning of the sixteenth century, the oppression of the peasantry by the landowners reached unheard-of extremes in the west, and particularly in the southwest.[12] The situation of the lower classes developed unfavorably in England, too, as a result of the enclosure policy that began in the fifteenth century. Thomas More tells us that the sheep "that were wont to be so meke and tame, and so smal eaters, now . . . . be become so great devowerers and so wylde, that they eate up, and swallow downe the very men them selfes. They consume, destroye, and devoure whole fieldes, howses, and cities." [13] The shift from agriculture to grazing, the rise of a capitalistic pasturage system with its resulting pauperization of large sections of the countryside, coincided with a general increase in the population of England.

The advantageous condition of the artisans was threatened by the immigation of dissatisfied peasants into the towns. It was noticeable everywhere that production was not keeping pace with the increase in population. The small area and population of even the larger towns did not allow for large-scale immigration of craftsmen and traders. Municipalities made it difficult, therefore, for strangers to obtain citizenship or membership in the guilds and closed their gates to newcomers.[14] Forced to remain on the roads, the latter became derelict vagrants, vagabonds, and beggars; their roving bands were a real plague. No consistent social policy was developed to meet such conditions. These people were left with but one recourse, to join the bands of mercenary troops which now came into existence. Ambitious princelings and other authorities found in this new and cheap supply of soldiers a means of consolidating and extending their power. In the middle of the fifteenth century, there was a slow but noticeable diffusion of mercenary troops from southern Germany which reached its peak about 1480.[15]

The cheap supply of mercenaries made the knights super-fluous and cost them an important part of their income. Some suffered doubly, especially among the lower ranks, because the exhaustion of the soil and the growing misery of the peasants made it impossible for them to pay their rents. Furthermore, the increase in the size of families in the course of generations meant a large number of younger sons of military caste having no prospect of inheritance, and this made matters still worse. Many of these hereditary, but landless, knights took to highway robbery just as their subjects were doing on a smaller scale. The main difference was that the destitute peasants had to rob openly, whereas the knights could conceal their aims under the pretext of legitimate warfare or of avenging the pauperized masses on the rich city merchants who had "ruined the populace bodily, economically, and morally, and by whom they felt themselves to be attacked." [16] Attempts were made to lower the birth rate by the prohibition of marriage and similar measures, but the only result was a rise in the number of illegitimate children.[17]

It was the exploitation of the pauperized masses of this period which gave rise to the huge fortunes amassed by the Fuggers and Welsers during the Middle Ages. A sufficient supply of labor was always available for the entrepreneurs of the various industries characteristic of the late medieval towns. At the end of the fifteenth century, the rate of accumulation of capital took a sharp turn upward.[18] Tawney describes the early Middle Ages as a time in which capital was the adjunct and ally of the personal labor of craftsmen and artisans. But in fifteenth-century Germany, and much earlier in Italy, it had ceased to be a servant and had become the master. Assuming a separate and independent vitality, as Tawney says, capital now claimed the right of a predominant partner to dictate economic organization in accordance with its own exacting requirements. These new forces left the form of existing institutions unchanged but altered their spirit and operation. The guild organizations in the larger cities, formerly a barrier to the encroachments of the capitalist, became one of the instruments which he used to consolidate his power. The rules of the fraternities masked the division of the brethren into a plutocracy of merchants sheltered behind barriers which none but the wealthy craftsman could scale and a wage-earning proletariat dependent for its livelihood on capital and credit supplied by its masters. This proletariat, as Tawney remarks, alternated between revolt and an ever-expanding morass of hopeless pauperism.[19]

The whole process can easily be traced in the history of wages. The drop of the wage rate shows the social changes of the period, that is to say, the development of a capitalist form of production and system of society, and the oppression of the urban and rural wage earner.[20] The researches of Beissel, Wiebe, and others indicate that real wages sank from 100 in the period between 1450 and 1499 to 48 in the period between 1550 and 1599.[21] We find struggles of a type which we tend to look upon as characteristic only of the nineteenth century: strikes for higher wages, journeymen laying down their tools and boycotting their masters, and masters retaliating with lockouts.[22]

Discontent among the poorer classes in town and country became more and more widespread during the course of the fifteenth century. An unfettered freedom of discussion made the people conscious of the defects in the social system. Is it surprising, asks Huizinga, that the people could see their fate and that of the world only as an endless succession of evils when we realize the prevalence of bad government, exactions, cupidity and violence on the part of the great, wars and brigandage, scarcity, misery, and pestilence?[23]

3. CRIMINAL LAW AND THE RISE OF CAPITALISM

The intense class conflicts in Flanders, upper Italy, Tuscany, and upper Germany which marked the transition to capitalist forms in the fourteenth and fifteenth centuries led to the creation of a harsh criminal law directed against the lower classes. The constant increase in crime among the ranks of the poverty-stricken proletariat, especially in the big towns, made it necessary for the ruling classes to search for new methods which would make the administration of criminal law more effective. The system of punishment, with its dual regime of corporal punish-

ment and fines, remained unchanged, however, except that
different applications were made according to the class of the condemned person. Variations in the treatment of different categories of offenses and offenders became more pronounced. The
private settlement of disputes involving dishonest acts, such as
theft, was no longer permitted. Even the right of asylum did not
apply to such cases. This did not mean that every form of offense
against property was regarded as a dishonest act. Dishonesty was
considered not from the angle of the property stolen or damaged
but rather from the angle of the person stealing or damaging:
he would be dealt with much more harshly if he happened to be
homeless or of low social status. As Radbruch remarks, social
and moral considerations were intermingled.[24] Since the majority
of criminals were members of the lower classes, the word "vil-
lain," originally applied to a member of a particular social class,
came to indicate a judgment of moral inferiority. This distinction clearly appears in Gandinus when he writes that the *poena
extraordinaria* must be determined by the judge with reference
to the nature of the offense and the offender (*secundum quali-
tatem delicti et personae*).[25]

When it was a question of damage done to property by member of the upper classes, legal opinion was not so severe. As late a
collection of laws and practices as the *Clagspiegel* contains the
statement that negotiations might be entered into and agreements reached in criminal cases for which the death penalty was
provided.[26] The conception of the feud offered a legal cover for
breaches of the peace and for all kinds of robbery by the upper
classes. Whatever disagreement there may be today over the
fields of application of Articles 128 and 129 of the Criminal Code
of Charles V regarding lawful feud and rebellion, it is certain
that the law did provide a large field of immunity for acts which
would be severely punished if perpetrated by members of a
lower class.[27]

The creation of a law effective in combating offenses against
property was one of the chief preoccupations of the rising urban
bourgeoisie. Wherever they had the monopoly of legislation and
jurisdiction they pursued this demand with the greatest energy.

Von Bar refers to the hard-hearted, money-minded bourgeoisie of south German towns, to whom property meant everything.[28] They even attempted to restrict the right of private settlement to offenses resulting from feuds. This could not be accomplished, however, and the upper classes continued to receive preferential treatment in a wide range of crimes, including offenses against property. In France, too, it was the bourgeoisie who always tried to obtain from the Crown an intensification of the repressive system. As early as 1353 they protested against the excessive use of the royal prerogative of mercy. In the Estates General of Blois in 1576, the third estate demanded not only greater guarantees of procedure for its members, but also a more energetic persecution of murderers and thieves. Chapter 105 of the royal ordonnance of Blois met their demands by providing for the dismissal of justiciaries and their officials and for a system of fines against villagers guilty of negligence in the fulfillment of their obligations. Chapter 108 abolished the royal right of annulling sentences, restricted the royal prerogative of pardon to noblemen, and provided that the courts should be competent to deal with petitions for mercy from all other offenders.[29] This right of pardon, which did not take into consideration the special circumstances of the case, that is, the degree of guilt, was widely exercised by the princes and constituted a kind of antidote against the harshness of the prevailing penal system. It is not difficult to see that such a practice, not based on a rational examination of the facts of the case and frequently influenced by special interests, was regarded with disapproval by the rising middle classes in their struggle for greater stability and rationalization of government. Cases are reported like that of the Duke of Burgundy, who pardoned a merchant in 1418 on the express ground that he was a good merchant who had long supplied the Duke with merchandise, and that the Duke owed him a considerable sum of money.[30] The bourgeois demands for increased efficiency in the administration of law were largely promoted by the growing centralization of the administration in the hands of a bureaucracy trained in Roman law.[31]

The fine had evolved from a compensation to the offended

party into a method of enriching the judges and justiciaries. In practice, it was reserved for the rich, whereas corporal punishment became the punishment of the poor. As crime increased among the masses, class differentiations in punishment became more marked.[32] The most important of the sixteenth-century codifications, Schwarzenberg's *Peinliche Halsgerichtsordnung,* sanctioned this process. Though it appears to set up a single and general system of capital and corporal punishment, those of its provisions which are of the greatest practical importance, Articles 158–175 dealing with larceny, open the door to a consideration of the wrongdoer's social standing. The term *ehrbar* (honest) used in those sections of the Code has found widely divergent interpretations.[33] The problem can hardly be solved by mere reference to the text of the Code and to historical sources, however. There can be no doubt that actual practice was based upon conceptions of class rather than of moral judgment. The legal freedom of choice between corporal punishment and fines may have contributed to this development. The harsh vagrancy statutes which we find everywhere in the sixteenth century clearly reveal the current interpretation of the term *honesty.* Besides the general differentiation between classes, which made the assessment of fines or corporal punishment dependent simply on the prisoner's capacity to pay, there were special estate privileges in various countries. Certain punishments were discarded for certain estates and replaced by others, or were applied with special modifications for members of the higher estates. We shall have occasion to return to this point later.[34] More important than these estate privileges, however, is the general privilege granted to the wealthy, the possibility, in a wide range of cases, of replacing capital and corporal punishment by fines, or, in more serious cases, by banishment.[35]

Thus, while those who had enough money to pay were able to buy exemption from punishment, offenders who were without means (and they made up the great majority in these hard times) were powerless to save themselves from the harsh treatment to which they were liable. By far the greater number of crimes were now crimes against property, committed by those who had no property, so that a fine would hardly have met the case. The exchequer could get nothing out of them, as Schmidt remarks.[36] He suggests a further reason for this important change of policy, namely, that "it had become a matter of paramount importance to suppress the bands of vagabonds, beggars, and robbers who were becoming a plague on the land. In one place after another the sluice gates would open and release a new and poisonous flood into the muddy sea of crime." [37] The poorer the masses became, the harsher the punishments in order to deter them from crime. Physical punishment now began to increase considerably all over the country, until finally it became not merely supplementary but the regular form of punishment. Execution, mutilation, and flogging were not introduced at one stroke by any sudden revolutionary change, but gradually became the rule with changing conditions. As time went on, punishment became harsher, not milder.[38] There was a theory that the punishment should be milder in case of doubt, but such humanizing tendencies did not meet with approval in practice. On the contrary, open war was waged between legislation and science in the matter of punishment.[39]

Legislation was openly directed against the lower classes. Even when criminal procedure as such was the same for all estates and classes, special procedures soon arose which affected only the lower classes. Thus, Schmidt says that there was one respect in which the old arbitrary justice could not be abolished, in the persecution of habitual lower-class offenders. The simplification of procedure in cases where the prisoner had been taken in *flagranti delicto* permitted the isolation of a class of outlaws for whom the provisions of the law, such as consideration of the gravity of the crime, could not fully apply. Execution, banishment, mutilation, branding, and flogging more or less exterminated the whole range of professional rogues from murderers and robbers to vagrants and gypsies. With the increase in the number of professional lower-class criminals in the later Middle Ages, this arbitrary justice, according to Schmidt, became more and more common and led to a profound change in the whole administration of criminal law.[40]

Until the fifteenth century, the death penalty and serious mutilation were used only in extreme cases to supplement the complicated and carefully differentiated system of fines, but now they became the most common measures. Judges resorted to them whenever they were convinced that the offender was a danger to society. The extraordinary increase in the number of death sentences in the course of the sixteenth century is well known. The data for England, which must be approximately correct, give us an idea of the situation prevailing throughout Europe. We are told that 72,000 major and minor thieves were hanged during the reign of Henry VIII, and that under Elizabeth vagabonds were strung up in rows, as many as three and four hundred at a time. And the population of England was then only about three million.[41] The Nürnberg executioner, Franz Schmidt, executed 361 people during his forty-four years in office (1573–1617) and inflicted corporal punishment on only 345. Both the absolute figures in proportion to the total population and the ratio of capital to corporal punishments offer a very significant indication of the prevailing severity of punishment.[42] Outwardly the death penalty remained the same, but it gained a new significance in principle. It was no longer the extreme penalty for serious offenses, but a means of putting allegedly dangerous individuals out of the way. In this kind of procedure, little attention was paid to the guilt or innocence of a suspect, as can be seen from the statement made by the Reichskammergericht to the Lindauer Reichstag in 1496 that innocent people were put to death without any just cause.[43]

Even the methods of execution became more brutal. The authorities were constantly devising new means by which to make the death penalty more painful.[44] The substitution of various forms of mutilation for capital punishment was hardly a mitigating measure, for mutilation usually served to identify criminals in much the same way as the modern criminal record file. We find removal of the hands, whole fingers, or phalanges, cutting off or tearing out of the tongue, putting out of eyes, severing of ears, and castration.[45] Apart from the actual suffering involved, it was very difficult for anyone thus punished to find honest employment again. He would therefore be forced back into the path of crime and would eventually fall victim to the harshest measures of the law.[46] Very often the mutilation left a mere travesty of a man, and even more often the victim died. When the law had prescribed only mutilation, however, a fatal outcome was ascribed to "natural causes."

Exile, a most common form of punishment at this period, frequently meant a far worse fate for lower-class victims than one might think. The exile escaped death in his own town, but, as often as not, the gallows awaited him in the town where he sought refuge. Exile for the rich, however, was not a very severe punishment. It meant travel for study, the establishment of business branches abroad, and even diplomatic service for the home town or native country, with the prospect of an early and glorious return.[47]

The whole system of punishment in the later Middle Ages makes it quite clear that there was no shortage of labor, at least in the towns. As the price paid for labor decreased, the value set on human life became smaller and smaller. The hard struggle for existence molded the penal system in such a way as to make it one of the means of preventing too great an increase of population. Von Hentig quite correctly applies the idea of selection to the penal system in this connection and he shows that the system acted as a kind of artificial earthquake or famine in destroying those whom the upper classes considered unfit for society.[48]

The people of the late Middle Ages, who could never hope for a kindly fate to raise them from their wretched condition, lived in an atmosphere of oppression, irritation, envy, anger, hatred, and desperation. Superstition was rife and the persecution of witches reached epidemic proportions. The lower classes vented their fury and grief on the alleged earthly representatives of the supernatural powers, on those who were suspected of dealing in the "black arts." The witches' crime might be nothing more than the attribution to them of certain powers which their personal appearance, eccentric habits, or vain boasting seemed to warrant, but they were persecuted not only by the masses who blamed them for misfortunes, but also by the authorities. No doubt sincere in their own hatred and fear of the supernatural, the latter saw in this new mass hatred, probably in a dim and semi-conscious way, the means of diverting responsibility from themselves.[49]

Jews were also subjected to blind persecution by the distressed masses. As the Jew became richer while they became poorer, it seemed obvious that he must be responsible for their impoverishment in some measure, especially by his money-lending activities. It was further alleged that by receiving stolen property Jews encouraged and in part gave rise to the epidemic of thefts which characterized the period. The victims of the economic decline could not be expected to perceive the true causes of crime, and the Jews were a very convenient scapegoat. Moreover, some churchmen and the ruling classes in general gave authority to the current legends of sacrilege and ritual murder, thus providing an adequate excuse for the dull hatred which broke out from time to time in organized persecution.[50]

Outlawed criminals, even more than the witches or the Jews, were the legitimate prey of anyone anxious to satisfy a lust for cruelty which the interests of society had forced him to hold in check. The great variety of punishments gave a maximum compensation of this kind. The masses who witnessed executions were constantly demanding new sensations. Huizinga relates that the citizens of Mons bought a brigand at far too high a price solely for the pleasure of seeing him quartered, and he comments upon the brutish and primitive enjoyment of such spectacles.[51] Publicity was officially believed to enhance the deterrent value of punishment. Thieves were more often left hanging in the air than buried in order that everyone might see them and fear a similar fate.[52] But the whole system was primarily the expression of sadism, and the deterrent effect of publicity was negligible. That is why the most morbid imagination today can hardly picture the variety of tortures inflicted. We read about executions by knife, ax, and sword, heads being knocked off with a plank or cut through with a plough, people being buried alive, left to starve in a dungeon, or having nails hammered through their heads, eyes, shoulders, and knees, strangulation and throttling, drowning and bleeding to death, evisceration, drawing and quartering, torture on the wheel, torture with red-hot tongs, strips being cut from the skin, the body being torn to pieces or sawed through with iron or wooden instruments, burning at the stake, and many other elaborate forms of cruelty. It is not surprising that practically every crime was punishable by death and that the vital question was the manner in which death should be inflicted.[53]

We find any number of such scenes depicted in contemporary art. When Hieronymus Bosch, Peter Breughel, Grünewald, and other painters depicted the frightful tortures of their martyrs, they were reproducing ordinary events in such a way as to conform to religious and esthetic requirements. Even the religious leaders of the time found little fault with the contemporary spirit of penal administration. Luther, for example, said that mere execution was not sufficient punishment and that rulers should pursue, beat, strangle, hang, burn, and torture the mob in every way. The use of the sword was a sacred duty of the ruler. "The hand that holds the sword and strangles is no longer a human hand, but the hand of God. It is not man but God who hangs, tortures, beheads, strangles, and makes war. . . ." [54]

Thomas More once asked: "What other things do you, than make thieves and then punish them?" [55] His laconic comment shows that he understood that the system of punishment constituted part of a vicious circle, but such insight was exceptional. Huizinga remarks that the Middle Ages knew nothing of all those ideas which have rendered our sentiment of justice timid and hesitant: doubts about the criminal's responsibility, the conviction that society is the accomplice of the individual to a certain extent, the desire to reform instead of to inflict pain, and, we may add, the fear of judicial error. Huizinga is largely justified, though he overstresses the criteria of nineteenth-century liberalism.[56]

Historians have differed sharply in their evaluations of this period of criminal law. Some have accepted the position of the then ruling classes and excuse their severity on the ground that stringent measures became necessary toward the end of the

Middle Ages in order to combat crime. The authorities, they argue, were obliged to get the better of the growing criminal bands and to uphold law and order at any cost, and they were, therefore, justified in adopting the most cruel forms of suppression.[57] Other criminologists condemn medieval methods as foolish and wrong. They believe that the history of punishment is to a large extent a history of human irrationality and cruelty.[58]

In reply to the first group, it has been pointed out that such a criminal policy met with relatively little success. It drove the outlawed, the maimed, and the branded from their homes and the society of honest people onto the high roads. The law itself thus served to swell the ranks of potential criminals, who later committed the many petty offenses that were becoming so common.[59] The second view is inadequate. Brutal punishment cannot be ascribed simply to the primitive cruelty of an epoch now vanished. Cruelty itself is a social phenomenon which can be understood only in terms of the social relationships prevailing in any given period.[60]

III

MERCANTILISM AND THE RISE OF IMPRISONMENT

1. THE LABOR MARKET AND THE STATE

METHODS of punishment began to undergo a gradual but profound change toward the end of the sixteenth century. The possibility of exploiting the labor of prisoners now received increasing attention. Galley slavery, deportation, and penal servitude at hard labor were introduced, the first two only for a time, the third as the hesitant precursor of an institution which has lasted into the present. Sometimes they appeared together with the traditional system of fines and capital and corporal punishment; at other times they tended to displace the latter. These changes were not the result of humanitarian considerations, but of certain economic developments which revealed the potential value of a mass of human material completely at the disposal of the administration.[1]

The rise of larger and wealthier town populations created an increased demand for certain consumer's goods. The steadiness of the demand and the growth of the financial system led to a constant extension of markets; the possibility that the entrepreneur would not be able to dispose of his products became almost negligible. Merchants from the countries which had been least affected by the new treasure were able to sell at a great profit to those which had been more strongly affected. Countries which had established trade relations with the Levant and Asia were able to export the treasure on extraordinarily profitable terms. The conquest of colonies not only led to greater importation of precious metals, with all its economic consequences, but also to an extension of markets for mass-consumption goods.[2]

The population, after the middle of the sixteenth century, failed to keep pace with this increase in the possibility of employment. In England and in France population growth was checked by the wars of religion and other internal disturbances, and it remained very small.[3] The most extreme case was that of Germany. As a result of the Thirty Years' War, population declined in the middle of the seventeenth century at a rate comparable only to certain local drops during the Black Death. An estimated fall from eighteen million to seven million, given by some authors,[4] may be exaggerated, but the more conservative estimates are impressive enough. Inama-Sternegg estimates 17.64 million in 1475, 20.95 in 1600–1620 and 13.29 in the middle of the seventeenth century.[5] A slow increase did not set in again until the second half of the seventeenth century, and in many cases a century or more was needed to make up the loss. In the period before the Thirty Years' War real wages fell while population increased, but from 1620 to 1670 real wages rose. As Elsas has recently formulated the relationship, real wages throughout the sixteenth and seventeenth centuries followed a course contrary to the movement of prices and population; in other words, real wages corresponded to the supply of labor.[6]

Spinoza's friend, De la Court, drew a vivid picture of Holland, where there was such a shortage of foreign labor that farmers were obliged to pay their hands at so high a rate that their own standard of living was very low in comparison with the laborer's. He describes similar conditions in the towns, where the apprentices and servants were less tractable and more highly paid than in any other country.[7] We hear similar complaints from Germany because of the destructiveness of the Thirty Years' War. There was often so great a lack of the least skilled manual workers that some enterprises were forced to close down altogether.[8] In Germany, as in Holland, there was a distinct improvement in the standard of living of both town and agricultural laborers.[9] Various factors aggravated the situation still more. Labor was quite immobile in France and England, and even more so in Germany, divided as it was into innumerable sovereign states. Scarcity of labor and high wages in one region could coexist with low living standards in others, without any interaction resulting. This is in contrast to the situation in our present society, in which, as Hauser says, markets tend to act like vessels communicating with one another.[10] Under the *ancien régime,* both the shortage of roads and the legislation prohibiting the circulation of grain blocked the tendency of prices to become interregionally uniform. A shortage which appears to be general may nevertheless spare some small local market cut off from the lines of communication.[11] The fact that extensive local poverty could coincide with scarcity of labor was due in part to the existing poor laws, which forced paupers back to their native towns and villages even when there was not the slightest possibility of their finding work at home.[12] These laws thus hindered the rational distribution of labor. Deterioration of local conditions, famine, war, and pestilence also drove newly trained hands back home almost automatically.

This lack of constancy in the labor supply and the low productivity of labor meant a tremendous change in the position of the owning classes. At the very time when the extension of markets and the increasing requirements of technical equipment called for more invested capital, labor became a relatively scarce commodity. Capitalists of the mercantilist period could obtain labor on the open market only by paying high wages and granting favorable working conditions. When one considers the diametrically opposed conditions of the previous century, one realizes what the change must have meant to the propertied classes. The beginning of the disappearance of the labor reserve was a severe blow to those who owned the means of production. Workers had the power to insist on radical improvements in their working conditions. Accumulation of capital was necessary for the expansion of trade and manufacture, and it was being severely hampered by the new wage and labor conditions. The capitalist was obliged to turn to the state for working capital and for the restriction of wages.

The ruling classes left no means unexplored in order to overcome the condition of the labor market. A series of rigorous measures restricting the liberty of the individual was introduced. These measures are mentioned in all the writings about the period, and they have been more or less thoroughly discussed.

But they are often evaluated merely as curious historical anomalies, paradoxical and absurd aberrations of the *Polizeigeist* of the time which were wiped out by a subsequent evolution.[13] Such a viewpoint fails to see their historical importance as measures aimed at the serious lack of labor that was threatening the very existence of the social order.

The most important measures of all were the attempts to increase the birth rate. Many writers have condemned them as signs of stupidity, shortsightedness, and even moral degeneracy. To contemporaries, however, nothing seemed more obvious. They would relieve the scarcity of labor by promoting a high rate of birth. The accepted theory during the whole of the eighteenth century was that the population of England was decreasing, and people talked of it as a fact which had actually been proved. Statesmen like Lord Shelburne and Lord Chatham publicly expressed the fears they felt on this score. The supposed evil was ascribed to a variety of causes: the excessive increase of armed forces, war, emigration, overtaxation, the rising prices of foodstuffs, the enclosure movement.[14]

Economists of the time thought it of supreme importance to fight this evil. Süssmilch, for example, said that a country's happiness, security, and wealth depend on the existence of a large number of subjects. One of the chief duties of the ruler is to see that his country is well populated; that function, in fact, includes most, if not all, of his other duties. It makes the ruler a father, a medical adviser, a shepherd, a God on earth. He must leave untried no means by which the population of his country may be increased. He must sweep all obstacles aside. He must see to it that his subjects have the means of subsistence; he must do everything in his power to combat poverty, so that all those who wish to marry may do so, and so that all parents may be eager to have many children.[15] The clergy itself was evidently quite ready to invoke religious arguments for a high birth rate. Süssmilch asked whether any theologian could possibly protest against his attempt to show that no man can rule wisely who has not the commandment of the Creator in his mind: Be fruitful and multiply and fill the earth![16]

Government and legislation followed these lines. In England, says Pribram, the Stuarts favored the rustic May Day festivities with all their bucolic joy and hilarity, because of the increase in population which resulted. Even if the maiden lost her virtue, the King gained subjects—specifically, soldiers. On these occasions, he probably took part in increasing the population himself, in order to merit the title of Father of His Country. It was for the same reason that the "Book of Sports" was read, continues Pribram, a very good example of the absolutist population policy which appealed to the lowest instincts of the masses in the interest of the omnipotence of the State.[17] In France, Colbert offered tax reductions for early marriages and large families. Systematic promotion of the birth rate was most significant in the Germanies, however. The consequences of the Thirty Years' War and the small size of the territories in comparison with their claims to political power had so great an effect on policy that German mercantilism has actually been named populationism.[18] In 1746 the Prussian clergy was forbidden to exact penance from unmarried mothers. The object of this step was to decrease the number of infanticides. In 1747 a proclamation was issued against the customary one year's mourning for widows. The edicts of Frederick II of Prussia of August 17, 1756, and February 8, 1765, forbade the consideration of illegitimate mothers as disreputable. The provisions relating to public morality were abolished. Frederick's opinions on the subject are expressed in a letter to Voltaire: "I think of them [the people] as a herd of deer in a great lord's park; their only function is to populate and fill the preserves." [19] We find the same tendencies in the great law codes of the time. The *Allgemeine preussische Landrecht* of 1794, for example, made the legal position of illegitimate children so favorable that the corresponding clauses of the Civil Code (*BGB*) of 1900 seem barbaric in comparison. The former entitled an unmarried mother to receive compensation from the child's father; she could even demand repayment of the costs of her confinement.[20]

Military strategy and methods of recruiting and of maintaining military discipline were determined by the scarcity of man power. In his evaluation of Frederick II's policy, Meinecke says that the barbaric elements of his military system and, above all, the recruitment of this scum of humanity were in such close accord with his carefully thought out demographic, financial, and economic system that everything would have fallen to pieces if he had removed a single stone from its foundation.[21] If one needed an army at the beginning of the Thirty Years' War, unemployed mercenaries would pour in from everywhere. As industry advanced, the living standard of the workers improved and they had the possibility of a life easier and quieter than the life of the soldier. It thus became more and more difficult for governments to outbid employers, who were offering rising wages, and to recruit soldiers for their service.

Press gangs had already made their appearance by the time of the Thirty Years' War.[22] Officers were instructed to seize passers-by and force them to sign for military service. Or local authorities were required to provide the regiments with a certain number of recruits.[23] Peasants were afraid to bring their produce to the towns, and large numbers of young people fled over the borders. Matters became still worse under Frederick William I. Local authorities in every province complained that people were being driven out of the country and that the whole economy was threatened. Recruits eventually became so expensive and rare that the Prussian king issued the famous *Kantonreglement* of 1733 in order to stop captains from quarreling with each other over recruits.[24] The value of soldiers is also shown by the extraordinarily high prices paid to the German princes by England when she was waging her colonial wars.[25] England fought her colonial wars almost entirely with foreigners, on the ground that her own able-bodied population could be more profitably occupied with the works and arts of peace.

The shortage of men eventually became so serious that the army had to be reinforced with criminals. In the great wars which England waged with France and Spain during the latter half of the eighteenth century it was difficult to find enough soldiers and sailors by any process of enlistment, impressment, or importation. Judges and gaolers were consulted about the fitness of convicts for military service, and the qualification was physical, not moral.[26] The army came to be considered a kind of penal organization suited only for ne'er-do-wells, spendthrifts, black sheep, and ex-convicts.[27] Countries even went so far as to take criminals over from other governments which did not know what to do with them.[28] Avé-Lallemant writes that the record of almost every criminal of the eighteenth century contained instances of recruiting and subsequent desertion. This was a very practical means of avoiding prosecution until time and circumstances became more favorable.[29]

Not only could the criminal cheat the gallows by enlistment, but he often received special treatment if he committed a crime while serving in the army. Special offenses of a military character were provided for in the statute books and very severe punishments were in law imposed upon soldiers guilty of any sort of crime, but in practice soldiers were frequently treated quite leniently. It was considered both unjust and inexpedient to execute a trained soldier or sailor.[30] In 1626, for example, four soldiers were condemned to death in Breslau for breach of military discipline; then they were pardoned with the understanding that they would be placed in particularly dangerous positions in case of war. Such leniency naturally had a significant influence upon army morality and upon the general security of life and property.[31]

The government policy of the mercantilist period shows a marked friendliness to the employer, for it was of interest to the forces of absolutism that industry should flourish. The state made numerous attempts to put undertakings on their feet by bounties, privileges, monopoly rights, tariffs, and restrictions on the guilds. Large-scale industry in France, for example, was almost exclusively artificial, and survived only with the help and patronage of the Crown.[32] Even England, despite its long history of flourishing capitalist enterprise and despite Puritan opposition to royal monopolies and similar "artificial" institutions, saw active governmental support of many industries under the Tudors and early Stuarts.[33] The continued growth of industry required the creation of a large labor supply. Workers offered them-

selves with considerable hesitation, partly because there was no
surplus and partly because of their opposition to the new conditions of labor and everyday life. The government, which had
often supplied considerable credit (the officials who negotiated
these loans were frequently rewarded with shares in the business),
was naturally eager to find cheap labor power and to enforce
factory regulations. The ruling class threw its whole weight on
the side of the employers. Levasseur is right in saying that from
the standpoint of the state there was no equality between employers and employees, for the law openly sought to maintain
the latter in a position of dependence.[34]

Emigration of labor was strictly forbidden by the state. A
French decree of 1669 provided for the arrest and confiscation
of the property of an emigrant worker, and a later decree of
1682 went so far as to introduce the death penalty for emigration and imprisonment for incitement to emigration.[35] Conditions for immigrants, on the other hand, were most favorable.
Each country jealously watched its own skilled workers and tried
to attract those of other countries. By 1786 no less than one-third
of the inhabitants of Prussia were either immigrants or descend-
ants of immigrants.[36] Becher rebuked statesmen who tried to
clear beggars out of the country, since all man power could be
used by the state. He even advocated the immigration of beggars.[37] Justi went further and reasoned that a state wishing to
increase its population should be an asylum for all the oppressed
and persecuted of other lands, and that it should never give up
any person who has fled to it for refuge. Such a policy, he said,
is not contrary to justice, for it is well known that hate, revenge,
and the spirit of persecution frequently lead to false accusations.
Even if the crimes are too heinous to be forgiven, one need only
offer clear proof of the offense and the new authorities will
themselves administer justice to the refugee.[38]

The state established maximum wage scales in order to halt
the rise of wages resulting from free competition in the labor
market. Wage policy was governed by the principle that a country
cannot become rich unless there is a large body of poor people
forced to work out of sheer poverty. This point of view was given

expression in contemporary economic theory, and reform proposals were all based on the idea that people can be made to work
only when wages are low. Mandeville says: "When Men shew such
an extraordinary proclivity to Idleness and Pleasure, what reason
have we to think that they would ever work, unless they were
oblig'd to it by immediate Necessity?" [39] A further incentive to
work was expected from the decline in real wages caused by
rising prices.

The observance of factory regulations became an urgent problem as a result of the scarcity of labor, especially of skilled labor.
Strict rules were introduced to control the activity of the worker
from morning prayers to the end of the day. Attempts were even
made to regulate his private life, with a view to protecting him
from influences likely to affect his productivity or discipline.[40]
The productivity of labor was low, and the difficulty was
heightened by the large number of holidays during the year.
Frequent laws were passed in order to regulate working hours,
which were being reduced by the growing power of the wage
earners. We hear of a twelve-hour day in Holland in the seventeenth century,[41] a short working day when compared with the
normal day of twelve to sixteen hours in seventeenth and
eighteenth century France.[42] The capstone of governmental
regulation of the labor market was the prohibition of working-
class organizations. Workers were severely punished for laying
down their tools for higher wages or any other cause.[43] Freedom
of combination was against the whole spirit of the law, which
held that labor questions were to be decided by the ruling authorities alone.[44]

Child labor was fostered in every way possible. The child was
put to work in the factory as soon as he could be of use. The
state provided manufacturers with children from the orphanages,
in which case the employer was sometimes obliged to provide
meals, but never anything else.[45] Occasionally, the state set up
its own establishments for the employment of orphans. All this
naturally increased the value of children *per se*. They became
an asset. Poor parents could hire their children out, or even ob-

tain a lump sum by relinquishing all claim to them and handing them over to a master for use in his factory.

The state of the labor market thus had its effects on education.[46] The underlying principle of all education was to train children for industry. There were all kinds of industrial schools, spinning schools, and sewing schools, where children were not only trained free of charge but were even paid a small wage for their work.[47] Theoreticians defended child labor vigorously, saying that it was the best way to keep them out of mischief and teach them to help their parents financially. Only isolated individuals raised a voice to protest against the physical dangers of working at too early an age, or to point out that such children would later become unfit for work, if they managed to survive at all.

The measures we have outlined were not always sufficient to counteract the harmful effect of the shortage of labor in industry.[48] In England we find forced labor as early as the Statute of Artificers of the reign of Elizabeth. We have already referred to the supply of orphans made available by the state, but apart from them the state began to engage workmen forcibly and placed them at the disposal of the entrepreneurs.[49] Even the soldiers and their families were required to do compulsory spinning. According to an Austrian decree of 1768, regiments were attached to flax, cotton, and wool mills, and were liable for all kinds of work in other factories and workshops as well. An earlier decree (1763) said that the object of the erection of factories throughout the country was to give idle people an opportunity of earning their living, and, if necessary, to force them to work by locking them up in workhouses.[50]

2. STAGES IN THE TREATMENT OF THE POOR

The man power which the state could best control was composed of persons exercising unlawful professions, such as beggars and prostitutes, and of people subject to its supervision and entitled to its assistance by law and tradition, that is, widows, lunatics, and orphans. The history of public policy toward beggars and paupers can be understood only in relation to poor relief on the one hand and criminal law on the other. Our discussion of the treatment of the poor is designed to show how this treatment reacted to changes in the social structure.

A fresco in the Church of St. Francis in Assisi, sometimes attributed to Giotto, portrays the allegory of Poverty. St. Francis places a wedding ring on the finger of Poverty, a woman wearing tattered garments, surrounded by thorns, and expressing renunciation. Christ stands between the two as though he were giving lady Poverty away to the bridegroom, and angels are watching reverently on either side. This painting illustrates the position to which it was socially possible to assign poverty during the Middle Ages.[51] Max Weber correctly remarks that medieval ethics not only tolerated begging but actually glorified it in the mendicant orders, and that even secular beggars were sometimes treated as an estate because they gave the person of means an opportunity for good works.[52] Of course, the church had voluntary poverty in mind, but it is difficult to distinguish sharply between voluntary and involuntary poverty, and even the duty and advantages of good works in the form of charity toward ordinary beggars were constantly reiterated. There was room both for the poor, living on alms, and for the mighty, living on income from property and able to fulfill their Christian obligations and to justify themselves in the eyes of God by doing good works. As Groethuysen says, the exercise of charity is an essential function of the powerful of this world.[53] The relation between these two contrasting groups, neither of which lived upon the product of its own labor, was expressed by the social teachings of the church in such a way as to utilize the desire of the wealthy for heavenly favor in order to promote material assistance for the poor.[54] This attitude was proper in a society in which one could always lead an existence not too far below the average worker's standard of living. Anyone who voluntarily chose the lot of a pauper was performing an act of heroic abnegation, so recognized by society. To give such people food and clothing was worthy of man and pleasing to God.

Care of the poor was regarded as the concern of the church.

The property accumulated by the church was justified as the property of the poor, the sick, and the aged. *Ad hoc* incursions of the state into this sphere were usually made with a view to keeping wages down and assuring a proper supply of labor. At a time when plague and war had carried away thirty to sixty percent of the population of Europe, wage policy consisted primarily in maintaining a low price level for the labor reserve, the paupers. If vagrants were forcibly employed on public works at low wages, the chief purpose was to force them into private employment at the prevailing rates. In other words, the basic aim of such measures was to overcome the shortage of labor without permitting a rise in wages, as in the French ordonnances of 1382 and 1535,[55] or the English statute of 1388.[56] These were only transitory measures, however, and they had no lasting success.

The related problems of labor and poverty underwent a complete change during the sixteenth century. The condition of the lower classes deteriorated, as we have already seen. Levasseur calls mendicity one of the sores of the century, and ascribes its rise to the dissolution of the feudal order.[57] Contrasting the sixteenth century with the fifteenth, Paultre notes that the authorities had no further cause to fear a shortage of labor, and that the mendicant and vagabond population was being augmented by many who sought work but were unable to find it.[58] Holdsworth concludes from all this that, with the rise of a large class of able-bodied vagrants, indiscriminate charity became positively dangerous and incapable of dealing with the problem of unemployment.[59] At the same time, the change in the position of the church and the confiscation of church property led to the complete disorganization of poor relief.[60]

The middle-class attitude toward labor and the poor differed sharply from that of the feudal ruling class. The Thomistic doctrine of the necessity of labor as an indispensable, natural condition of life meant that man has a duty to work only to the extent required for the preservation of the individual and society.[61] Labor is not the chief content of life or even highly desirable, but merely a necessary factor. This conception corresponds to the static medieval system of society. For the powerful lord who lived on the labor of others or on war, the necessity of working for a living was a calamity comparable to the straits of a propertyless man obliged to work, yet conscious of the fact that his labor would never carry him to a higher social position. The bourgeois, however, succeeded in becoming prosperous through his industry. It is highly doubtful whether his road to wealth and power can be compared with the work required of a member of the lower class, but as far as current ideas of merit were concerned, his activity was esteemed and glorified as work. Wealth thus lost the mark of sinfulness, and the idea of voluntary generosity toward the poor as absolution for the sin involved in wealth became meaningless. The bourgeois justified his life not by good works but by his everyday conduct. His existence, behavior, and success in this world were his justification. His charitable activity could be taken as the measure of his moral worth because it was his ability which explained his worldly success in the first place.[62] Not everyone could display the same ability, of course, but anyone who honestly applied himself to his work could earn his daily bread. The typical argument of the wealthy, that the poor are too lazy to work and that the opportunities for work are plentiful, finds a strong defender in Luther. He writes that one need only prevent the poor from dying of hunger or cold, and that no one should live upon the labor of another. No one who wants to be poor should become rich, he continues, but anyone who desires wealth has only to toil.[63]

The bourgeois attitude received its clearest formulation in Calvinism. The Dutch and English middle class did not have royal and colonial monopolistic privileges and they did not enjoy the same capital resources as the old trading companies. They found in Calvinism a theoretical foundation for their ascetic attitude and for their concept of the calling, an attitude to economic problems which was a necessity for them. With such a small capital reserve, luxury and heavy expenditure would have led to ruin. One had to work and save if one wished to get on or even to maintain a bare subsistence level.

Calvinism was only a contributing factor in the rise of capitalism, however. The fact that it was England and Holland which ushered in the new era, and not the old trading aristocracies of Venice and Florence, was the result of external material conditions, particularly the rise of new trade routes. We shall have occasion later to note the fact that Catholic authorities adopted the very measures in the field of poor relief which we are tempted to regard as typically Calvinist. There can be no doubt, however, that the Calvinist doctrine did provide a welcome intellectual foundation for the bourgeois attitude toward social problems. The useful virtues which help production and restrict consumption, especially the consumption of luxuries, were the Puritan's massive, earthy pillars, says Kraus, and rationalization and standardized methods marked the bounds of his inspiration. Sober denial of sensual pleasure and renunciation of the vain joys of this world were his portion. Kraus is correct in linking this ethical ideal with the chief tenet of the mercantilist period, that all must be sacrificed to production and export, that imports and consumption must be reduced, in order to bring as much precious metal as possible into the country and preserve a favorable balance of trade.[64]

The religious ideas of the middle class took on an ascetic coloring in the same degree as economic conditions forced them to lead an ascetic life. A characteristic Calvinist business ethic grew up, encouraging great business acumen together with life-long self-denial. Protestant worldly asceticism acted powerfully against the spontaneous enjoyment of property, but at the same time it freed the acquisition of property from the inhibitions of traditional ethics. It not only legalized the "impulse of acquisition," but deemed it to be directly willed by God.[65] This religious attitude helped pave the way for one of the necessary conditions of the rise of modern capitalism, the accumulation of capital. It far surpassed older church doctrines in providing the employer with a welcome justification for his attitude toward the lower classes. Weber writes that the bourgeois entrepreneur, conscious of the fullness of God's grace and of being visibly blessed by Him, could follow his pecuniary interests as he would and feel that he was thus fulfilling a duty, so long as he remained within the bounds of formal correctness, so long as his moral conduct was spotless and the use to which he put his wealth was not objectionable. His consciousness gave him the comforting assurance that unequal distribution of the goods of this world is a special dispensation of a Providence that pursues secret ends unknown to men.[66] This justification of his social position enabled the employer to set himself up as a moral judge of others and to impose his own habits of work as general rules of conduct for the less fortunate. The hardships accepted by the dominant classes were expected of the lower classes to a still greater degree. When the supply of labor is low, special means of forcing people to compete for work become necessary if the level of capitalist profit is to be maintained. Calvin's frequently quoted saying that the people, that is to say, the masses of laborers and craftsmen, remain obedient to God only when they are poor, is to be understood in this sense. Weber is quite right when he remarks that the interests of God and the interests of the employers are curiously harmonious in a conception which finds the criterion of the worker's saintliness in his conscience about his duty, not in his external confession of faith.[67]

Such a philosophy was naturally unable to leave anything over for the beggars and it opposed the Catholic practice of indiscriminate almsgiving. The religious principle which endorsed the support of beggars who were capable of work and whose laziness was merely increased by alms must have seemed as stupid to the sober Calvinist as the worldly principle of wiping them off the face of the earth. The Calvinist knew a better way to use this unexploited source of wealth, and he justified his practice by condemning beggary as the sin of slothfulness and as a violation of the duty of brotherly love.[68]

In the sixteenth century, more and more emphasis was placed on the distinction between able-bodied beggars and beggars unable to work. The former were regarded as proper subjects for a rational system of social welfare, the latter as subjects for criminal policy.[69] This is fully confirmed by the regulations of the German towns dealing with poor relief within the framework of local administration. The municipal regulations of

Wittenberg and Leisnitz (influenced by Luther) introduced inadequate arrangements, but the large free imperial cities (Nürnberg, Augsburg, Strassburg) set up thoroughly rational systems covering all the aspects of poor relief. In theory these systems represented a marked advance. The Nürnberg statute, for example, thought of everything: prohibition of beggary, provision of work and tools, advances of money to poverty-stricken craftsmen, distribution of alms, begging licenses for those unable to work, and so on.[70] But in practice they rarely achieved success and their attitude compared badly with former church measures, as can be seen from the following complaint made by a priest in 1534:

I accuse them of almost completely destroying the establishment for the relief of the poor built up by our fathers at great expense, and of rendering it useless. In former times, there were Christians who so loved the poor that they called them fathers and sons, washed their feet, prepared meals for them, served them at table as did our Lord Himself. Now they are forbidden to enter the towns and are driven away, men close their doors against them as though they were wrong-doers and public enemies.[71]

Although the doctrines of the Reformation, and particularly the radical rejection of good works, may have strengthened the trend toward a new treatment of beggary, they were not the principal causes of the change. At the instigation of Vives, for example, the Catholic town of Ypres introduced poor laws exactly like the measures of the Protestant towns.[72] It was the economic situation, the general deterioration of living conditions as reflected in the enormous increase in beggary, which obliged the towns to make new rules at the beginning of the sixteenth century. The treatment of beggars as criminals is one indication of the helplessness which the authorities felt in handling this superfluous human material and of the resulting harshness of their measures. An English statute of 1547 provided that all vagrants who refused to work or who ran away could be adjudged slaves of their masters for two years; second offenders could be sentenced to slavery for life, and third offenders to death.[73] In France, the first half of the sixteenth century saw the introduction of public works, such as the construction of fortresses and road making and cleaning, for the employment of vagrants.[74] The problem of beggary remains unsolved, however, because none of these schemes provided sufficient employment, and the authorities were actually forced to legalize mendicity by granting a certain number of begging permits.[75]

From the end of the sixteenth century, the increasing scarcity of labor forced a change in the treatment of the poor, a change which is reflected in the attitudes toward beggary expressed in contemporary writing. In a pamphlet of 1641, which bears the significant title, *STANLEY'S REMEDY: Or, the Way how to Reform Wandring Beggers, Theeves, High-way Robbers, and Pick-pockets: Or, an Abstract of his Discoverie; wherein is shewed, that Sodome's Sin of Idleness is the Poverty and Misery of this Kingdome: By some Well-wishers to the Honour of God, and the Publike Good, both of Rich and Poore,* a robber who was pardoned by Queen Elizabeth after having received a sentence of death calculated the loss sustained by the commonwealth as a result of the idleness of 80,000 beggars who could be put to useful work.[76] The characteristic complaints of the later Middle Ages about the offenses against property and other serious crimes committed by despairing creatures who had no means of subsistence give way to complaints about the laziness of beggars and the resulting loss to the country.

The people who tramped and begged their way through the country and streamed into the towns during the mercantilist period in search of favorable living conditions were not always unable to defend themselves against social oppression, except in times of unusual distress. If the conditions offered by employers seemed too harsh, they threw themselves upon private charity in preference to regular employment. At this time, the beggars' income, like government unemployment benefits today, was the limit below which wages could not sink. Workers often became beggars when they wanted a holiday for a longer or shorter period of time, or when they sought a breathing spell in which to find more congenial or more profitable employment.

Everywhere there were bitter complaints about the shortage of labor caused by mendicancy.[77] The repressive poor laws took this problem into consideration. In contrast to the policy at the beginning of the sixteenth century, with its chief aim the elimination of beggary, the new program was more directly economic in purpose. It sought to prevent the poor from withholding their labor power, as they used to do by begging in preference to working for low wages.[78] A Brussels decree of 1599 established penalties for able-bodied beggars, domestic servants who left their masters, and workmen who left their employment in order to become beggars. A French decree of 1724 justified the punishment of able-bodied beggars on the ground that they really deprived the poor of bread, since they withheld their labor power from town and village.[79] The definitions of rogue, vagabond, and sturdy beggar in an English statute of 1597 are further evidence of the change in attitude, for these terms included all laborers who refused to work at prevailing wages.[80]

We are therefore led to the conclusion that the adoption, at the end of the seventeenth century, of a more humane method for the repression of vagrancy, the institution of the house of correction, was also the outcome of a change in general economic conditions. The new legislative policy on begging was a direct expression of the new economic policy. With the help of its legislative and administrative machinery, the state used the labor contingent, which it found at its disposal, for the prosecution of its new aims.

3. THE RISE OF THE HOUSE OF CORRECTION

The earliest institution created for the specific purpose of ridding the towns of vagabonds and beggars was probably the Bridewell in London (1555).[81] The act of 1576, which we have already mentioned, provided for the establishment of similar institutions in every county.[82] England thus led the way in time, but the development reached its peak in Holland for a number

of reasons.[83] At the end of the sixteenth century, Holland had
the most highly developed capitalist system in Europe, but it
did not have the reserve of labor power which existed in England after the enclosure movement. We have already referred
to the high wages and favorable labor conditions prevailing in
Holland, with its unusually short working day. Innovations
destined to reduce the cost of production were naturally welcome. Every effort was made to draw upon all the available labor
reserves, not only to absorb them into economic activity but,
further, to "resocialize" them in such a way that in the future
they would enter the labor market freely.

This approach was strengthened by Calvinism. How could a
society which accepted a thoroughly rationalized asceticism as
its official creed allow the lower classes to disregard its commandment to labor? People who were satisfied with the earnings of a
four-day week and who preferred to spend the rest of their time
as they chose were asked to believe that the duty of work is
itself the true aim of life. Obviously, many workers could not
be persuaded to accept the new theory voluntarily, nor was the
strict discipline set forth in the Catechism always sufficient to
solve the social problems. More extreme measures were necessary, hence the houses of correction, where those who were un-
willing were forced to make their everyday practice conform to
the needs of industry.

The example of Amsterdam was studied and followed everywhere in Europe, particularly in the German-speaking countries.[84] The essence of the house of correction was that it combined the principles of the poorhouse, workhouse, and penal
institution. Its main aim was to make the labor power of un-
willing people socially useful. By being forced to work within
the institution, the prisoners would form industrious habits
and would receive a vocational training at the same time. When
released, it was hoped, they would voluntarily swell the labor
market.

The usual inmates were able-bodied beggars, vagabonds,
idlers, prostitutes, and thieves. Only petty offenders were received at first, and later men who had been flogged, branded,

and sentenced to long terms.[85] As the reputation of the institution became more firmly established, citizens began to intern their ne'er-do-well children and spendthrift dependents. In general, the composition of the houses of correction appears to have developed along the same lines everywhere.[86] A number of towns went further and admitted the poor and needy, when they could not earn a living.[87] This last category occupied a particularly important place in the French *Hôpitaux généraux*, which even fed and gave work to widows and orphans. The first *Hôpital général* was founded in Paris in 1656, and others soon came into existence all over France as a result of the energetic activity of the Jesuits Chauraud, Dunod, and Guevarre.[88]

The labor power of the inmates was utilized in one of two ways: either the authorities ran the institution themselves or the occupants were hired out to a private employer. Occasionally the whole establishment was hired out to a contractor. Male inmates were occupied chiefly in rasping the hard woods used by the dyers, a practice first introduced in Amsterdam. This was particularly difficult work, requiring considerable strength and stamina. Prisoners worked in pairs with a twelve-bladed saw, and the normal week's output for two men was three hundred pounds of wood. One hundred pounds had to be delivered every other day.[89] In the eighteenth century, the Dutch found wool manufacture to be more profitable and introduced it into several houses of correction.[90] The women inmates, chiefly prostitutes and beggars, were engaged in the preparation of textiles.[91]

In France, as in Amsterdam, most of the work was performed under the direct management of the establishments. In the London Bridewell, hiring out was more frequent, often accompanied by special provisions for the training of apprentices.[92] Bremen, Lübeck, and Hamburg appear to have followed the Amsterdam model both in management and in the nature of the work performed. In Brandenburg, where the lease system was more frequent and where whole establishments were rented to private individuals,[93] the economic side of the system came to the fore most strongly. Some light is thrown on this point by the contract of Küstrin of 1750, which contained a clause recommending clemency for offending inmates. The sole reason offered was that they should not be rendered incapable of continuing their spinning.[94] The decree of 1687 which founded the Spandau House of Correction frankly announced that the object of the institution was to promote the production of textiles and to remedy the lack of spinning wheels in the country.[95] Whenever the hiring system was practiced, as in Holland for example, the economic interest of the lessee meant the depression of the condition of the prisoners to the lowest possible level.[96] In order to assure the financial success of the institution itself, the inmates were usually required to continue working for a considerable period after they completed their training, and thus to repay the cost of board and education.[97]

Criminals were often admitted from abroad, especially from little neighboring states where the small number of inmates made it inexpedient to use the prisons for forced labor.[98] Outsiders incapable of work, however, were not accepted unless their sponsors paid considerable sums of money. Their reception was not legally obligatory and they would only be a burden on the budget. Payment was always required from parents introducing miscreant children and from persons introducing spendthrifts or other undesirable relatives.[99]

Training of efficient workers was the chief preoccupation of the authorities, and that met with fierce opposition from the guilds. From the very beginning the guilds considered prison labor an infringement of their monopoly. It was therefore difficult to persuade them to provide the institutions with teachers,[100] and the state often turned to so-called *Freimeister*, that is to say, nonguild artisans who were given master privileges. We hear of lawsuits brought by the guilds in Bremen and Troyes in an attempt to stop the whole system.[101] The authorities maintained their position, however, especially in Brandenburg, where decrees of 1710 and 1716 required the guilds to accept workers trained in the houses of correction.[102] The French *Hôpitaux généraux* occupied themselves with the improvement and application of new methods of production. The directors of the various *Hôpitaux* exchanged notes on their experiences, and they encouraged one another to adopt new methods and to make use of all the available human material to this end. It was even proposed to marry inmates trained in complementary occupations, in order to transmit special technical abilities.[103]

In reply to the accusation of unfair competition with private enterprise, a house of correction occasionally offered to accept work for a business firm on the institution's premises and at its low rate of wages.[104] Private enterprise, on the other hand, did not hesitate to use prison labor in order to destroy competition. The honorable body of lens grinders of Nürnberg, for example, adopted the plan of underselling their competitors of Fürth by exploiting the labor in the *Lochgefängnis*.[105]

The Jesuit Father Dunod, in his introductory address recommending the establishment of *Hôpitaux généraux*, said: "They are at once a religious institution, a seminary, and manufactories." [106] Despite the differences of creed between Amsterdam and Germany on the one hand, and the France of Louis XIII and Louis XIV on the other, the use of religion as a means of inculcating discipline and hard labor was an essential feature of these institutions everywhere. The first clause of the section on discipline in the regulations of the Amsterdam house, compiled between 1599 and 1603, contains the words: "In the first place, every inmate must render thanks . . . . to God the Lord, morning, noon, and night, according to the ancient tradition; the first failure to comply will be punished by loss of a meal, the second according to the discretion of the authorities." [107] The general provisions required attendance at Sunday and Saint's Day services.[108] The curriculum of the French *Hôpitaux généraux* was similar; the everyday life of the inmates was regulated with the utmost precision.[109] In order to increase the productivity of their labor, they were given a share of the profits. Article 19 of the French edict of 1656 phrases it in this way: "In order to make the occupants work with greater zeal and affection in the manufactories, they will be given a third of the proceeds of their work." [110] The fact that the productivity of labor was a primary consideration becomes still clearer when we learn that religious duties had to give way whenever they threatened to reduce efficiency. If mass coincided with the early hour fixed for the beginning of work, it was celebrated still earlier and the catechism was omitted.[111]

The erection of new buildings and, what was more frequent, the adaptation of old buildings were usually paid for by the authorities. There were occasional private endowments, however, such as the *Spinnhaus* for dishonest persons erected in Hamburg in 1669. The *Spinnhaus* charter reveals the middle-class philosophy of the period after the Reformation, with its characteristic attitude toward welfare work. It reads in part:

Mr. Peter Rentzel of revered memory, Doctor of Civil and Ecclesiastical Law and Councillor of this town, who experienced many cases during his councillorship in which punishment levied on wrongdoers bore little fruit, really hardening offenders in their evil doing, conceived the very Christian idea of erecting a *Spinnhaus* at his own cost and endowing it with a sum of 10,000 Marks, to the greater glory of God and for the salvation of the souls of many evil men, so that all such evildoers may be enclosed therein, brought to the fear of God, and put to work and saved from temporal and eternal damnation.[112]

The authorities frequently levied a special tax for a house of correction. This was done in Pforzheim, for example, in the hope that the institution would ultimately render the local poor relief fund unnecessary.[113] It is not clear whether the wealthy really profited by those establishments, for which they had to pay costs and taxes. De Morangis, the intendant of Caen, wrote to Colbert in 1683: "These establishments suppress mendicity and idleness, and the astonishing thing is that the wealthy admit that when their alms are given with order and justice, they are less than when given to passing paupers and professional beggars." [114] The satisfaction was sometimes more ephemeral in character, however, as in England where the creation of these establishments did not lead to the expected reduction in poor rates.[115]

One way of getting around the financial difficulties was to pack the administrative council of the institution with wealthy men who were expected to advance the funds needed to set it on its feet.[116] It was a recognized principle in France, at least in the earlier stages, that no one should be placed on the council who might seek to profit personally. Article 65 of the ordonnance of Blois required the appointment of men of property, merchants, and laborers on the ground that they would be economically minded and trained in business methods.[117] At the end of the *ancien régime*, however, appointment to an administrative position in one of the *Hôpitaux généraux* was regarded as a sure road to wealth.[118]

In Brandenburg, the administration shifted the operating costs by leasing the establishment and requiring the lessee to pay his rent in advance. The lower officials were paid by the state or municipality, and their small wage was supplemented by the brandy monopoly.[119] It is apparent from this example that the state placed its own financial interests ahead of the reform of the inmates. In some cases, an attempt was made to provide the establishments with permanent sources of income by granting them certain monopolies and the proceeds of certain taxes. The Amsterdam *Zuchthaus* (for men) received the fines imposed upon town councilors for being late at council meetings. The fines for adultery went to the *Spinnhaus* (for women).[120] Every official in Delft had to make a contribution to the house of correction upon his appointment or promotion.[121] In Bremen, the administrators complained about the large advances they had made and they were twice permitted to organize lotteries.[122] A Paris decree of Feb. 26, 1752, assigned the proceeds of the custom duties on wine to the institutions.[123]

The most valuable of all these sources of income was probably the wood monopoly of the Amsterdam house. First granted in 1602, it carried with it the sole right to rasp hard wood for commercial purposes. The other Dutch establishments were allowed to rasp hard wood only for the use of local authorities. As the latter activity did not pay while the former was quite profitable, the monopoly rights were often violated by other institutions, especially in Leyden and Rotterdam, and by private individuals. A lawsuit between Leyden and Amsterdam arising from such an infringement was argued before the courts in 1676–77, and decided in favor of Amsterdam. The monopoly could not be maintained for practical reasons, however, since the Amsterdam house did not have enough inmates to satisfy the requirements of the whole of Holland.[124]

It is impossible to draw any general conclusion about the success of the houses of correction from a purely business standpoint. Account must be taken of time, place, and character of the inmates, and efficiency and mentality of the administration. The French *Hôpitaux généraux,* with their heterogeneous population and their corrupt administration, ran into debt in the second half of the seventeenth century. In 1657, the income of the Paris *Hôpitaux* was 589,536 livres, and their expenses 586,- 966 livres, but by 1667 the expenses had risen to 895,222 livres, the income to but 776,869. The development in the provinces was much the same.[125] The *Hôpitaux* cannot be taken as typical, however, for the general economic conditions of France were deteriorating in this period. A Hungarian traveler, Martin Csombor, visited the Amsterdam establishment in 1619 and received the impression that the town derived excessive profits from it.[126] Other contemporary writers, such as Bornitius and Döpler, marveled at the enormous income.[127] Some of these statements may be exaggerated, but it is certain that the possibility of profits was a decisive motive for the institution of houses of correction. Henelius, one of their most active protagonists, argued for replacing the death penalty by confinement on the ground that execution may be cheap from a short-term view, but it is unproductive and therefore expensive from a long-term view, whereas the new form of punishment forces those who had injured the state to work for its profit.[128] The importance of the profit motive is well illustrated by the curious *Zucht- und Arbeitshaus, sowie Kriminalinstitut* of the Imperial Count Schenk von Castell zu Oberdischingen im Kreis Schwaben.[129] German constitutional law did not give him the right to erect prisons, but he built one anyway, and then went on to collect the rogues of all Württemberg, exceeding the legal limits of his jurisdiction. After imprisoning them, he initiated proceedings against them in the hope of finding some valid ground for their further detention and profitable employment.[130]

Wagnitz, who had first-hand knowledge of eighteenth-century houses of correction, argued that since an able-bodied man could find enough work to earn his keep, the Prince would have no expenses apart from the initial outlay, and there would even be a surplus for the support of aged and decrepit paupers. Without too great an effort, elderly and feeble people can spin enough yarn to cover their keep, entirely apart from the advantage that the state would gain from the manufacture. Wagnitz pointed out further that the inmates actually produced a considerable surplus, from which the institution derived profits.[131] Writing in the first half of the nineteenth century, Füsslin gave the industrious Netherlanders the credit for having introduced houses of correction as early as the sixteenth century, although their motive was less ethical than material. It was sad, he thought, but common throughout history, that improvements in the life of a nation or of mankind in general do not come about without the stimulus of some temporary advantage. The barbarity of the penal system had become more and more hateful to advancing civilization, but what the philanthropist and the spread of enlightenment had failed to accomplish was achieved in a moment by the financial value of the house of correction, and he regarded the latter as an undesirable accompaniment of reform.[132] Hippel's valuable study on the evolution of the modern prison is especially representative of this viewpoint. He accused the founders of allowing pecuniary advantages to outweigh the more important consideration, the educational value of prison work.[133] This attitude overlooks the fact that the reform of any human institution depends upon the value attributed to the individual within a given society.

A Swiss report of 1803 illustrates the difference between the seventeenth- and eighteenth-century conception of the house of correction as a center of production and more recent views. The report states that the inmates have generally taken to crime as a result of idleness, and that work is the greatest of evils for them.

Confinement without labor would be no punishment, and the first requirement, therefore, is to force the inmates to work under strict discipline. If the government finds itself financially unable to carry out a particular branch of production, the prisoners should be put to work on less expensive material. Food should be given only in return for work done.[134] The report was written at a time when people were beginning to regard it as the duty of society to look after those of its members who were in distress. Treatment of the inmates is the central problem. Work is not examined in its relation to national production, and the productivity of labor receives a secondary position because it is taken for granted that the administration will bear the costs.

The seventeenth and eighteenth centuries knew little of such a conception. Policy toward the poor was haphazard and criminal policy was purely repressive and shortsighted. The institution of houses of correction in such a society was not the result of brotherly love or of an official sense of obligation to the distressed. It was part of the development of capitalism. Hallema, the historian of the Dutch prison system, is right, therefore, when he says that the houses of correction were primarily manufactories, turning out commodities at a particularly low cost because of their cheap labor.[135] It is probable, then, that they were generally paying concerns. That was clearly the intention of their founders.[136]

It is equally certain that the houses of correction were very valuable for the national economy as a whole. Their low wages and their training of unskilled workers were important contributing factors in the rise of capitalist production. Contemporary writers and economic historians were agreed on this point. In Döpler's description, for example, great stress is laid on the enrichment of the national economy which accompanied the work of rehabilitation. The moral and material advantages of "modern" imprisonment, he says, arise because the inmates are turned aside from their wickedness to piety, from vice to virtue, from the road to destruction to the straight path of salvation, from the sloth that makes men stupid and sleepy to work that is useful for themselves and for society. When they are reformed, they will know how to earn their bread, and it is advantageous to the state that the idlers and rogues who will not work or improve their situation of their own accord should not be a burden on the industrious workers, but should be compelled to work against their will, by flogging and other means. Finally, Döpler points out, their labor in the production of useful goods will repay the initial investment.[137] Modern students of economic history also have emphasized the economic role of the house of correction. Kulischer writes that, like orphanages, they were to be trade schools and nurseries of industry, spreading all kinds of useful things throughout the country. He argues from this that the industries begun in the houses of forced labor were regarded as contributions to the industry of the country.[138]

It is interesting to note that the success of the Amsterdam institution led to the publication of a pamphlet which describes the wonderful miracles performed daily in the House of Correction of the world-renowned town of Amsterdam.[139] The author, a militant Protestant, gives his account the character of a polemic against Catholicism, and he ridicules the miracles of the Church by comparing them with the miracles actually performed in the houses of correction. The twelve-bladed saw for rasping wood appears as St. Raspinus, and other forms of hard labor appear as St. Ponus and St. Labor. Together these three saints perform their miracles on the patients, who pay with great devotion. The examples sited in the pamphlet clearly reveal the confidence which was placed in the methods used, for cases of laziness, debauchery, and malingering are confused with real illness, for which St. Ponus always has a remedy.

As for the problem of Catholic and Protestant influence on the institutions, it is true that the theoretical justification of the new ethic of work was essentially Calvinist in origin. But, just as French Catholicism went a long way in its theoretical concessions to the philosophy of the rising bourgeoisie, it also played a major role in the establishment of the *Hôpitaux généraux*. It was the Jesuits who introduced the *Hôpitaux* into the provinces. Joret says that Louis XIV's campaign against poverty might have been partially unsuccessful without the energetic support of several Jesuit Fathers.[140] It would be more correct to say that the condition of the poor under Louis XIV would have been even worse if not for the activity of certain Jesuits. The fact that both the old and the new religious doctrines collaborated in the actual development of the new institution goes to prove that purely ideological viewpoints took second place to economic motives as driving forces in the whole movement.[141]

IV

CHANGES IN THE FORM OF
PUNISHMENT

I N THE foregoing chapter we have seen how certain economic changes helped to bring about an increase in the value placed upon human life and led the state to make practical use of the man power at its disposal. The idea of utilizing the potential labor of the criminal was not new. From time to time thoughtful men had come to the same conclusion as the inhabitants of More's Utopia, that it is unwise to execute offenders because their labor is more profitable than their death.[1] But this idea could not be put into practice unless the dominant tendencies of the age were favorable to it. Until then, people who believed in it were considered cranks, and public practice followed those who advocated cruelty. Earlier thinkers were resurrected and hailed as misunderstood "forerunners" only after the conditions had changed.

1. THE GALLEY

Galley slavery persisted even after the end of the economic system based upon slavery, because the strenuous and hazardous nature of the work made it difficult to recruit free men. The need for rowers became particularly urgent toward the end of the fifteenth century with the onset of the period of naval wars among the Mediterranean powers, Christian and Mohammedan. These wars gave added impetus to the old practice of drafting oarsmen from among prisoners. The number needed for a single ship was very large, three hundred and fifty for one of the big galleys, called a *galéasse*, and one hundred and eighty for a smaller boat.[2] Decrees of Charles V and Philip II of Spain introduced this form of punishment for major offenders as well as for beggars and vagabonds. An edict of Margaret of Parma organized vagabond hunts in the Netherlands at the instigation of Philip

II who was unable to procure large enough crews for his galleys.[3] The practice was widespread in France from the sixteenth century on. In 1771, when Joussé wrote his *Traité de la justice criminelle en France,* galley servitude was the punishment for forgers, thieves sentenced for the second time, and beggars for the third, among others.[4]

Galley servitude was introduced into the Austrian part of the Holy Roman Empire at about the same time. In 1556, Andrea Doria received letters of patent from the Emperor Ferdinand giving him the right to take men from the Bohemian prisons for the Turkish war. The Emperor preferred this punishment of robbers and murderers to the death penalty, he said, because in this way they could do greater penance for their sins, while being profitably employed against the Turks.[5] Similarly in Spain, Spinola approached Duke Albrecht of Bavaria and the authorities of the south German towns for criminals to be used in the galleys in order to reduce transport costs. An agreement between Spinola's representative, Panzer, and the Nürnberg town council stipulated that Spinola should be responsible for the expenses and risks of transporting them, while the city promised not to pronounce sentences of less than three years. To the end of 1573, Nürnberg supplied about forty men who ranged from common thieves and vagrants to murderers.[6]

In spite of new letters of patent from Maximilian II in 1570, and in spite of concentrated efforts by the city authorities, the attempt to get rid of prisoners by sending them to the galleys was rendered difficult by the high cost and long delays involved in transporting them, which made the traffic unprofitable for the entrepreneurs.[7] The south German towns tried to remedy the situation by selling their prisoners to the Italian cities, as some Swiss city authorities had been doing for a long time. In 1571, for example, a treaty was contracted between Bern and Savoy for the delivery of prisoners.[8] The Thirty Years' War interrupted this traffic, at least as far as Germany was concerned. Later, transport arrangements became cheaper and more efficient when they were carried out between the governments directly, without the aid of middlemen.[9]

What is significant in the development of the galley as a method of punishment is the fact that economic considerations alone were involved, not penal. This is true for both the sentence and its execution. The introduction and regulation of galley servitude were determined solely by the desire to obtain necessary labor on the cheapest possible basis. In Colbert's France, for example, the administration brought strong pressure on the courts for enough prisoners to maintain the crews at full strength. A letter of February 21, 1676, directs the attention of the public prosecutor of the Paris *Parlement* to the presence in the *Conciergerie* of a large number of prisoners capable of serving in the galleys. The letter says quite bluntly that,

since His Majesty urgently needs more men to strengthen His rowing crews . . . . to be delivered at the end of the following month, His Majesty commands me to tell you that He wishes you to take the necessary steps in His name in order to have the criminals judged quickly.[10]

The courts hastened to comply, as the following report of the public prosecutor at Bordeaux reveals:

You have frequently done me the honor of writing to me in connection with the supply of prisoners for the galleys and of transmitting to me the express orders of His Majesty relating to the use of such prisoners in the execution of His glorious projects. You will be gratified to learn that this Court has twenty prisoners who will be chained together this morning and sent off.[11]

The administration sometimes went to the length of organizing man hunts for oarsmen. Thus, the intendant of Orange writes that he is particularly eager to catch Huguénots who had behaved insolently during a religious procession.[12]

In the actual management of the galleys, the predominant aim was again to obtain the greatest possible benefit from the labor. A French decree of 1664 sets the minimum galley sentence at ten years. The argument is that the men must first get their sea legs, and then it would be foolish to free them just when they had begun to be useful to the state.[13] A Venetian decree of 1588 approaches this simple economic problem in another way.

It rules that galley servitude for life should be reduced to twelve years, because the convicts are unable to perform the required work for a longer period, and then they would have to be clothed and fed without adequate return in the form of labor power.[14] Contemporary opinion agrees that release from the galleys—if the convict survived at all, which was rather problematical—was determined in practice solely by the question as to whether the prisoners were still able-bodied or not. There were explicit rules that they should not be held beyond the expiration of their terms and that they should carry a copy of the sentence with them as evidence. These rules were frequently violated, however.[15]

Galley servitude declined in the eighteenth century for various reasons. In France, the great technical improvements in the art of sailing led to the substitution of forced labor in the *bagno* (Toulon and Marseilles).[16] An Austrian decree of 1724 tried to extend the use of galley servitude, but this only led to an excessive supply of labor. In 1728, for example, eighteen hundred convicts were assembled, and could not be absorbed in the galleys. The Austrian government then sought other outlets for these prisoners, such as the mines, but the Breslau town council, for one, objected that the free laborer's standard of living would be affected much too adversely. An Austrian decree of 1762 finally abolished galley servitude altogether.[17]

Seventeenth-century opinion generally held that the galleys were more humane than previous criminal practice, since such punishment served the interests of the convict as well as the state. The author of the article "Galérien" in Diderot's *Encyclopedia* wrote: "The introduction of galley slavery was a wise measure. It keeps men, whose crimes would have exiled them or led to capital punishment, in the service of the state without danger to society. Furthermore, it is in accord with the dictates of humanity." [18] A modern author adopts a similar viewpoint when he writes that the utilization of men in the galleys was a means of combining loss of liberty with forced labor while serving the interests of retribution, keeping the criminals out of mischief, and reforming their character at one and the same time—in other words, the galley system combined the main features of the prison system.[19] These opinions have been strongly disputed, and quite correctly, on the grounds that galley service had much more in common with corporal punishment than with imprisonment.[20]

The texts of the decrees and orders make it quite clear that the substitution of galley labor for the death penalty was a result of the need for more oarsmen and not of humanitarian considerations. They provide for commutation only on the basis of bodily strength, not special personal circumstances justifying clemency. A particularly drastic order was sent to the public prosecutor in Paris on September 11, 1677, at the command of Louis XIV:

His Majesty has instructed me to inform you that in the cases of prisoners who are over fifty-five years of age or who have lost an arm or a leg or are disabled or incurably sick, His Majesty does not wish His judges to invoke this order in order to exempt prisoners from sentences which they really merit.[21]

The attitude of the convicts is revealed by the frequency of self-mutilations inflicted for the purpose of avoiding the galleys. The practice became so extensive that a French decree of 1677 established the death penalty for it.[22]

Sixteenth- and seventeenth-century opinion was well aware of the terrible fate of the galley slaves, but nothing was done to better their condition. Thanks to his position as former tutor in the Gondi family which had purchased from Louis XIII the general command over the galleys in the seas and armies of the Levant, St. Vincent de Paul was able to devote himself to the spiritual salvation of the oarsmen. He became general almoner for all galleys and prisons in 1619, but he could not effect any real improvement in their material situation.[23] The hospital for old and disabled galley slaves, which he founded in Marseilles in 1643 with the support of Richelieu, could not alter the fact that galley labor was tantamount to a slow and painful death.[24]

In sum, sentence to the galleys was the most rational way to procure labor for tasks for which free labor could never be found, even when economic conditions were at their worst. Reformation of the convicts played no role in the establishment or further development of galley servitude.

2. THE EARLY HISTORY OF THE TRANSPORTATION OF CRIMINALS [25]

Another way of utilizing the labor power of convicts was to ship them to colonies and distant military settlements. Spain and Portugal were doing this as early as the fifteenth century, but then abandoned the practice because man power was urgently needed for the galleys. England became the first country to introduce systematic transportation of criminals, a method of punishment made necessary by her colonial expansion. The purpose of the following brief discussion is to show how this innovation in penology is analogous to galley servitude in that the need for labor power was the driving force in both cases.[26]

Overseas colonies had huge tracts of land available for cultivation and there was a great demand for the colonial products in Europe. Each colonist, says Adam Smith,

is eager . . . . to collect laborers from all quarters, and to reward them with the most liberal wages. But those liberal wages, joined to the plenty and cheapness of land, soon make these laborers leave him, in order to become landlords themselves, and to reward, with equal liberality other laborers, who soon leave them for the same reason that they left their first master.[27]

There was thus a constant shortage of labor in the colonies and the search for workers became a pressing problem. Settlers attempted to enslave the natives but the latter too often fled in groups to the vast open spaces of the colonies. The native population was quickly decimated by war, compulsory labor of unusual severity, and disease. The only alternative was to import workers, and that meant forced labor, in the main. The demand was so great that a new crime came into being—kidnaping. In the middle of the seventeenth century there were numerous instances of organized bands of kidnapers in the seaport towns seizing children, generally of the poorer classes, and selling them into slavery in the colonies.[28]

In England, however, transportation was held to be contrary to the interests of the mother country, where workers were needed so badly. Colonization, Furniss relates, was condemned because it reduced the number of working hands and robbed the country of their contribution to the wealth of the nation. It was export of the prime material of the country's wealth without a sufficient return.[29] As one contemporary phrased it,

they have drained us of multitudes of our people who might have been serviceable at home, and advanced improvements in husbandry and manufactures; that this kingdom is worse peopled, by so much as they are increased; and that inhabitants being the wealth of a nation, by how much they are lessened, by so much we are poorer than when we first began to settle those colonies.[30]

The simplest way to supply the needs of the colonies without prejudice to the interests of the mother country was to send out convicts who would normally be executed. Referring to the example of Spain, Governor Dole of Virginia wrote to the King in 1611, asking that prisoners under sentence of death be sent to the colony for three years. This, he thought, would be a good way to populate the new country.[31] Prizes were even offered in order to encourage the importation of convicts.

The Vagrancy Act of 1597 legalized deportation for the first time by providing that "such rogues as shall be thought fitt not to be delivered shall be banyshed out of this Realme and all the domynions thereof and shall be conveied to such partes beyond the seas as shall be at any tyme hereafter for that purpose assigned by the Private Counsell." [32] Batches of dissolute persons were sporadically transported to Virginia from its foundation in 1606. An Order in Council of 1617 granted reprieve and stay of execution to those persons convicted of robbery and felony who were strong enough to be employed in service beyond the sea.[33] This decree resembles the order of Louis XIV and the decree of Margaret of Parma on the commutation of death sentences to galley servitude, in that it calls for consideration of bodily strength before allowing commutation. It also mentioned correction of the prisoners as a motive, but that had no real meaning because of the implication that only criminals

who were strong or had special abilities were capable of rehabilitation. Or must we assume that the author subscribed to such
a radical theory of selection that the only proof of capacity for
improvement was the possibility of "profitable service to the
Commonwealth in partes abroad"? [34] Commutation of sentence
to transportation was very profitable for the judges and clerks
involved, and at least 4,431 prisoners "benefited" between 1655
and 1699.[35]

A further extension came with the statutes of 1718 and 1720.
Transportation now became the regular sentence for larceny and
felonious stealing and not merely a commutation at the discretion of the judge. The reason given for the change was the great
need for servants to develop the colonial plantations.[36] Transportation cost the government little. Until 1772, the contractors
received a grant of five pounds per convict. Later, they did not
charge anything because, having become owners of the convicts,
they were able to derive enough profit by disposing of their
labor. Male laborers in Virginia and Maryland were worth ten
pounds each in the course of the eighteenth century, females
eight to nine, artificers between fifteen and twenty-five. The
wealthier prisoners could buy themselves off and thus convert
the sentence into mere banishment.[37] The number shipped to
North America was very considerable. The Old Bailey alone
supplied at least 10,000 between 1717 and 1775.[38]

The only difference between the deported convicts and slaves
was that the former were under constraint for a limited period
of time, after which they were freed. In other words, they were
not sold but were hired out for the duration of their sentence.
The general view in the colonies was that their importation did
not really constitute a punishment, since the more capable, at
any rate, had never lived so well or so easily in England. A
number, including some who had been labeled "incorrigible
rogues," became reformed characters in their new surround-
ings. Many indentured servants ultimately became independent
farmers and planters, in some cases even acquiring considerable
wealth. To what extent that was also true of transported convicts

is not clear. There was certainly room for abuse and oppression by the individual master.[39]

With the introduction of Negro slavery in the last decades of the seventeenth century the conditions of the white colonial servants began to deteriorate. From 1635 on, importers of Negroes also were given a bonus, and the spread of the plantation system greatly increased the demand for slave labor. There were only 2,000 slaves in Virginia in 1671, whereas white servants numbered about 6,000. By 1708, however, there were 12,000 slaves, and about fifty years later 120,156.[40] Just before the American Revolution there were 192 ships engaged in the slave trade, and they had a gross yearly freightage of 47,000. Such a huge supply of workers considerably alleviated the "labor famine" in the colonies, and the transportation of convicts ceased to be a paying proposition, for Negro slaves tended to bring a higher price than criminals whose labor was available for only a limited period of time.[41]

Once transportation ceased to pay, the colonists realized that it was a shameful business unworthy of them. They took steps against the "humiliating obligation of receiving every year an importation of the refuse of the British population." [42] Furthermore, most of the colonists consisted of people who had crossed the ocean because they were dissatisfied with conditions at home. They based their freedom and independence on their own work, and were therefore bitter opponents of the large plantation owners who relied on forced labor. Their discontent was opposed by the financial interests of the English court, however. A great many people in England who were interested in the new colonies considered it advantageous to increase the labor supply and to drive wages down by transporting criminals. The colonists fought back by means of statutes which levied a duty on the import of poor and disabled persons as well as on persons convicted of heinous crimes.[43] The Declaration of Independence and the Revolutionary War ended the problem by making it impossible to send any more criminals to America.

Francis Bacon once made the following pessimistic prophecy:

It is a shameful and unblessed thing to take the scum of people, and wicked condemned men, to be the people with whom you plant; and not only so, but it spoileth the plantation; for they will ever live like rogues, and not fall to work, but be lazy, and do mischief, and spend victuals, and be quickly weary, and then certify over to their country to the discredit of the plantation.[44]

After quoting this passage, Holtzendorff, a nineteenth-century German authority on criminal policy, comments that experience proved the very opposite.[45] We may add that the reform of convicts achieved under the favorable social conditions in the North American colonies proves conclusively that the categories good and bad, honest and criminal, are strictly relative.

3. THE EVOLUTION OF THE PRISON SYSTEM

Carcer enim ad continendos homines non ad puniendos haberi debet (Prisons exist only in order to keep men, not to punish them).[46] This was the dominant principle all through the Middle Ages and in the early modern period. Until the eighteenth century, jails were primarily places of detention before trial, where the defendants often spent several months or years until the case came to an end. The conditions defy description. The authorities usually made no provision for the inmate's upkeep, and the office of warden was a business proposition until the end of the eighteenth century.[47] The wealthier prisoners were able to purchase more or less tolerable conditions at a high price. Most of the poor prisoners supported themselves by begging and by alms supplied by church fraternities founded for the purpose.[48]

Sentences to imprisonment do occur, but only exceptionally.[49] The largest group of prisoners not awaiting trial probably consisted of members of the lowest classes who were jailed for their inability to pay a fine. That led to a vicious circle. Men were imprisoned because they could not pay fines, and they could not leave the prison because they were unable to repay the jailer for maintenance. The first task of a liberated prisoner was frequently the repayment of his debt to the jailer, which explains why the conception of the sturdy beggar in the English Vagrancy Act of

1597 includes ex-convicts who beg for their fees.[50] What created this appalling state of affairs was not so much intentional cruelty as the universally accepted administrative method of operating prisons on a commercial basis.[51]

The idea of exploiting the labor power of prisoners, as against the jailer's way of deriving income from them, already existed in the *opus publicum* of antiquity, a punishment for the lower classes which persisted through medieval times.[52] The smaller states and towns saw in this institution a method comparable to the galleys for disposing of prisoners. They transferred their convicts as cheaply as possible to other public bodies who employed them in forced labor or military service. But the modern prison system as a method of exploiting labor and, equally important in the mercantilist period, as a way of training new labor reserves was really the outgrowth of the houses of correction.

A theoretical distinction can be drawn between a house of correction (*Zuchthaus*), a prison for duly sentenced thieves, pickpockets, and other serious offenders, and a workhouse (*Arbeitshaus*), an institution for the detention of beggars and similar people who had run foul of the police, until they mended their ways. In practice, however, the recognition of this distinction took a slow and uneven course.

The minutes of the Amsterdam town council of July 15, 1589, read:

Whereas numerous wrongdoers, for the most part young persons, are arrested in the streets of this town daily, and whereas the attitude of the citizens is such that the juries hesitate to condemn such young persons to corporal punishment or life imprisonment, the mayors have asked whether it would not be advisable to set up a house and decree where vagabonds, wrongdoers, rogues, and the like, may be shut up and made to work for their correction.[53]

No differentiation is proposed for the various categories of offenders. An administrative order sent to the managers of the *Tuchthuis* on March 27, 1598, ruled that persons not handed over by court sentence could be accepted only upon approval of the mayors. This was a mere matter of form, however, for the same order proceeded to instruct the regents to arrest all able-bodied persons found begging without the permission of the authorities.[54] Real differentiation was hardly to be expected, for a respectable Amsterdam merchant would find little distinction between an idler arrested by the regents' officers and a thief duly tried and sentenced. Both were guilty of violating the principles of Calvinist ethics. When the council decided on November 12, 1600, to enlarge the establishment and to subdivide it according to new principles, the division was not made between condemned criminals and persons arrested for administrative reasons. The new establishment erected in 1603 housed the children whom their parents, respectable citizens, interned for correction.[55] Elsewhere we find the same failure to divide condemned persons from other inmates. The rules of the Bremen house of correction of January 26, 1609, did draw a line between various categories, but there is no indication that they were actually handled separately.[56]

The regulations of the Lübeck house drew no distinction, but it is worth noting that the administrators constantly refused to accept prisoners who had been condemned by the courts.[57] Was this due to pedagogical considerations and practical objections or simply to a bureaucratic conflict between the administration of the houses and the council, as the correspondence of the council leads one to suspect? In opposition to the latter's policy of sending more and more criminals to the house, the administration wished to uphold its honorable character. The same situation developed in Hamburg, where the necessity of wider application of prison sentences led to the establishment of a spinning house for dishonorable persons in 1669.[58] In Danzig, beggars, idlers, and persons interned by their relatives were separated from convicts as early as 1636 when the house of correction was instituted. In 1690, the courts proposed the erection of a special house for the incarceration and employment of serious offenders against whom the death sentence could hardly be applied and who could not be reformed by other punishments.[59] These instances show that the practice of sending criminals to the houses of correction did occasionally lead to a separation. Since the exploitation of labor power was the decisive consideration, however, local conditions, and particularly population problems, usually determined whether the separation indicated for pedagogical reasons would be carried out in practice.

As late as the end of the eighteenth century it was common to combine the most widely different purposes in the same institution. The Pforzheim house, supported with such affection and care by the princes of Baden, was an orphanage, as institution for the blind, deaf, and dumb, a lunatic asylum, an infant welfare center, and a penal colony, all in one.[60] The Leipzig house bore the following inscription: *Et improbis coercendis et quos deseruit sanae mentis usura custodiendis* (In order to correct the dishonest and to guard the lunatic).[61] In 1780, only 148 of the 283 inmates of the Ludwigsburg institution were convicts; the rest were orphans, paupers, or lunatics.[62] The same variety was to be found in the *Hôpitaux généraux,* although only minor criminals were included at first, because of the harsh sentences under the *ancien régime.* They, too, gradually took on the character of prisons, but without abandoning the practice of admitting the aged, the insane, and children.

The early form of the modern prison was thus bound up with the manufacturing houses of correction. Since the principal objective was not the reformation of the inmates but the rational exploitation of labor power, the manner of recruiting the inmates was not a central problem for the administration. Nor was it an important consideration in the matter of liberation. We have already seen how the period of detention in the case of young or newly trained inmates was determined solely by reference to the needs of the institution or its lessees. Valuable workers whose maintenance and training involved considerable expense must be retained as long as possible. The length of confinement was, therefore, arbitrarily fixed by the administrators in all cases except those voluntarily committed by their relatives. We hear of houses in Brandenburg where, in the absence of determinate sentences laid down in the judgment, some inmates were set free after a fortnight while other minor offenders were retained for years.[63]

The gradual rise of imprisonment was implemented by the

necessity for special treatment of women and for differentiation in the treatment of the various social strata. The majority of the women in the *Hôpitaux généraux,* for example, were guilty of crimes punished by galley slavery in the case of male offenders.[64] Incarceration in a *Hôpital* or house of correction was often employed in order to spare members of the privileged classes the humiliation of corporal punishment or galley slavery.[65] Thus, a son of a wealthy citizen of Bremen was tried for housebreaking in 1693 and sentenced to the house of correction for life at the request of his father. He was released on August 20, 1694, on condition that he go to India and not return.[66] The *poena extraordinaria,* which allowed the judge arbitrarily to increase or decrease punishments, everywhere paved the way for a broad extension of the practice of incarceration in the houses of correction.[67]

An especially interesting privilege is found in the decisions of the Tübingen faculty of law and in Württemberg decrees of the seventeenth and eighteenth centuries. The practice had developed of replacing capital or corporal punishment and banishment in the case of craftsmen by public works or confinement in houses of correction. Confirmed by several ducal decrees, this practice had two grounds. One grew out of considerations of social policy, as shown by an edict of 1620—a dishonorable judgment would have condemned the craftsman and his family to ruin by depriving him of the right to exercise his trade. The second motive was the desire to use trained craftsmen in the service of the state, and one decision explicitly justifies a sentence to public works by reference to the shortage of labor power.[68] The same motive was responsible for the replacement of banishment by the houses of correction. The legislator who exiles evil-doers is not a good householder, people argued, for every subject is a treasure and no sane man would throw a treasure away.[69] Furthermore, it was becoming clear that banishment was the least effective method of suppressing crime. It merely led criminals to shift their fields of activity and had no more utility than present-day expulsion of aliens.[70]

The tendency became rather general to replace even physical

punishment by forced labor, and to retain only those forms which "gave old Adam as much pain as possible without doing the slightest damage to a single limb of his body." [71] The necessity of keeping the state supplied with labor power was complicated by the desire not to withdraw labor power from the employers. As a result, economic considerations occasionally led to the opposite of the prevailing tendency, that is, to the retention of corporal punishment, especially in agricultural regions. An additional argument in the case of farm servants arose from the fact that imprisonment was no deterrent when their conditions were so bad. Knapp relates that in Upper Silesia as late as the end of the eighteenth century many punishments administered to farm laborers and gardeners failed to stop their stealing. When the master threatened them with hard labor, they would tell him to his face that they preferred ten years of that to one year on his lordship's estate. [72] The landowners drew the conclusion that some form of punishment should be chosen for serfs which did not entail a loss to the landowners themselves. [73] It must be emphasized that these were exceptional cases created by the social and political situation of the eastern farm laborer, which temporarily increased the value of corporal punishment.

The increasing proportion of sentences to houses of correction was brought about by judicial practice and by the sovereign's prerogative of confirmation and mercy, not by general rules. [74] It was commonly, but mistakenly, assumed that the reduction and attenuation of statutory punishments would be very dangerous from the point of view of deterring prospective criminals. All laws carefully avoided too precise statements of the punishment in order not to weaken their efficacy. [75] Thus, in as late a code as the *Allgemeine preussische Landrecht,* the Prussian government played hide and seek with the people, as Dilthey says. [76]

A certain uniformity was attained in the administration of criminal law which in turn affected the extension of prison sentences. [77] Schmidt describes this process as the reverse of that which had made medieval penal administration so harsh. In the sixteenth century, he says, the tendency was to apply to petty offenders as well the normal punishments (even death) for serious criminals. That is to say, the small fry shared the fate of the great because of the "dangerous trend of their mentality." But the tables were turned when the tentative efforts to punish vagrants by more humane methods, such as banishment, forced labor, and galley slavery, became oriented to prisons, workhouses, and houses of correction. The minor criminals were now brought into these convenient and comfortable houses for society's worst elements, and they gradually drew the more serious offenders after them.[78]

Seventeenth-century writers favored this development because of the useless character of the prevailing system of punishment and because of the anticipated value of the new establishments. Henelius's called for the restriction of the death penalty to criminals guilty of the most heinous offenses.[79] The good record of the Amsterdam house of correction was widely broadcast as a concrete example of the efficiency of the new system and the uselessness of the old. Henelius's principle, *Mittantur igitur fures ad Sanctum Raspinum, non ad Carnificem,"* [80] was accepted by everyone. Complete abolition of capital punishment was, of course, inconceivable at this time, but the number of executions diminished considerably. In the seventeenth and eighteenth centuries, the mere existence of certain forms of punishment, like galley slavery, transportation, and incarceration in houses of correction, limited the use of the capital sentence. As Stephen correctly remarks,

in the days of Coke it would have been impossible practically to set up convict establishments like Dartmoor or Portland, and the expense of establishing either police or prisons adequate to the wants of the country would have been regarded as exceedingly burdensome, besides which the subject of the management of prisons was not understood. Hence, unless a criminal was hanged, there was no way of disposing of him. Large numbers of criminals accordingly were hanged whose offences indicated no great moral depravity.[81]

Of all the forces which were responsible for the new emphasis upon imprisonment as a punishment, the most important was the profit motive, both in the narrower sense of making the establishment pay and in the wider sense of making the whole penal system a part of the state's mercantilist program.[82] The secondary interest that the state took in criminal justice was largely due to the fact that the state did not expect to profit by the penal system and sought to deal with the prisoners in the most inexpensive way possible. The state was not expected to make any important outlays apart from salaries, which often amounted to interest payments on the purchase price of a job, as in France. The salary bill of the Paris *Parlement* under Henry III, for example, amounted to 100,000 livres, whereas the payments which, according to an ordonnance of March, 1498, covered general items, such as transportation and maintenance of prisoners and expenses and wages of several lower officials, came to a total of 1,000 livres.[83] The evolution of this unprofitable judicial business into a system which was partially self-supporting from the standpoint of the treasury and a successful part of nation industry from the standpoint of mercantilist policy paved the way for the introduction of imprisonment as a regular form of punishment. It is highly significant that prisons used primarily for the detention of prisoners awaiting trial and therefore not susceptible to commercial exploitation remained in a very bad condition until well into the nineteenth century.

The ideology which accompanied this development in the system of punishment did not find much support in the penal theories of the seventeenth and eighteenth centuries. It is true that the idea of correction is stressed as a plausible justification for new practices along with the deterrence and material profits, but it was never really developed by the leading authorities of the period.[84] The Benedictine Father Mabillon first drew attention to the many theoretical problems connected with imprisonment in his essay, "Réflexions sur les prisons des ordres religieux," published posthumously in 1724.[85] It is no coincidence that an eminent member of the Catholic Church should have been the first to treat the purpose and character of the prison systematically, for the Church was faced with the problem at an early date. It had criminal jurisdiction over clerics, but once it was not allowed to sentence them to death, it was forced to turn to imprisonment and corporal punishment. Furthermore, the *privilegium fori* was conferred with the tonsure. A large number of people entered the lower orders of the Church merely to profit by the *privilegium,* and they intensified the problem of criminal clerics. In sum, the Church was confronted at an early date with problems of imprisonment which did not occupy the temporal authorities until much later.

Confinement in the monasteries proved unsuccessful, partly because the convicted clerics escaped too easily and partly because many monasteries refused to accept them. As early a pope as Alexander III felt obliged to include the clause *si fieri potest* in his order for monastery confinement of the clerics who had participated in the assassination of Thomas à Becket, and Boniface VIII allowed temporary or life imprisonment in separate establishments for clerics.[86] Life imprisonment was limited to cases for which the temporal authorities would apply a qualified death sentence. It frequently meant death because of the possibility of withholding food.[87] Punishments were increased in various ways in order to emphasize the unpleasantness of prison sentences. Solitary confinement was common, since it was supposed to serve the basic purpose of punishment, reformation of the prisoner. The material problem of the exploitation of labor power was of little importance; Mabillon insisted that the prisoners work, but only for the moral value of working.[88] The task before the Church was to strike a balance between a disinterested consideration of the spiritual welfare of the delinquent on the one hand and the requirements of Church discipline on the other.

Mabillon's consideration anticipated modern discussions of the problem of imprisonment to a striking degree. From his comparison of the severity of secular justice with the charity which ought to play a decisive part in ecclesiastical justice, he concluded that punishment should be proportionate to the gravity of the offense and to the bodily and spiritual strength of the offender.[89] The duration of the sentence, he said, should be considered in relation to the character of the individual criminal. The system of favors was closely associated with penitence; more and less desirable locations at mass were awarded according to the degree of regeneration attained by the prisoner.[90] The refined disciplinary conceptions of a close community demanded reformation which meant not simply outward conformity to the rules of society but inner conversion. Once this difficulty inherent in the peculiar character of the Church was overcome, Mabillon could solve his problem rather easily. Penitence and pardon represented readmission into the community, which was both a spiritual home and the place of work. The problem thus ended at a point where, outside the Church, the grave question of readjustment to society first began.

V

DEVELOPMENTS IN CRIMINAL THEORY AND LAW DURING THE AGE OF THE ENLIGHTENMENT

THE roots of the prison system lay in mercantilism, and its promotion and elaboration were the task of the Enlightenment. We have seen how, far into the eighteenth century, the houses of correction accepted convicts, vagrants, orphans, the aged, and lunatics without distinction. Little discrimination was shown in committing people. Wherever imprisonment had been introduced, those in power used it to remove "undesirable" characters. Often no definite procedure was laid down. Prisons and galleys were filled with unfortunates who discovered the crimes they were charged with only after they had been imprisoned, and then only from the nature of the punishment inflicted.[1] Krohne is quite right when he concludes that the confusion about the purpose and nature of imprisonment made it possible to incarcerate all who were deemed undesirable by their neighbors or betters. It became so difficult to distinguish justice from individual caprice, he continues, that penal administration lost prestige in the eyes of the people.[2] There were no definite criteria for fixing the duration of punishment, for there was no adequate conception of the necessary relationship between punishment and crime. Sentences were sometimes absurdly short but more often absurdly long, if the term was stated at all.

Alongside the agitation against the stupidity and harshness of punishment which led to the acceptance of imprisonment as the normal penalty for offenses of every kind, there arose another movement, directed against the uncertainty of punishment and the arbitrariness of the criminal courts. Ever since Montesquieu's *Lettres persanes,* reformers demanded the abolition of such out-of-date conditions. The classic formulation appears in Beccaria's *Essay on Crimes and Punishments*.[3] Continuation of the piece-meal reform of the system of punishment suddenly found itself raised to the rank of a major political issue.

The question of the nature of punishment concerned the lower classes primarily. Meanwhile, the problem of a more precise definition of substantive law and of improved methods of criminal procedure was brought to the fore by the bourgeoisie who had not yet won their struggle for political power and who were seeking legal guarantees for their own security. These were two quite distinct and independent issues, united in the tracts of contemporary reformers by the historical circumstances that the productive system had to contend with a shortage of workers during the period of the rise of the bourgeoisie. Until the beginning of the twentieth century, the bond between the protection of the material foundations of bourgeois society and an apparent equality and humaneness in the administration of criminal justice for all classes of society was never openly attacked. Everywhere the political opposition to absolutism condemned a criminal justice which did not seem to be governed by fixed rules, even where no definite objections were raised against its contents, such as the use of imprisonment. The fact that many punishments were inflicted under laws which gave the judge arbitrary power to fix penalties as he thought fit was attacked, together with vague formulations of the law. That type of judicial administration frequently brought material advantages to the poorer classes, as in the case of the Star Chamber, and it was now berated bitterly. The pioneers of reform were thus concerned first and foremost with limiting the power of the state to punish (both the means employed and the extent of their use) by creating fixed rules and subjecting the authorities to rigid control.

The separation of law from ethics, and a strict legal formulation of the idea of criminal culpability by placing it in close relationship with a legally defined fact, were already accomplished by Hobbes: "A CRIME, is a sinne, consisting in the Committing (by Deed, or Word) of that which the Law forbiddeth, or the Omission of what it hath commanded. So that every Crime is a sinne; but not every sinne a Crime." [4] Hobbes still passed moral judgment on human action, but its sphere of application was now limited and clearly distinguished from deeds punishable by law. The separation was facilitated by the principle that "no Law, made after a Fact done, can make it a Crime: because if the Fact be against the Law of Nature, the Law was before the Fact; and a Positive Law cannot be taken notice of, before it be made; and therefore cannot be Obligatory." [5] Here Hobbes applied the principle of nonretroactivity to criminal law. It was strongly upheld by Beccaria,[6] and incorporated in Article XIV of the Constitution of the Year III and in the Prussian *Allgemeines Landrecht.*[7]

The formalization of both procedure and substantive law was one of the chief preoccupations of Montesquieu and Beccaria. Montesquieu's contemporaries used the arguments of Book XI, Chapter VI of the *Esprit des lois,* "De la constitution de l'Angleterre," and of Book VI, Chapter V, "Dans quel gouvernement le souverain peut être juge," against *Kabinettsjustiz* and against all other forms of arbitrary administration of criminal justice.[8] Beccaria vigorously attacked all decisions based on the "spirit of the laws." [9] The contemporary passion for mathematics combined with the bourgeois desire for security to identify justice with calculability. "If mathematical calculations could be applied to the obscure and infinite combination of human actions," he writes, "there might be a corresponding scale of punishments." [10] The demand for a strict correlation between crime and punishment was finally worked out to the last detail by Bentham.[11]

Montesquieu's triumphant cry, that all arbitrary treatment ceases once punishment is determined by the nature of the particular crime,[12] was taken up by all criminologists of the day, but it is rendered somewhat hollow by the fact that the way in which the criminal shall make restitution must be chosen from a multitude of possible alternatives, and still more by the fact that the results of punishment are not mechanical, but vary with the degree of sensibility and the social standing of the individual involved. Beccaria, more cautious than most of his contemporaries, admitted this, but he went on to argue that the punishment is an automatic consequence of the offense. He thus found himself adopting the liberal dogma of the purely formal nature of equality, though he saw that equality of punishment can never be more than external. Recognition of the purely external character of equality compelled him to oppose legal class privileges in criminal law.[13] This did not prevent criminal legislation and practice of the later eighteenth and early nineteenth centuries from disregarding the thesis of its most revered authority and it pretended that privileges were accorded not to the aristocracy of wealth but to an aristocracy of culture. Article 11 of the Hessen *Strafgesetzbuch* of 1841, for example, reads: "Upon careful investigation of the social conditions and cultural level (*Bildungsstufe*) of the culprit, the court is allowed to order the execution of the *Correktionshausstrafe* in a fortress or similar place." [14]

The idea of proportion was concretized in a legally recognized graduation of punishments according to the gravity of the offense. That became one of the most powerful arguments in the struggle against too frequent use of the death penalty. Both Beccaria and Voltaire repeated the popular distinction between simple robbery and robbery accompanied by violence as proof of the necessity for varying the punishment according to the facts in each case.[15] This problem was the *raison d'être* of the formal definitions so numerous in Continental jurisprudence. Starting from the crude definitions already in existence, much thought was now concentrated on developing an elaborate system of legislation which would recognize all the fine distinctions between the various motives and ways of committing the same crime. Methods of punishment then had to come in for considerable attention in view of the prevailing harshness of penalties in general and the indiscriminate use of the death penalty in particular.

The passage in which Beccaria emphasized the distinction between robbery and robbery with violence runs as follows:

The punishment of robbery, not accompanied with violence, should be pecuniary. He who endeavors to enrich himself with a property of another should be deprived of part of his own. But this crime, alas! is commonly the effect of misery and despair: the crime of that unhappy part of mankind, to whom the right of exclusive property, a terrible, and perhaps necessary right, has left but a bare existence. Besides, as pecuniary punishment may increase the number of poor, and may deprive an innocent family of subsistence, the most proper punishment will be that kind of slavery, which alone can be called just; that is, which makes the society, for a time, absolute master of the person and labor of the criminal, in order to oblige him to repair, by this dependence, the unjust despotism he usurped over the property of another, and his violation of the social compact.[16]

This passage is significant in the first place because it calls for fines in the interest of property. But since the payment of a fine is not possible for the lower classes, imprisonment is recommended in its place. The deprivation of liberty is considered a natural result of the invasion of property, that is to say, property and personal liberty are assigned equal value.

Beccaria and Voltaire were also conscious of more practical reasons for the use of imprisonment. Both realized the effects of public executions, especially in France where the frequent and unjust execution of domestic servants for the pettiest thefts led to dangerous disturbances.[17] Beccaria's conclusions are summarized in an imaginary conversation: "What are these laws that I am born to respect, which make so great a difference between me and the rich man? . . . . Who makes these laws? The rich and the great who never deigned to visit the miserable hut of the poor. . . . . Let us break those ties, fatal to the greatest part of mankind, and only useful to a few indolent tyrants!" [18] This is an argument against the traditional use of the death penalty based on an open fear that it did not serve the desired purpose of defending existing property relations, but, on the contrary, encouraged a direct attack on the propertied classes. The attenuation of punishment thus becomes a practical measure of defense against social revolution as well as against individual acts.[19]

Not all writers were as frank as Beccaria in admitting the immutable bond between larceny and the prevailing social order based on private property. Of the many contemporary authors who wrote on the subject, we shall mention two whose notions were not without practical influence. The idea that society also has a responsibility appears in a letter of Frederick II of Prussia to D'Alembert, in which he gave a theoretical justification for theft in certain circumstances: "The good of society is based upon reciprocal service, but if society is composed of persons without pity, all obligations will be broken and there will be a return to the pure state of nature where the strength of the strongest decides everything." [20] Frederick held misery to be the consequence of individual mercilessness, however, and he did not appreciate its deeper social implications. That enabled him to add that there are always people who occupy themselves with the care of the poor, and he generally followed the line of Beccaria, even when he passed a decree ordering that offenses committed out of thoughtlessness or poverty should not be punished with the maximum severity.[21]

The same conception is to be found in Marat's *Plan de législation criminelle,* which was in some respects the model for the criminal legislation of the French Revolution. Instead of Frederick's private benefactors who reëstablish the harmony of society, Marat introduced the idea of public workshops to provide vagrants and beggars with work and education. Such workshops would theoretically put an end to unemployment and would, therefore, destroy the moral justification of thefts, relieving the legislator of the task of providing different punishments for rich and poor, which might violate the cherished principle of proportion. As Marat says, the shades of difference which fortune introduces between men are too difficult to ascertain and too slight to receive legislative consideration.[22] The French Revolution, like the Reformation, began by suppressing existing welfare organizations; it threw them into financial disorder, but that did not prevent the revolutionary legislators from developing criminal law on the basis of a fictitious equality between rich and poor.

In order to understand the direction taken by the upper-class enthusiasm for reform, it is significant to note that both Beccaria and Voltaire were satisfied with very short dissertations upon larceny, and then turned to the attenuation and elimination of punishment for religious and moral offenses. Here at any rate the emancipated bourgeoisie in France received a sympathetic response from the *noblesse de robe*. Other demands, such as suppression of property confiscations and curtailment of the existing libel laws, grew out of the same general conception. The bourgeoisie favored stringent punitive action by the law only when the social order itself was menaced. Where no such menace was envisaged, freedom, essentially freedom of movement for the upper classes and only an indirect advantage to the lower classes, should not be restricted. It is the certainty of punishment rather than its severity which is again emphasized in Beccaria's concluding remarks.[23] The rising bourgeois society was more interested in the completeness, rapidity, and reliability of criminal justice than in its severity. These qualities could only be attained by a rationally functioning administration. The latter goal thus overshadowed the problem of the harshness of an administration of justice which was constantly being delayed and diverted by incompetence and corruption.[24]

These demands for changes in the substantive law were accompanied by complaints against the deficiencies of legal procedure, a central problem, as the *Cahiers des états généraux* of 1789 show.[25] Public trials, free choice of a lawyer, trial by jury, suppression of torture, a clearly defined law of evidence, protection against illegal imprisonment—these demands in the name of humanity and human progress were to benefit all classes alike. But experience has shown that the effects of the new procedure differed widely among the various classes despite a certain tendency to increase the general guarantees. It served to protect, among others, those members of the bourgeoisie and aristocracy who were least entitled to protection to guarantee them against encroachments on their liberty of movement and thus to facilitate their disreputable activities. The lower classes, on the other hand, could seldom avail themselves of the complicated trial machinery which the law set up for them as for the wealthy, since they lacked the necessary knowledge or financial resources.

The independence of the judiciary has two functions. Positively, it guarantees freedom and equality before the law;

negatively, it conceals the power of the law-making judge. This problem took on one form when it was a matter of a new power asserting itself and another when an established power was seeking to conserve or extend its influence. In eighteenth-century England, the question of controlling the administration of justice had already been settled. The first of the modern European revolutions, the Great Rebellion in England, saw the victory of the bourgeoisie and put into their hands the penal code under which they had suffered. The judiciary received life tenure, that is, their term of office depended solely on good behavior, and that meant that they had been weaned away from the Crown. The innovation had little to do with a formal separation of powers, however, in view of the complete corruption of the judges, who could be bribed by the King as well as by private parties to a suit.

The formal and rational system which was now developing for the regulation of disputes among the bourgeoisie had little to do with the actual administration of criminal justice.[26] The latter was still dominated by *ad hoc* legislation, leading to undue intricacy and many loopholes in substantive law and procedure.[27] At the same time, there was little flexibility in the choice of punishments. Death or transportation was the rule for most offenses, and this very harshness and crudity added to the general insecurity of criminal administration because courts frequently drew back from the severe penalities required by law and refused to impose any punishment.

The English local courts presided over by the justices of-the peace, on the other hand, handled the petty offenses of the masses with an informality unknown on the Continent. The expense of legal proceedings made it extremely difficult to appeal decisions of the justices of the peace, so that Max Weber can speak of a denial of justice to the lower classes.[28] Blackstone thought that the justices, the representatives of the landed gentry, "have heaped upon them such an infinite variety of business . . . . that the country is infinitely obliged to any worthy magistrate that without sinister views of his own will engage.in this troublesome service." [29] But the evaluation of the justices of the peace is not a problem of their personal integrity, but of the class interests of the landed gentry whose tools they were. The Hammonds have shown that the rural magistrates became most effective organs in the system of repression against which the proletariat was too weak to protect itself. In actual practice, the fundamental civil rights to which every English citizen was legally entitled were denied to the poor, chiefly by abuse of the vagrancy laws.[30]

The political situation had thus placed judicial administration in the hands of the propertied classes. The power of the landed gentry was disproportionally great, but they saw in the administration of criminal justice the common interest of all the upper strata; the conservation of property was the main business of society. Since the personal liberty of the upper classes was fully recognized by the existing law, reform could benefit only the common people and the movement for greater leniency faced strong resistance. As late as 1770, the House of Lords rejected the abolition of the death penalty for gypsies and army deserters as immoral and subversive.[31] Much time was to pass before the attacks of Paley, Romilly, and Bentham on the futility of the prevailing system were to result in change and before Bentham's proof of the economic advantages of his own proposal was to take effect.

In France, as elsewhere on the Continent, the class situation was much more complicated. Montesquieu's *Esprit des lois,* which had become the program of the entire liberal bourgeoisie, was itself the product of an ambiguous situation. The French monarchy was losing ground and trying to find its way between the landed aristocracy and the bourgeoisie. Its weakness was openly revealed when it was unable to carry out Maupeou's judicial reform program against the temporary alliance between the *noblesse de robe,* defending its position, and the bourgeoisie, preparing to take power. Under these conditions, the judiciary could pose as the protector of freedom against tyranny and brutal force, and the *noblesse de robe* was able to hold its political position for a few more years by pretending to be the standard-bearer of sovereignty at one moment and the protector of civil liberties at another. Furthermore, the government could never have accepted the resignation en bloc of the members of the *Parlements* because the royal exchequer was unable to return the price paid by the magistrates for their office.[32]

Faced with the popular sovereignty, these antiquated institutions died quietly when the Revolution broke out. After the vicissitudes of the revolutionary period, the courts became about what they are today, relatively independent branches of the administration which have often represented the permanent interests of the bourgeois social order more consciously than the government did, and even sometimes in opposition to it. The *Code pénal* of September 25, 1791, was in theory the complete realization of the program developed by Marat in 1778:

The infliction of punishment should attempt to repair the offense as much as to expiate it. This is the triumph of justice; this is also the triumph of liberty, because then punishment no longer arises out of the will of the legislator, but out of the very nature of crimes. Man is no longer committing violence against man.[33]

Lepeletier St. Fargeau, reporter of this bill for the Committee for Constitutional and Criminal Legislation and subsequently an official martyr of French republicanism because he was killed by the royalists, was an enthusiastic follower of Beccaria.[34] The idea of providing a fixed punishment for each offense was carried out to its logical conclusion. That is understandable as a political move, but the principle met with great difficulties in practice. Of the various forms of punishment, transportation was accepted in theory, but the galleys and bagnos were rejected because of the danger of arbitrary application and because of their nondeterrent character. Whipping and branding were rejected as incompatible with the temporary nature of punishment. Incarceration in an *Hôpital* or prison was retained. The strong desire for a careful demarcation between acts punishable by law and morally reproachable but not punishable conduct can be seen in the fact that prostitution was not a crime. The only serious debate was over the question of capital punishment, but the arguments for its abolition, especially the remarkably firm attitude of Robespierre, remained without real influence on the later use of this penalty. The romantic conception of honor, strongly emphasized in the public debates of the period and part of the vogue of imitating classical antiquity, led to the reintroduction of punishment by public exposure. This tendency left no deep mark on criminal practice, but it is significant as a reflection of the conscious break with the mercantilist conception of prison work. Prison work now came to be regarded as a favor granted to the prisoner, so that he might improve his standard of living, which was deliberately kept below the minimum level. This depression of the living standard has remained one of the guiding principles of French criminal practice until today.[35]

In the German territories, the firm control over the administration of justice exercised by the princes, in conjunction with the judicial practice in the hands of the law faculties, permitted a more even, though slower, development of criminal law. Toward the end of the Holy Roman Empire we find two great territorial codifications, the *Codex Juris Bavarici* of 1751 and the Austrian *Constitutio Criminalis Theresiana* of 1768, which, as Köstlin says, combined different territorial legislations in a primitive stage.[36] The official commentary to the Bavarian criminal code of 1814, hardly progressive insofar as the system of punishment is concerned, contains the following remark about its predecessor:

No scientific researches had then spread their benevolent light over the criminal law; severity was still assumed to be the best means of achieving the aims of good criminal legislation. The recently ended, long and disastrous war had increased the number of crimes and encouraged the idea that this general corruption could be mastered only by rigid criminal laws.[37]

The requirements of the time are not considered either in criminal procedure or in the selection of punishments.

It was the *Allgemeine preussische Landrecht* which took a decisive step forward. Prussian criminal practice under Frederick II, who retained the right of final decision in criminal cases, had already introduced the principle of proportion and had seriously limited capital punishment. The main motive for this policy of clemency was the desire to recruit soldiers, as we have already stated. We find another characteristic anticipation of nineteenth-century trends in the tendency to limit usury fines to fifty percent of the capital, so that the maximum penalty no longer served as a deterrent.[38] The *Allgemeines Landrecht* agreed with the French code of 1791 in sanctioning the mitigation of the system of punishment and in reducing the importance of religious offenses. Characteristic of this law, as compared with the French revolutionary legislation, is its attempt to formulate in legal definitions the entire economic and social policy of the state. The code of an absolute monarchy was not obliged to worship the doctrine of equality before the law. Poor people were exempt from the payment of fines, whereas the imprisonment of criminals of higher social rank depended chiefly on the nonpayment of fines.[39] It is clear that the legislative practice of absolutism can afford to prepare the way for the future capitalistic rationalization of criminal law more easily than the proponents of the doctrine of the legal equality of classes.

SOCIAL AND PENAL CONSEQUENCES OF
THE INDUSTRIAL REVOLUTION

THE movement for the reform of criminal law gained real momentum during the second half of the eighteenth century. The first edition of Beccaria was published in 1763, the *Allgemeine preussische Landrecht* in 1794. But the basis for the new system of punishment, the need for man power, was disappearing during the same period. We have already indicated that the reform found fertile ground only because its humanitarian principles coincided with the economic necessities of the time. Now, when attempts were being made to give practical expression to these new ideas, part of the base from which they arose had already ceased to exist. That situation was reflected in the conditions of prison life, as we can see from the descriptions in the fourth edition of Howard's *State of the Prisons in England and Wales*. Visiting the Osnabrück prison, he completely disregarded the warden's information—we are vividly reminded of similar cases today—after he saw the misery expressed in the faces of the prisoners.[1] In Ghent, his inquiries led him to the same conclusions.[2] We have similar evidence from Thuringia in the second half of the eighteenth century, where there were not enough instructors nor adequate markets for the commodities produced in the prisons. Lack of space made it necessary to herd people together. The report of the Weimar *Zuchthaus,* for example, said that conditions were "thoroughly bad." [3]

Historians agree that the houses of correction had passed their heyday, when they were clean and tidy and well managed, and that, after spreading throughout Europe, the system gradually decayed "until finally the deplorable state of affairs characteristic of the eighteenth century was reached." [4] They have tried to account for this development in different ways, but, operating from the idea that progress is a necessary element in evolution, they have generally restricted themselves to moral judgments. Thus, Hippel has nothing but extravagant praise for the Amsterdam methods, but subsequent developments dissatisfy him. In this connection, he writes that the prison system might have developed and prospered if the authorities had followed the Dutch example, built the necessary houses of correction in every town, and really used them as places of punishment. But the development in that direction was only partial. It is true, he continues, that we find houses of correction established in growing numbers from the middle of the seventeenth to the end of the eighteenth century. We find further that imprisonment continued to take the place of physical forms of punishment and the death penalty until, by the end of the eighteenth century, it predominated. At the same time, we find the deplorable tendency to make houses of correction perform the functions of charitable institutions and poorhouses, and to deprive them of their real aim by combining them with orphanages and asylums in which the most heterogeneous elements were herded together. In these institutions, we look in vain for the spirit of the earlier houses of correction with their organization of prison life on a definitely educational basis. Neglect, intimidation, and torment of the inmates became the rule of the day, and they were given work only for their discomfort or for the profit to be gained. Hippel notes with misgivings that the chief aim of the later houses of correction was to increase the income of the exchequer, and that the argument was raised that they need not be as expensive as they were in Amsterdam.[5]

Hippel seeks to explain these facts, which he deplores, by reference to the political situation of the time. The Thirty Years' War, he says, apparently ended that advance of civilization which had begun with such high hopes for culture as for other spheres. After the Reformation, the original houses of correction had developed into well-appointed, flourishing institutions under a strong but humane civil administration. The impoverished and brutalized race of men left by the Thirty Years' War lacked both the means and the finer sensibilities necessary to establish institutions of equal value. The idea of improvement of the inmates of the houses of correction had become a mere phrase, understood partially if at all.[6] This explanation might be accepted for the special German situation alone. But even there the effects of the Thirty Years' War had diminished in the course of the eighteenth century. Germany, too, displayed a remarkable trend toward the reformation of criminal law and punishment, but it was throttled in the last decades of the eighteenth century. Even for Germany, therefore, the causes must be sought in general social developments rather than in particular events.

The house of correction grew out of a social situation in which the conditions of the labor market were favorable to the lower classes. But this situation changed. The demand for workers was satisfied and a surplus eventually developed. The population of England increased by one million in the first half of the eighteenth century, and by three million in the second half. It was 5.1 million in 1720, 6 in 1750, and 9.18 in 1801. Between 1781 and 1800 the rate of increase was 9 to 11 percent, and between 1801 and 1820, 14 to 18 percent.[7] The population of France was 19 million in 1707, 24 in 1770, and 26 in 1789.[8] What the ruling classes had been seeking for over a century was now an accomplished fact—relative overpopulation. Factory owners need no longer hunt for men. On the contrary, workers had to search out places of employment. The rapidly growing population could not support itself on the land, especially after certain changes had taken place in agricultural production, resulting in enclosures and large estates.[9] From the beginning of the eighteenth century agricultural workers began to stream into the towns, a movement which reached its climax in the first decades of the nineteenth century.[10]

The introduction of machinery at such a time was bound to have catastrophic effects. It began in the textile industry. Home spinning, which used to occupy entire districts, had been unable to satisfy the demand of the textile mills for yarn. The introduction of the spinning machine now increased the output per worker to such a degree that it became possible to develop the textile industry to meet the needs of all possible markets without relying on hand-spun yarn. The consequence was that spinning ceased to be one of those subsidiary home industries by means of which the poorer English people had managed to supplement their insufficient returns from the land. All the spinning was now done in factories, and men frequently found it impossible to compete with women and children. The same process of industrialization gradually spread from the cotton mills to all other enterprises. More and more people were thrown out of work, steadily increasing industrial unemployment.

1. THE END OF THE MERCANTILIST SOCIAL POLICY

The organization of industry was revolutionized by the new condition of the labor market. Formerly only those enterprises which received government assistance could hold their own, but now anyone with a little capital could establish some sort of business. The middle classes were coming into their own, and they felt themselves seriously hampered by those privileged groups who used their monopolies and other advantages to keep them out of business. The bourgeoisie demanded freedom of manufacture and freedom of trade. They spread the ideals of liberal optimism; free competition was to be the guarantee of harmony among conflicting interests. Strongly influenced by Adam Smith, this agitation against the old system of state regulation also affected the relationship between employer and employee. At first the generally accepted view was that the interest of the worker himself required that freedom of employment should replace the former rule and regulations limiting the terms of the contract.[11] "Laisser faire, laisser passer, le monde va de lui-même" was the new motto, and both employers and employees saw the key to the millennium in this principle of pure individualism. The effect of this freedom on the condition of the workers, however, was quite different from what its proponents had expected. If there had still been a shortage of labor, the worker would certainly have benefited from the new freedom, for he would have been able to raise the price of his labor. But since the labor market was oversupplied, the workers were more downtrodden than ever and wages lower. Marshall remarked that this period saw the working class fall into the greatest misery it had ever suffered, at least since the beginning of trustworthy records in English social history.[12]

It is not necessary to examine the different steps in the impoverishment of the lower classes and in the rise of the modern proletariat. The facts are well known and they are available in any textbook. The process was neither continuous nor parallel in all countries, but the course of development was generally the same on the Continent as in England, though delayed. There, too, the change brought about the impoverishment of the lower classes. We do not have the same reliable records on the condition of the German workers, but, as Neumann has pointed out, there can be no question about the sharp widening of the gap between rich and poor in Prussia. While the number of people of moderate means was rapidly decreasing, the number of the extremely rich and the extremely poor was increasing.[13]

The ruling classes had no further need for the coercive measures employed in the mercantilist period to make up for the absence of economic pressure on the working class. The exhaustive system of laws and regulations designed to check rising wages became obsolete. The English laws restricting freedom of movement from one job or trade to another had begun to go out of use in the eighteenth century and they finally disappeared altogether. The justices of the peace refrained from fixing wages. In fact, the machinery for the assessment of fair wages virtually disappeared toward the end of the seventeenth century.[14] It was originally created to fix maximum wages, and that was no longer necessary.

Although the idea that poverty is one of the best spurs to hard work began to be disputed,[15] every move to fix minimum wages for the benefit of workers came to nothing. Burns states that in the early years of the nineteenth century in England the provision of the Act of 1536, whereby wages were to be regulated according to prevailing conditions, appeared to offer some protection to workers adversely affected by the Napoleonic Wars and by the changes taking place in the organization of industry.

But the only result of the attempt to claim the support of this provision was its removal from the statute book in 1813.[16] Formerly it had been a crime punishable by imprisonment to give or receive wages higher than those set by the justices of the peace, and court records show that this law was no dead letter.[17] Now it was taboo to talk of the regulation of wages.[18] The new doctrine is well illustrated for France by a letter of October 4, 1790, from the Committee of Trade of the Assembly to the authorities of Beauvais, who had intervened in a wage dispute. They overruled this intervention on the ground that wages would be regulated by natural laws.[19]

The wage fund theory provided the theoretical foundation for this viewpoint, maintaining as it did that any sort of artificial increase of wages can only be made at the expense of capital investment and must eventually lead to a result contrary to the one intended. It must destroy, or at least reduce, the only means of employing workers profitably. The Malthusian notion in its later form, the so-called iron law of wages, went still further and alleged the impossibility and senselessness of such plans. Wages must remain at the bare subsistence level. The moment they rise above it, an undue increase in the population will follow and the ensuing competition will force them down again. Thus, liberalism seems to have degenerated into ruthless pessimism in the period from the *Wealth of Nations* to the first effective factory law.

The whole mercantilist population policy could now be abandoned. Under the influence of Malthus, people believed that the population was steadily increasing to a point at which the surplus millions would be driven by starvation to crime and every kind of vice.[20] The "population fanatics" of the previous period were ridiculed,[21] and the artificial method which enabled the state to boast of its *faciamus homines* was condemned. Interference into the "holiest relationships of life" was insupportable despotism, bringing men down to the level of animals. All the measures introduced to encourage the poor to marry, it was argued, could only fill the land with beggars and paupers, whose children must be destined to a life of vice and shame.[22]

Theorists demanded that steps be taken to check illegitimacy and to require government consent for marriage.

It is interesting to note how the new conditions of the labor market were reflected in the history of the *Allgemeine preussische Landrecht*. The preparatory work for this code dates back to 1736, a time when the country was underpopulated. That condition had been overcome by 1794, however, when the code was promulgated and the paragraphs dealing with illegitimate children were never rigidly enforced and often disregarded entirely. Later, they were openly attacked both in theory and in practice. Finally, a law of April 24, 1854, thoroughly revised the *Landrecht* by depriving an illegitimate child of the support of the father if the mother was a person of disreputable character. The mere fact that she received money or gifts in return for her consent allowed the judge to account her disreputable.[23]

During the French Revolution, an effort was made to insure more equitable treatment of illegitimate children. Not only was the old right to claim support from the father maintained, but laws of June 4 and November 2, 1793, went further and granted bastards the same rights of succession as legitimate children. Offspring of adulterous relations were allowed one-third of the inheritance to which they would have been entitled if born in wedlock. These reforms did not last, however. The *Code civil* virtually destroyed the hereditary position of the illegitimate child, while children born in adultery were deprived of all rights of succession.[24] In explaining this part of the bill before the tribunal, Huguet criticized the humanitarian and philanthropic work of the revolutionary legislation on the grounds that it tended to weaken the social order.[25]

It was no longer necessary to erect artificial barriers against emigration, and all legislation restricting freedom of movement was withdrawn.[26] Emigration is a good measure of the pressure of social conditions. In Germany it reached its peak during the years 1820 to 1880, and the years 1845 to 1855 marked the worst period for the working class in many parts of the country.[27] Between 1847 and 1855 alone, Germany lost more than a million of its citizens through emigration.

The whole system of public relief broke down. A good example is provided by the Hamburg poor law reform of 1788. In order to keep the poor at work, the poorhouses founded factories of their own and industrial schools for the children. The immediate results were most satisfactory. The board of governors of the poorhouses could say in their report for 1791 that there were no longer any beggars in the streets of Hamburg, and that no one in the city could starve.[28] But such enterprises began to collapse with surprising rapidity. By 1801 the main poorhouses had a deficit of over 60,000 marks, and the deficit increased year by year. The same development occurred everywhere. The reduced demand for spinning after the appearance of machinery which did the work of several men made it increasingly difficult to keep able-bodied inmates of the poorhouses at profitable work.[29]

In France on the eve of the Revolution, with the situation of the lower classes deteriorating steadily, the *Hôpitaux généraux* no longer fulfilled their task. They were equally unfit as prisons and as poorhouses. Mirabeau's judgment on the *Hôpital de Bicêtre,* that "this institution which is used at the same time as a hospital and as a prison seems a hospital for infecting the sick and a prison for breeding crimes," is a reflection of the prevailing opinion.[30] The Committee on Mendicity of the Constituent Assembly rendered a devastating judgment, exposing both the technical shortcomings and the mistaken principles underlying the *Hôpitaux.* Its report emphasized the fact that not one of the mass of administrative regulations dealt even remotely with the type of work to be introduced in the institution or with the employment of the labor power.[31] This shows that they had lost their character as industrial schools and model workshops.

During the mercantilist period, the shortage of hands had always prevented the problem of able-bodied paupers from becoming too acute, and poor-law reform was at a standstill during the period from 1650 to 1800. The mercantilist theory of involuntary unemployment was clearly stated by Justi, who said that it is not impossible to discover rare cases where industrious and willing men failed to procure employment and were committed to a poorhouse through no fault of their own. He went on to say that he did not think that there were really countries in which trade did not flourish and in which so little employment was available that people willing to work were forced to beg. He never saw people of such inclination begging in his own country, at any rate.[32]

The formula that every man willing to work can find employment was still a popular slogan in the early nineteenth century, but Justi's confidence was no longer shared by the well-informed. There were still bitter complaints about the lazy people who would be maintained in their idleness with the help of poor relief, but such complaints went unheard against the argument raised long before by Petty that "the public should keep the beggars though they earned nothing, for if there be but a certain proportion of work to be done and the same be already done by the non-beggars about, it will but transfer the want from one hand to another." [33] Mirabeau remarked that, although the number of *Hôpitaux* had nearly doubled, the number of vagrants and beggars was steadily increasing, and he concluded that the insecurity of the working class was only a part of the general insecurity of the age.

We all have a precarious existence today. I would add, a subsistence based on the future. Those who have the means devour them by the pursuit of a fortune, but the men obliged to live by the work of their hands, who expect nothing from the government, business, or inheritance, lean upon the idea of public charity, and the saying that the *Hôpital* is not for the dogs has taken the place of the industry of the ants.[34]

The emphasis is no longer on the unlimited opportunity to work, but on the necessity of considering the working class as a part of the social system, in which it must take its risks independently.

The question of the criminal character of beggary also underwent a significant transformation. Logically one should reach the conclusion that begging is a crime only when it is voluntary, that is to say, when there is no industrial reserve army. Nearly

every reply to the circular of the Academy of Chalons, requesting suggestions for the best means of destroying begging in
France while making the mendicants useful to the state without
rendering them unhappy, insisted that begging is not a crime.[35]
The archbishop of Aix used the common argument, that where
there is no crime there is no proportional basis for inflicting
punishment.[36] The same opposition to the punishment of beggars developed in England.

Humanitarian reasoning cannot hide the fact that it was the
new economic system and the pressure of increasing population
which revolutionized the poor-relief problem. Absolutism and
its successor, democratic national sovereignty, reacted in the
same way by declaring it to be the duty of the state to assist the
poor; then the state had the right to proceed against beggary by
punitive measures. The *Allgemeine preussische Landrecht* held
that it is the business of the state to feed and support those citizens who are unable to gain a living for themselves and who
cannot be supported by other persons who are bound to do so
by special laws. Those whose inability to earn a living is due
only to lack of opportunity shall be employed at some task which
suits their strength and abilities.[37] The French constitution of
1793 recognized the right to work when it stated that society owes
subsistence to its unfortunate citizens either by providing work
or by securing the means of existence for those unable to work.
The assignment of the burden of existence to the state was a
counterweight to the seizure of the estates of the *Hôpitaux*,
which had led to a severe crisis in poor relief when the state
failed to fulfill the obligations. The experiment ended with the
abandonment of centralized poor relief.[38]

England requires special consideration. According to Colquhoun, poverty in London was so great that more than 20,000
miserable individuals rose every morning without knowing how
they were to be supported through the day or where they were to
lodge on the succeeding night, and cases of death from starvation
appeared in the coroner's lists daily.[39] It was in this atmosphere
that Malthus came forward with his doctrine that the living
standard of paupers can be raised only at the expense of the

remaining members of the working class, and that the benevolent intentions of the poor-law reformers must lead to an increase in population and hence to the creation of more misery.[40] He is thus a significant example of the impact of the newly created industrial reserve army upon theoretical considerations. But even Malthus never drew the conclusion that people in distress should be allowed to go hungry, and such a policy was inconceivable to English statesmen merely in the interest of social peace. Clapham goes so far as to say that the poor laws were the only means of preventing discontent and despair from giving rise to revolution.[41] Because of the industrial reserve army, it was no longer necessary "by savage punishments to discipline the whole propertyless class to the continuous and regular service in agriculture and manufactures," so that increasing pauperization of the masses was accompanied by more lenient treatment of the poor.[42]

The outcome was a tremendous increase in the poor rates. In 1775, the cost of public assistance was more than a million and a half pounds, and the sum rose rapidly until it reached nearly eight million in 1817, an amount which remained fairly constant to 1834.[43] The propertied classes began to rebel against this expense, and a royal commission appointed in 1832 formulated the principle that all outdoor relief to the able-bodied should be abolished in favor of workhouse relief so that the situation of relief recipients should not be "so eligible as the situation of the independent labourer of the lowest class." [44] This principle, incorporated in the Poor Law of 1834, is the leitmotiv of all prison administration down to the present time.

Changing conditions turned into a right what had once been taught to the masses as their duty and from this time on the question never disappeared from the political programs of the working class. No problem was dealt with in the socialist pamphlets of the time so frequently as this right to work. After the February Revolution, the Paris proletariat forced the provisional government to issue the proclamation of February 25, 1848, in which it guaranteed work to every citizen. In order to quiet the people, the government accepted the formulas of Considérant and Fourier, without any intention of keeping them. A decree was passed on February 26, 1848, instituting national workshops.[45] Prison labor was abolished on March 24, and foreign labor was expelled from Paris. The government used every available resource to hinder the experiment and, after the defeat of the proletariat, the workshops were shut down and prison labor was reintroduced.[46]

A temporary victory of the working class in its fight for the right to work thus found expression in the abolition of prison labor. This is a significant indication of the new situation. Instead of an upper class eager to obtain labor power from any source whatsoever, we find a working class mounting the barricades to secure official acknowledgment of their right to work. The factory replaced the house of correction, for the latter required large outlays for administration and discipline. Free labor could produce much more and it avoided the drain on capital involved in the houses of correction. In other words, the house of correction fell into decay because other and better sources of profit had been found, and because with the disappearance of the house of correction as a means of profitable exploitation the possible reformatory influence of steady work also disappeared.

2. THE INCREASE IN CRIME AND ITS EFFECTS ON THE THEORY AND PRACTICE OF PUNISHMENT

The increasing sharpness of the struggle for existence brought the living standard of the working class to an incredibly low level. In England, the height of pauperism was reached between 1780 and 1830. Throughout the first half of the nineteenth century, behind the picture of growing starvation, immorality, and drunkenness we find the threat of revolution. The newly created proletariat was ready at any moment for rebellion and violence. The slogan "Bread or Blood" spread through the English factory districts in 1810, and in 1831 the silk weavers of Lyons inscribed on their banner the motto, "Vivre en travaillant ou mourir en combattant." [47]

More and more of the impoverished masses were driven to

crime. Offenses against property began to increase considerably at the end of the eighteenth century,[48] and matters became still worse during the first decades of the nineteenth. The London statistics for the period 1821–27 give a vivid picture of the decisive part played by larceny in the general increase of convictions (Table 1).

TABLE 1. *Larceny in London, 1821–27*

YEAR	TOTAL CONVICTIONS	CONVICTIONS FOR LARCENY
1821	8,788	6,629
1822	8,209	6,424
1823	8,204	6,452
1824	9,452	7,550
1825	9,964	8,011
1826	11,095	8,962
1827	12,564	9,803

Source: C. Lucas, *Du système pénitentiaire en Europe et aux États-Unis* (Paris, 1825), I, p. 53.

The yearly average of convictions by Assizes and Quarter Sessions in England rose as is shown in Table 2.

TABLE 2. *Convictions by Assizes and Quarter Sessions, 1805–33*

YEARS	CONVICTIONS
1805– 6	2,649
1807– 9	2,843
1810–12	3,411
1813–15	4,443
1816–18	7,937
1819–21	9,205
1822–24	8,613
1825–27	11,212
1828–30	12,596
1831–33	14,408

Source: E. Ducpetiaux, *Statistique comparie de la criminalité. . . .* (Bruxelles, 1835), p. 41.

During this period, then, the number of convictions increased by 540%. Engels commented: "Want leaves the workingman the choice between starving slowly, killing himself speedily, or taking what he needs where he finds it—in plain English, stealing. And there is no cause for surprise that most of them prefer stealing to starvation and suicide." [49] This general development was not limited to England by any means, as the French criminal statistics of Table 3 show.[50]

TABLE 3. *Larceny in France, 1825–42*

YEAR	TOTAL CONVICTIONS	CONVICTIONS FOR LARCENY
1825	35,214	7,132
1828	41,120	9,400
1832	45,431	13,463
1836	54,976	14,601
1842	72,490	20,022

Source: Compiled from the annual *Compte général de l'administration de la justice criminelle.*

We thus see what tremendous proportions crime reached during the great industrial crisis. Such far-reaching crises were unknown during the mercantilist period in spite of all the disturbances due to war or natural causes. In describing the close connection between the crime rate and economic conditions, Pike says that the English Criminal Tables from 1810 on indicate that hard times, increased competition, or diminished demand for labor were followed by an increase in convictions for larceny and graver offenses, whereas better times were accompanied by a decrease. The year 1815, when the troops returned home and began to compete with other laborers, saw a marked increase of convictions, and so did 1825, the year of the great commercial depression. In 1835, on the other hand, a sharp drop in the price of corn, continuing the price fall of the three previous years, was accompanied by a considerable decrease in the number of prison commitments.[51]

The ruling classes were tempted to return to the premercantilist methods of treating criminals. A demand for harsher methods became widespread, and the liberal use of imprisonment to replace the traditional forms of punishment was severely criticized. People declared that the penal system had become a humbug, and that punishment should once again become something that the wrongdoer felt to the very marrow of his bones, something that tortured and destroyed him, as the penal laws of Charles V expressed it. The ax, the whip, and starvation ought to be reintroduced in order to root out the criminals.[52] Wagnitz stated that, although he would not advocate the gallows and the wheel as other writers had done, he would insist on permanent confinement for those miserable people who showed by repeated offenses that they were too weak to withstand the temptation of crime and were therefore incurably diseased in spirit.[53] In 1802 the Helvetian Department of the Interior sent out a questionnaire concerning the results of the criminal code drawn up on the lines of the French code of 1795. In reply, a Zürich judge, Meyer, bitterly attacked the humanitarian effeminacy of the age and made ironic remarks about the dream of a possible elevation of mankind. He recommended the reëstablishment of a qualified death penalty and corporal punishment.[54] That his opinion was fairly representative can be seen from the fact that some cantons returned to the *Peinliche Halsgerichtsordnung* of Charles V when they regained their sovereign legislative power.[55]

The same complaints appear in France. Debry, formerly a member of the Convention and later an administrative official under Napoleon, said that there could be no doubt that the high frequency of thefts and robberies, especially in the rural areas, was due to the weakness of the legislation on which court practice was founded. Punishments were not heavy enough. Special police and court martials were established, and the campaigns of "pacification" led to a virtual slaughter of poor outlaws, especially in the southern departments.[56] The same tendencies were manifested in legislation. The *ad hoc* laws which had already intensified the repression in the time of the Consulate, especially the law reintroducing branding for recidivists and forgers, reached their climax in the code of 1810. This codification deviated still further from the liberal system of punishment of the revolutionary legislation. In introducing the bill before the *Tribunat*, Treilhard expressed the new official attitude toward crime when he judged the revolutionary legislation in the following language: "This famous assembly, which has distinguished itself by so many useful ideas, which has done away with so many abuses, and which has without doubt shown the best intentions, has not always guarded itself against the enthusiasm of human kindness." [57] Garraud characterized the new system correctly when he remarked that it was particularly noteworthy for the excess of its severity, that its only interest was to strike the guilty, and that the idea of correction had no place in it.[58] The death penalty remained unchallenged and life imprisonment was frequently applied. Excessive punishment, barbaric mutilations, and unjust penalties like confiscation of property and loss of civil rights were its chief characteristics.

The situation had become reversed in Germany, too. Conservative students of criminal theory stated with satisfaction that the principle of retributive justice was beginning to have a salutary effect on the penal system.[59] They returned to the view that one can get at a thief only through his skin, and whipping became a favored form of punishment once more, for it was cheap and avoided overcrowding the prisons.[60] The most important step in this direction is represented by Anselm Feuerbach's Bavarian Criminal Code of 1813. In legal technique it was a distinctly progressive step, as compared with the eighteenth-century codifications, but in its system of punishment it followed the harsh tendencies of the period. The death penalty, life imprisonment in chains, and the house of correction were the basis of the system.[61]

Prussian criminal practice, based on the *Allgemeines Landrecht,* had been comparatively mild. But, Mittelstädt relates, the Prussian authorities soon came to the conclusion that they had entered far too deeply into the dangerous arithmetic of imprisonment as far as proletarian criminals were concerned, and that it was high time to lead these criminals back to the right path. The whip and the rod, the pillory, the branding iron, and confinement with deprivations were restored in order to control the growing number of footpads and thieves.[62] The Prussian circular decree of 1799, formulated in order to strengthen the law in suppressing theft, established corporal punishment for first offenders, but with characteristic exceptions for convicts of higher social standing.[63] There was a year-long fight over the Prussian penal law reform. A rough draft ready in 1830 eliminated the cruder forms of intimidation, but for this very reason it found no favor with von Kamptz, Minister of Justice, and he prepared a new draft in which intimidation remained the dominant principle (aggravated forms of the death penalty, public flogging, etc.).[64] It was not until all citizens were given equal political rights in 1848 that flogging was abolished and replaced by appropriate terms of imprisonment.[65] In Austria, mild and humane criminal practice came to an end with the Penal Code of September 3, 1803, a vigorous manifestation of bureaucratic reaction against "Josephinism." The qualified death penalty was reintroduced and the use of capital punishment in general was extended.[66]

The intensification of the system of punishment which followed deteriorating economic conditions and the consequent increase in crime left the essential achievements of the Enlightenment untouched. The same criminal codes, like the Code Penal of 1810 and the Bavarian Criminal Codes of 1813, which contained the most severe systems of punishment, were epoch-making in the development of the liberal theory, the basis of modern criminal law until the rise of Fascism. They introduced a more effective separation between moral and legal conceptions than did eighteenth-century criminal legislation, which arose in a period when bourgeois society was still struggling with mercantilist conceptions and with extensive administrative regulation in all private spheres.

The safety of the state and of the individual requires an absolute separation of law from morality, according to Feuerbach.[67] This doctrine found its chief expression in the attempt to achieve a precise formulation of the facts. Elimination of analogy, development of a formal legal concept of culpability by concentrating on the act and not on the person of the wrongdoer, accurate determination of punishment in proportion to the damage inflicted—all these achievements were theoretically applicable to every citizen.[68] The forces behind this development became quite clear when we note that Feuerbach included usury and bankruptcy along with offenses against public morality as mere breaches of administrative regulation.[69] Not only was the protective function of criminal law largely shaped by the requirements of the bourgeoisie, but the old class differentiation was retained by the new criminal legislation in the application of punishments. Talk of equality before the law could not prevent the same facts from having different meanings for different classes. The decisions couched in official language would seldom admit this point although it was constantly followed in practice, and still more rarely would it be expressed so naïvely as in the opinion of an Auxerre judge in 1811, when the penalty in a rape case was under consideration: "I vote for the minimum. We have to consider that the victim is a farm servant. If we were dealing with a girl from the higher social ranks, if we were dealing with your child or mine, I should vote for the maximum. I consider it important to mark a distinction between better society and the common people." [70]

The theories of Kant and Hegel provided a better philosophical foundation than a utilitarian penal theory for linking the conception of the *Rechtsstaat* to a harsh system of punishment.[71] The idealistic philosophy of criminal law provided a scientific basis for the retribution hitherto exercised without much reasoning, at least in the German-speaking countries and other countries under the intellectual influence of Germany.[72] The starting point of Kant and Hegel was a refutation of the theorem that punishment can be justified by pure utility. Kant's well-known remark about the necessity of executing the last murderer even in a community which is in the process of dissolution [73] expresses the denial of all teleological elements in punishment. Hegel expresses a similar viewpoint:

The criminal is honoured as reasonable, because the punishment is regarded as containing his own right. The honour would not be shared by him, if the conception and measure of his punishment were not deduced from his very act. Just as little is he honoured when he is regarded as a hurtful animal, which must be made harmless, or as one who must be terrified or reformed.[74]

By removing all subjective elements from the legal relationship between the particular criminal act and the general rule of criminal law to be applied to the particular case, idealism paved the way in practice for the liberal conception of criminal law.[75] The main demand of the bourgeoisie with regard to criminal law, the formulation of precise calculable standards of conduct, is fulfilled in the idealistic program, which is based on legality at all costs on the one side, retributions and nothing but retributions on the other.[76] The automatic correlation between culpability and punishment and the rigid exclusion of all teleo-logical elements oriented penal law toward the exact definition of all legal relationships.[77] The doctrine of Feuerbach, the chief theorist of criminal law in the early nineteenth century, is a combination of utilitarian conceptions with Kantian ideas.[78] Punishments are provided by the law in order to deter prospec-tive criminals; but once a crime has been committed, the punish-ment has no utilitarian value and is conceived as an automatic consequence of the transgression. Feuerbach writes:

Shall we attempt to fix the culpability of his act, whether he has not already improved himself, whether he really does threaten the state with new dangers, whether it is necessary and useful to protect oneself against him? I find none of these things in my consciousness, and I find as little in the consciousness of others. The transgression of the law is itself sufficient in order to hold him deserving of punish-ment.[79]

The rejection of all teleological considerations tends to give idealistic conceptions of penal law some of the resplendence inherent in the abstract idea of justice independent of human caprice. German idealism, therefore, was better suited than the criminology of other European countries for an important position in the process of developing a metaphysical structure. Western European criminology, in its first principles more closely bound to reality, always makes the class function of crimi-nal law transparent, and openly admits it at times.[80]

3. NEW AIMS AND METHODS OF PRISON ADMINISTRATION

Imprisonment became the chief punishment throughout the western world at the very moment when the economic founda-tion of the house of correction was destroyed by industrial changes. English developments are particularly interesting in this connection, as they show that imprisonment was much the most frequent form of punishment even when transportation was at its height.[81]

TABLE 4. *Distribution of Punishments in England, 1806–33*

PUNISHMENT	NUMBER OF SENTENCES			
	1806–12	1813–19	1820–26	1827–33
Capital punishment	2,800	6,584	7,659	9,457
Transportation for life	76	564	1,000	2,979
21–35 years	—	—	—	13
14 years	291	1,012	1,196	4,287
10, 9, 4 years	—	3	3	3
7 years	3,660	7,823	10,828	16,221
Imprisonment with or without other punishments				
3 to 5 years	—	99	79	46
1 to 2 years	13,413	1,698	2,343	1,673
6 months to 1 year	—	5,644	8,088	9,050
Less than 6 months	—	21,737	31,988	47,620
Whipping and fines	1,027	1,487	1,832	2,225
Total	21,277	46,651	65,015	93,579

Source: Ducpetiaux, *op. cit.*, p. 51.

In 1837–39, the ratio of transportation to imprisonment was 23.5 to 100, and in 1844–46 only 15 to 100.[82]

Imprisonment took various forms and gradations according to the gravity of the crime and the social position of the convict.[83] It has already been indicated that class differentiations in the system of punishment were not abolished in the first half of the nineteenth century. The upper classes were not yet convinced the advantages of sacrificing to the ideology of justice and equality those of its members whose position could no longer be maintained, as in the case of Hatry and, more recently, Whitney. The official commentary on the Bavarian Criminal Code of 1813 actually attempted to justify the introduction of *Festungshaft* for the upper classes on the ground that it was not a violator of liberal ideas. It argued that the principle of equality is not abandoned when minor punishments are adapted to personal conditions as long as modifications of severe punishments are not permitted to turn into the privilege of immunity.[84] The argument that the upper classes are more sensitive to punishment and that there is greater likelihood of suffering on the part of their families, already rejected by Beccaria,[85] was again drawn upon to save the traditional privileges of the aristocracy. The privilege of separate confinement for the upper classes was retained in all the German countries, and especially in Prussia. Only in the second half of the century did the pressure of the Rhineland lawyers and parliamentarians, representatives of a more highly developed section of capitalist society, change *Festungshaft* from a privilege of the upper strata to a particular form of punishment for specific crimes.[86]

The existing prisons did not meet the new requirements. To a large extent, the buildings previously utilized for prisoners awaiting trial were now used for the execution of prison sentences. The increasing number of condemnations, especially in the twenties, led to overcrowding in the main European prisons. Krohne says that there was neither time nor money available for the construction of new prisons and the old ones were not large enough, even when filled to the bursting point. The only alternative was to equip other buildings as emergency jails.[87] Furthermore, at the very time when the prison population was growing, the governments were reducing the total amounts allotted for the upkeep of prisoners, a measure for which the French budget reporter of 1827 congratulated the administration.[88] The conditions were therefore deplorable and the governments were slow in developing a sense of responsibility. We hear that in Belgium under the Napoleonic regime, for example, feeding the prisoners was not held to be a real obligation of the state, and an order was issued ruling that bread was to be supplied only in cases of extreme need.[89] The president of the administrative council of the Namur prison said in 1817 that all the prisoners were herded together in dark filthy places, that laziness existed everywhere along with open depravity of speech and conduct, and that nothing could be found which reminded man of his destiny.[90] We may conclude that no new policy in dealing with prisoners had been developed after the degeneration of the houses of correction. We learn from the detailed report of a political prisoner that the Paris prisons in the first decade under Napoleon were commercial enterprises of the jailers and police officials, who supplied bad merchandise to the solvent prisoners at high prices, leaving the rest to their fate—sickness, starvation, and death.[91] Even where some understanding of the need for reasonably equipped new buildings did prevail in the administration, the legislatures often refused the funds required for the most urgent construction work.[92]

The increase of commitments led to the same situation in England.[93] Buxton visited the prisons in 1818 and found hardly one that was not overcrowded, cold, damp, full of vermin, and exuding the most unbearable stench. The prisoners complained of rheumatism and there was no way of avoiding infection when a sick man was interned. The food was inadequate, often consisting of no more than half a pound of bread daily, and the prisoners, most of whom were kept in chains, had no opportunity to work.[94] Jorns concludes that anyone who found himself in jail because of some trifling offense ran the risk of paying for his error with lifelong illness.[95] Peel's desperate exclamation that the number of convicts was too overwhelming for proper and effective punishment is easily comprehensible.[96]

Contemporary reformers attributed the shortcomings of the prison system at the beginning of the nineteenth century to incompetent and often ineffective administration, the operation of prisons as private enterprises of the jailer, the internment of convicts together with men awaiting trial, and the internment of men with women. All these abuses gradually disappeared in one country after another,[97] but the crucial question remained: according to what principles and by what methods should prisoners be treated? Writers emphasized the fact that the great majority of prisoners came from the lower ranks of society.[98] The question, then, was to devise treatment which would even have a deterrent effect on those strata. This seems to have been a very difficult task, for we find complaints everywhere that the slight difference between prison conditions and normal existence was a major reason for the rapid increase of the prison population.

As early as 1802, the anonymous author of a pamphlet entitled *Warum werden so wenig Sträflinge in Zuchthaus gebes sert?* (*Why Are So Few Prisoners Improved in the House of Correction?*) commented that conditions in the Leipzig house of correction were too good, and that the inmates themselves were aware of that fact and expressed the desire to remain instead of returning to their customary life outside. This, he asserted, was a very bad state of affairs, for what could be more opposed to the true purpose of imprisonment than for a convict to feel that the comforts of prison life made up for the loss of freedom. And one need not wonder that they feel that way, the pamphlet concludes, when one compares their freedom from care, their light and pleasant work, the pocket money which they could save or spend as they wished, their daily meals, and their good clothing with the life to which they were accustomed, dressed in rags, condemned to work hard, feeling the eternal torment of trying to buy enough food with their inadequate earnings, unable to save a penny for a rainy day or for amusement, often unable to protect themselves against frost and disease.[99] The result was that many people who had committed a crime were not afraid of the house of correction, and some actually offended in order to be sent there and then begged to be allowed to remain permanently.[100] Impoverished citizens and journeymen were saying quite correctly: "Convicts are better off than we are; they throw more bread away than we can earn; they live a carefree life, feasting and drinking while we live in misery and cannot improve our lot." [101]

Béranger, an influential French writer and parliamentarian, remarked in 1836 that the administration should guard itself against exaggerating a rather untimely philanthropy which sought to increase the well-being of convicts. He warned that if prisons provided a more comfortable existence than the laborers in town and country could attain through their work, the prisons would cease to have a deterrent effect and released convicts would be induced to commit new crimes in order to return to jail.[102] Lucas expressed the same notion in the progressive ideology of the time when he said that prisoners are entitled to a share in the improvements of civilization, but to a lesser degree than the rest of society.[103] Füsslin, director of the

Bruchsal house of correction, took a modified position and emphasized the fact that the bad conditions outside rather than the relatively comfortable conditions in the prisons (the worst possible for warding off disease, he says), induce the poor to envy the lot of prisoners.[104]

In like manner, the 1825 report on the prison of the canton Waad, one of the most valuable documents of the whole prison literature of the period, insisted first of all that mere deprivation of liberty is no effective punishment for the lower classes. The conclusion was reached that the necessary condition for the prisoner's reëntry into society is unconditional submission to authority, a conclusion which has remained unshaken by reform programs and tendencies up to the present. If the prisoners resign themselves to a quiet, regular, and industrious life, punishment will become more tolerable for them. Once this routine becomes a habit, the first step toward improvement has been taken. As far as possible there must be a guaranty that the improvement will continue after the prisoner has been released. Obedience is demanded not so much for the smooth functioning of the prison but for the sake of the convict himself, who shall learn to submit willingly to the fate of the lower classes.[105] That is a difficult task. Obedience to the law is simple and self-evident for the upper classes, but it is almost hopeless to lift the ragged and starved prison inmates to such a level.[106] The chances of success were not considered very good, but the report indicated a practical method. To induce the convicts to economize, they were credited with the value of as much bread as they were able to refrain from consuming immediately. The saving was about 50 quintals a year, which went to the profit of the criminals without any added expense to the administration.[107] The convicts learn to economize even in times of want and misery, in preparation for worse times yet to come.

All agreed that nothing beyond the barest minimum should be supplied to the prisoners. In discussing the reproduction costs of labor power as the determining factor in wages, Marx remarked that political economy deals with the worker only in his capacity as worker.

Political economy therefore does not take account of the idler, the member of the working class, insofar as he finds himself excluded from the process of production. The scoundrel, the rogue, the beggar, the unemployed, the miserable, the starving, and the criminal, occupied in forced labor, are types which do not exist for it, existing only for the eyes of the physician, the judge, the grave digger, and the prison commissioner—ghosts outside of its realm.[108]

In the period when houses of correction were centers of production, the necessity of providing for the reproduction of labor power was extended to prisoners too. Now, however, this need no longer exists, or, as Marx put it "political economy does not take notice of them." [109]

The upper margin for the maintenance of the prisoners was thus determined by the necessity of keeping the prisoners' living standard below the living standard of the lowest classes of the free population.[110] The lower margin, accepted everywhere and explicitly prescribed by a Royal English Commission in 1850, was set by the minimum requirements of health.[111] But the possibilities of variation between these two were merely theoretical. Wages in the first half of the nineteenth century were frequently lower than the minimum necessary to reproduce the labor power of the workers. In other words, the lower margin prescribed by prison regulations was often not attained by free men. That means that the miserable conditions of the working class reduced the standard of prison life far below the officially recognized minimum level.

The old and once satisfactory arrangement whereby the feeding and care of the prisoners was entrusted to entrepreneurs who were financially interested in their physical well-being and capacity for work now had very distressing consequences. As rations were cut down to the very minimum, we hear a great deal about starvation in prisons, about the eating of candles and even of refuse.[112] Voit reports that it was considered sufficient to buy the cheapest foodstuffs available and to cook them in the simplest way, at least in most European countries, so that prisoners were virtually limited to a vegetable diet of mashed potatoes and bad bread in large quantities, clearly one of the chief causes of the poor health and the high death rate in the jails.[113] There was no medical attention even where special sick rooms were set aside for the prisoners, since the superintendent often had to pay doctor's bills and the cost of medicines out of his own small salary.[114] It is not surprising that sixty to eighty percent of the prison deaths were the result of tuberculosis,[115] even according to official figures.

Chassinat discovered that the life expectation of middle-aged convicts was reduced by 32 or 33 years in the *bagni* and by 36 years in the prisons, so that a galley convict of 30 had the same life expectation as a free man of 62 or 63. The mortality among prisoners was colossal when one considers that most of them were in their early manhood. Wappäus noted that if one took the average age of inmates as 40, a high estimate, one would see that their mortality was three, four, and even five times as great as that of the free population. According to Engel, the annual mortality in the Prussian prisons from 1858 to 1863 averaged 31.6 per 1,000. This was the death rate for men between 58 and 60 among the free population, whereas the average age of prisoners was not over 35 to 38, and their normal mortality would have been about 10 per 1,000.[116] Finally, we must remember that many prisoners were released in such poor health that they died soon after.[117]

4. THE NEW ATTITUDE TOWARD PRISON LABOR

Bad as prison conditions were because of the deliberate policy of starving the prisoners and because of the steadily increasing number of convicts without a corresponding increase in the funds available, they were made still more intolerable by the change in the system of convict labor. It was not necessary for a cruel tyrant to appear and turn the houses of correction into places of torment. The simple fact that they were no longer paying propositions was sufficient. The profit which had accrued to prison managers when men were scarce and wages high disappeared, driving them into bankruptcy or forcing them to abandon the enterprise; and, further, the revenues were no longer sufficient for the upkeep of either prisoners or warders.

The Webbs correctly emphasize the fact that the industrial revolution was making it more and more difficult to obtain any real profit from the demoralized and indiscriminately assembled prisoners.[118] The development of machinery had so destroyed the value of work by hand that it was entirely out of the question to support a remunerative system of nonmachine labor in the jails, as Sir G. O. Paul stated in his speech before a House of Commons committee in 1819.[119] The same report said that it had long since been discovered from English experience that, whatever the means used to encourage or stimulate work, goods could seldom be produced in a prison with any reasonable prospect of gain, or even without serious risk of loss. In parts of the country there might be a few prisons to which people would be willing to send raw materials from the neighborhood, paying for the labor when they received the manufactured articles; but such employment would necessarily be precarious and apt to cease at any moment. It could never be prudent for those who managed houses of correction—or poorhouses—to manufacture articles in large quantities for sale throughout the country, owing to the uncertainty of finding a market, among other reasons.[120]

On the basis of French experience, Lucas drew the general conclusion that the European prison system everywhere was operating under the hypothesis that the state could not meet the costs by the products of convict labor.[121] Houses of correction suddenly found themselves entirely dependent on subsidies. An attempt was naturally made to keep the subsidies as low as possible. There were two ways of doing this. One was to continue farming out the prison, no longer to the highest bidder but to the manager who requested the smallest subsidy for overhead and for feeding the prisoners. The other way was for the government to operate the prisons itself. The administration of prisons could be combined with the maintenance of retired army men. Krohne, discussing Prussian prison conditions, writes that there arose a useful and cheap source of officials in the form of retired officers.[122] In this way, too, military order and discipline were introduced into the prisons.[123]

With the new economic conditions, the competition on the open market between the products of prison labor and free labor became a serious problem. There had never been a time when people did not complain about it. In the mercantilist period the corporations placed difficulties in the way of convict labor, especially by refusing to accept apprentices from the prisons.[124] This opposition could not accomplish its purpose, however, because there was a shortage of labor and because prison-made goods were often superior. Now matters had changed, and convict work was vehemently attacked by the working class and employers alike. Beaumont and Tocqueville emphasized the difficulties in determining the precise moment when manufactories, or any system of productive labor, might be established in the jails without detriment to free citizens.[125] They maintained that the system prevailing in American prisons, which was to make the labor of the convicts as productive as possible, was quite correct in that country where the price of labor was high and where there was no danger that the establishment of prison manufactories would injure the free workers. It is generally to the interest of a nation, they continued, that the mass of production should constantly increase, because prices fall in proportion to the increase in volume, and the consumer would thus grow richer. In countries where the expansion of production has already reduced the price of commodities to its lowest level, however, production cannot be further increased without harm to the working class. Production is presumed to be at its lowest price when the wage of the workman allows him to purchase the bare necessities of life. The prison works to diminish its expenses, not to profit; and so it can lower prices at will without endangering its existence. If prices fall, the contractor pays less for the labor of the prisoners and the government has to pay more for their support. The ordinary workman, on the contrary, can live only when he earns money, and if the price of the commodity is too low to yield a profit the establishment must close down. After all, they argued, the capital of the free manufactory is limited and cannot withstand all losses, whereas the capital of a prison—the public treasury—is infinite.[126]

We have seen that the houses of correction used to spur the inmates to greater industry by paying them according to their work or by giving them a share of the profits. They were punished only if they failed to perform their task, whether from lack of skill or from laziness.[127] Now that it no longer paid to employ prisoners, however, they were frequently left with nothing to do. This raised the whole problem of the purpose of imprisonment, and brought its repressive, deterrent side to the fore. The way was open for the realization of the programs of reformers like Pearson and Mittelstädt, who sought to make the prisons rational and efficient means of deterring the lower classes from crime, means which would not allow the convict to perish, but which would impress him once and for all by fear and terror.[128] England, with its large industrial reserve army, led the way. Work was introduced as a form of punishment, not as a source of profit, and moral arguments were brought forward as a justification. One experienced administrator explained in 1821 that work which was to produce profit would interfere with discipline and moral improvement, because, for purposes of manufacture, the taskmaster would seek to assemble prisoners who would otherwise not be permitted to associate with each other.[129]

Prison labor became a method of torture, and the authorities were expert enough in inventing new forms; occupations of a purely punitive character were made as fatiguing as possible and were dragged out for unbearable lengths of time.[130] Prisoners carried huge stones from one place to another and then back again, they worked pumps from which the water flowed back to its source, or trod mills which did no useful work. A simple form of treadwheel, easily applicable to all prisons, was devised by William Cubitt about 1818 for use in the Suffolk County Gaol at Bury, and it was from this example that the practice spread. The cheapness and simplicity of the "stepping-mill" or "everlasting staircase," as it was called, the severe physical exertion required, and the hatred engendered by "wheel-stepping" commended the new device to Quarter Sessions, and models were set up in every reformed prison, grinding corn or grinding nothing, raising water, supplying power for hemp-beating, cork-cutting, or other machines.[131] Not only was the treadwheel regarded as a success because it afforded a cheap and easy method of forcing prisoners to work, but also because it deterred persons who might use the gaol as a place of ultimate refuge.[132]

The prisoners tried desperately to avoid such punishments.[133] A strong outside opposition also developed on the ground that the treadwheel was so exhausting as to destroy the prisoner's health and that it often amounted to actual torture. Furthermore, it was argued, such punishment counteracted every effort to reform the prisoner's character.[134] But official English opinion continued to favor strictly punitive labor, and it spread from prison to prison despite the attacks of the humanitarians. It was even to be found in the colonial penitentiaries of Hobart Town and Sidney.[135]

These developments also attracted attention outside of England. A German writer insisted on the infliction of penalties having a humiliating effect; if corporal punishment is abolished, he argued, there must be a substitute like the treadmill, which would soon come to be regarded as humiliating.[136] Mittelstädt welcomed the changes because they indicated a realization that the principles of justice demanded that imprisonment should be something more than mere deprivation of liberty and hence should entail a certain amount of positive pain and hardship.[137] German penal practice adhered to this conception until the middle of the nineteenth century. Judges did not trouble to distinguish between different degrees of imprisonment or to fix the term according to definite principles. Legislators and judges were indifferent to prison conditions. They were content to assume that hunger, flogging, and hard labor would do their work, and that there could be no one so poor and miserable but that fear and shame would ultimately force him to do everything in his power to stay outside the prison walls. The possibility that imprisonment could lose its intimidating effects lay beyond the realm of rational thought.[138]

VII

THE ABOLITION OF TRANSPORTATION

1. TRANSPORTATION TO AUSTRALIA

W HEN the American Revolution ended the transportation of convicts to North America,[1] the dilapidated English prisons were unable to stand the strain. They could not house the thousand or more prisoners who had formerly been shipped to North America every year.[2] The government began to look about for a solution. A law was passed in 1776 which temporarily replaced transportation by hard labor for the public benefit. Prisoners were occupied in raising sand, soil, and gravel from the River Thames for three to ten years (women and the more infirm males might be kept at hard labor in the county where convicted). The House of Commons was not satisfied with the working of the "hulks" (the ships where these convicts were lodged), and a committee was appointed in 1878 to inquire into the operation of the new statute. Duncan Campbell, the former contractor for transportation to America and now overseer of the prisoners working on the Thames, reported that 632 men had been received between August 1776 and March 1778, and that 176 had died, 24 had escaped, and 60 had been pardoned.[3] In 1179, a second commission found considerable improvement, but still no satisfactory solution. Howard visited the ships on several occasions and condemned the indiscriminate association of so many criminals as destructive of all morality.[4] New schemes for transportation were put forward against the arguments of those who feared the depopulation of the country. The East and West Indies, the Falkland Islands, and the remainder of British North America were all mentioned as possibilities. Australia was mentioned for the first time in a House of Commons debate on February 5, 1779,[5] but the suggestion went unheard for the moment. An attempt to ship a batch of prisoners to America in 1783 failed miserably. It had become evident in the meantime that the hulks, conceived as the first part of a transportation sentence, were nothing but reservoirs of criminals and were making matters worse. The new prisons of which the reformers spoke were not likely to be erected in the near future.[6]

These difficulties, together with the bad economic situation, led to a severe crisis in the administration of criminal law in the eighties. Madan's *Thoughts on Executive Justice* (1785) and Paley's *Moral and Political Philosophy* (1785) insisted on strict and impartial execution of the law.[7] They condemned the steady increase in pardons and commutations as weakening the whole legal structure. In 1786, the City of London petitioned the King for "a speedy and due execution of the law both as to capital punishment and as to transportation." The Pitt government gave in. Botany Bay in Australia was selected, the authorities were instructed to provide for the conveyance of 750 convicts, and Governor Philipp went out with the first convoy on May 3, 1787.[8] Since contractors were paid according to the number of prisoners embarked, not for the number landed, the mortality en route was very high, especially on the second transport.[9]

Conditions among the new Australian colonists were very bad in the first year, and the mortality rate was high. They had to depend on England for all their food, and the contractors preferred to ship expensive merchandise for sale to the officials and free settlers rather than the cheap articles supplied by the government for mass consumption.[10] The convicts were occupied on public works, clearing forest land and building barracks and roads, or they were assigned to settlers in return for food and clothing. When the official work day was over, they could hire themselves out to private employers, and in view of the scarcity of labor, the progress of agriculture can be attributed largely to the voluntary and paid labor of the prisoners.[11] An enabling act of 1790 gave the governor the right to remit sentences for good behavior. Other forms of indulgence grew up in later years, such as the ticket of leave and the conditional pardon. Governor Philipp began to make grants of land to the freed convicts, as well as tools, seeds, and foods for a specified period.

Philipp's departure in 1792 was followed by great social unrest throughout the growing colony. The food shortage became
less serious with the increased acreage under cultivation, and
there was less dependence on supplies from England, but the
army men had gained the upper hand and were exploiting their
power in order to enrich themselves. They arranged to have the
government pay for the upkeep of the convicts assigned to them,
and then sold the products of the convicts' labor to the government stores. They monopolized the liquor trade. Far too many
convicts were assigned to private individuals and public works
came to a standstill. All in all, the military rule proved disastrous
for thousands of convicts who were directly dependent on government support, but it was a stimulus to private enterprise.[12] Many
of the freed convicts failed to take advantage of the possibilities
available—the military liquor monopoly and the shortage of
women [13] played an important role—but Hunter's testimony before a select committee in 1812 correctly emphasizes the fact
"that there are many men who have been convicts and are now
settlers there, who were as respectable as any people who have
gone from this country." [14] Furthermore, the reactionary Pitt
government shipped a large number of political prisoners to
Australia, and they often held responsible posts as officers, doctors, schoolmasters, and businessmen.

By about 1800, the colony had gone through its worst period.
New South Wales had a population of nearly five thousand and
the area under cultivation had grown considerably.[15] Although
many ex-convicts were of no great use to the community and
many left after the expiration of their terms, the number of
emancipists who became satisfactorily adjusted proves that the
experiment was not a total failure. Many who had come into
conflict with the law in England were really given a fresh start
when they were sent to Australia. The liberal policy of free land
grants followed until 1830 gave transported convicts the opportunity to become colonists as soon as they had served their
terms. Even the unskilled had good prospects, for they too could
settle on the land as respected, though humble, squatters unless they had the misfortune to fall into the hands of a bad master,

whose mistreatment could shorten their lives or force them into the chain gangs. The prospects of the trained and educated convicts were of course much better. Able men were well paid and often worked their way into partnership with their masters. The emancipists became a strong moral force in the country because of their real prospects of making a living and their newly awakened feeling of independence. Every convict who was willing to work found employment in New South Wales even if he had no particular skill, and that was impossible in England. Unemployment and insecurity were virtually unknown. Men like Howard, who foretold the collapse of the whole scheme, were completely refuted in the course of half a century, while others were much too enthusiastic and overlooked the dark sides of early colonial life in Australia. It is incontestable that the opportunities of those convicts who survived the hardships of transportation and the occasional mistreatment by a private master or overseer of public works were very bright in comparison with the possibilities in the mother country.[16]

England had at first been much too absorbed in the war with America and in European affairs to pay much attention to Australia. But now people began to take an interest in New South Wales. With its increasing wealth and prosperity it began to offer opportunities both for capital investment and for new settlers. The result was a serious change in the structure of the colonial population. Of the total population of 23,939 in 1820, only 1,307 were free and 1,495 were born in the colony.[17] By 1828, there were 36,598 inhabitants of whom 4,673 were free and 8,727 native.[18] The proportion continued to change still more rapidly; 1,300 free immigrants arrived in 1835, and 18,581 in 1841, far exceeding the number of convicts.[19]

The minority of free settlers, the government officials, the army men, the free farmers, and businessmen soon developed a distinct aristocratic pride. They were "good society" and it was degrading to mix with people who "bore the brand of crime." [20] The Australian Patriotic Association, founded by the old aristocracy, was primarily directed against the continued immigration of free settlers which threatened to destroy their social monopoly. This aristocracy welcomed transportation as a source of cheap labor. The chief reason for the introduction of auction sales of land at minimum prices in 1831, sponsored by Wakefield to replace the free land grants, was to prevent laborers from becoming landowners at once. Wakefield made a sharp criticism of the prevailing colonization methods because in New South Wales, unlike England, it was impossible to find laborers for the large estates. The reason, he thought, was that the lower classes, who had to hire themselves out in England, could acquire property of their own in Australia. He considered it a great misfortune that people who came to the colonies as craftsmen were able to become landowners, and that labor was as expensive as land was cheap. His proposal was to turn Australia into an aristocratic country. Propertyless workers from England could be sent out to work for the benefit of the colony. At Wakefield's suggestion, the proceeds from the sale of Crown lands were used in part to pay for the passage of poor immigrants.[21]

The position of the emancipists underwent a serious change. They had once had the opportunity to become independent farmers, having learned the trade while serving their terms, but now that land was no longer free they were shut out from acquiring the very land which, but for them, would have remained uncultivated for a long time. One of the aims of the new policy was to help provide the big landowners with sufficient labor power. Having thus lost the prospect of becoming free settlers, many emancipists began to leave the farms for the towns, where they could obtain lighter and more pleasant employment.[22] In other words, they returned to the ranks of the laboring class from which most of them had originally come. The newly arrived free immigrants found it necessary to do away with the cheap labor of convicts and emancipists in order to maintain high wages for themselves. They joined in demanding the abolition of transportation. Opposed to them were those emancipists and "exclusives" (old free settlers) who were employers and who profited from cheap convict labor. The steady stream of free immigrants, eager to maintain a high standard of living, left no doubt about the eventual victor. After extensive parliamentary debates, transportation to New South Wales was discontinued in 1840.[23]

There were several interesting divergences in the development of Van Diemen's Land, the most important transportation district in Australia next to New South Wales.[24] Governor Arthur (1824–36) made a deliberate effort to maintain the penal character of this settlement. From the very beginning of his term of office, he tried to introduce a thoroughly hierarchical system, carefully separating the convicts from the free settlers. With its perfect police organization, its unlimited exploitation and subjugation of the convicts, and its attempt to control the whole of the free population by economic pressure—the free colonists were in his eyes nothing but "amateur gaolers to be coerced into efficiency" [25]—Arthur's system was severely criticized by contemporaries. Even official reports speak of the ordeals and evils of his methods.[26] As in New South Wales, the chief advantage to the free settlers lay in the assignment of convicts; and the disproportion between supply and demand gave Arthur a welcome means of pressure on the settlers.[27] In the second place, the penal colony was a market which they supplied; the costs were borne by England until 1840. Thus, when an address was presented to the Secretary of State in 1835, in which the petitioners sought "to remove from the Colony of Van Diemen's Land the degradation and other unspeakable evils to which it is subjected in consequence of its present penal character," it was easy for Arthur to explain in a postscript that this petition was framed by a meeting "entirely composed of residents of Hobart Town and therefore of the class least dependent on convict labor." [28] Arthur even hindered the influx of free people into the towns (unlike New South Wales) for he realized that they were a threat to the very existence of the penal colony. He blocked the movement toward the towns by free distribution of all available land, so that there was not enough left for the new land sale policy which was to provide the money for further immigration.[29]

The English working class was still comparatively well off in the period when transportation to Australia began. As time went on, however, their situation became worse until it reached the level of utter destitution at the end of the Napoleonic Wars. During the first phase, the long and tedious journey to an unknown destination and the lifelong exile were regarded as a harsh punishment in themselves, especially for convicts coming from the soil, for whom, as experience showed, transplantation conveyed an additional horror. The mere fact of exile lost much of its terror as soon as the journey became more familiar and the poor or "criminal" classes, as they were called, began to have friends and relatives on the other side.

> "Let us haste away to Botany Bay,
> Where there is plenty and nothing to pay." [30]

Such a verse shows a new attitude which is easy to understand. In England a free worker met almost insuperable difficulties in the way of finding ordinary manual labor, even in the industrial districts, and conditions in Australia were much better.[31]

The instructions of the government to Commissioner Bigge in 1819 already reveal a fear that the deterrent effect of transportation might not be strong enough.[32] Governor Arthur received the following instructions for severity (unnecessary for a man of his disposition) in dispatches from Colonial Secretary Bathurst on March 31 and April 23, 1826:

It appears very essential to the ends of Justice that no practicable means should be neglected of keeping up in the minds of criminals that salutary apprehension of transportation which originally existed. . . . Any measure which with a due attention to legal powers with which you are invested will enable you to enforce a stricter discipline, should be resorted to.[33]

Arthur was of the opinion that the "criminal classes" should be officially informed of the real fate which awaited transported convicts. It was difficult, however, to convince the lower classes that New South Wales and Van Diemen's Land were not the promised land they imagined, for ex-convicts were sending back "glowing accounts," as the report of the 1838 committee demonstrates.[34] Even the extreme terror and disciplinary system of Arthur, which was limited by the economic needs of the colony, had little success in overcoming the attractiveness of transportation as compared with the miserable conditions of the lower classes in England.

Specific concrete interests, not abstract feelings of justice, thus led people to realize that there was a false proportion between guilt and punishment and that transportation had no real deterrent effect on crime. The very factors which were responsible for the changes in the administration of the houses of correction also had considerable weight in the negative attitude that developed with regard to transportation. As early as 1833, the committee investigating the demands for the abolition of transportation proposed the discontinuance of the existing arrangements. Its president, Molesworth, wrote to his constituents that they were "inefficient, cruel and demoralizing, full of absurdity and wickedness." [35] Russell made special reference to the point that the extent of guilt was not sufficiently considered in the treatment of the convicts. In his opinion, it was a case of confusing questions of colonial profit and loss with the problem of justice.[36] Colonial society, for its part, treated the convict according to his usefulness and the personal sympathy of the master, and not according to his guilt. In other words, the possibility of using his labor power determined the value and fate of the prisoner just as in the criminal policy of mercantilism.

The continued English and Australian objections prompted the 1838 committee to take a stand for the abolition of the existing system. Its report, however, stressed the poor results in the improvement of the convicts rather than the weak deterrent effect. The failure of the convicts to "improve" was the fault of a system that produced a peasant class which, in the words of the report, was "without domestic feelings or affections, without wives, children or homes; one more strange and less attached to the soil they till, than the negro slaves of a planter." [37] It was a peasant class which lived in a condition of virtual slavery. Furthermore, the reformatory aims were less important than the interests of the free colonists and still less important than the real or presumed interests of the criminal policy of the English ruling class. A new method of procedure was therefore recommended, one which would both relieve the colonies and strengthen the deterrent aspects. This policy, which the committee considered to be cheaper and more to the point, consisted in a system of grading, ranging from solitary confinement in an English prison to public work in ports and labor colonies and finally to ticket-of-leave transportation.[38] This system was to have the advantage of destroying the dreams of the lower classes for free passage to a land without unemployment and at the same time of partially satisfying the desire of the colonies for the discontinuance of transportation. It was to make the life of prisoners less comfortable than that of the poorest free laborer in England.

In spite of the slow rise of its free population—the percentage of convicts was 46.8 in 1824, 41.6 in 1830, and 39.6 in 1838 [39] —Van Diemen's Land would have retained its character as a penal colony if the home government had not radically changed its policy in 1840. The assignment system was discontinued although convict shipments increased when New South Wales stopped accepting them. The same reform made the penal colony self-supporting by requiring the convicts to grow their own food.[40] These two changes, the decline of cheap labor and the decline of the market, destroyed the interest of the settlers in maintaining the penal character of the colony. The result was the same as in New South Wales. Financial support was withdrawn and the interests of free labor were brought more strongly to the fore. Agitation against transportation grew to such a degree that transportation was finally discontinued in 1852.[41] A new outlet for ticket-of-leave holders was then found in West Australia, which literally begged for compulsory labor, and 9,718 were sent there between 1850 and 1868.[42]

The history of English transportation gives us a clear and straightforward picture of the effects of changing social and economic conditions on criminal policy. The starting point was the impossibility of accommodating the increasing number of criminals in the existing prisons at a time when the labor market was oversupplied. If they were not to be executed, a policy opposed by prevailing population theories even before humanitarian principles made themselves felt, the only way to dispose of them was to banish them from the country. For a time, this solution coincided with the need for labor power in the colonies. But American conditions had already demonstrated the limited possibilities of absorbing convict labor. The colonial economic system made its continuance impossible long before political conditions finally put an end to transportation. In New South Wales and Van Diemen's Land it was shown that convict labor with financial assistance from the mother country was a possible foundation for further development, but that convict labor could not compete with free labor the moment the latter began to assume appreciable proportions.

Michaud, an official in the French colonial office in the second half of the nineteenth century, gave a fairly good description of this development when he said that the role of transportation was that of a pioneer who opens up hitherto unexplored lands. It would be just as harmful, however, to permit transportation into already organized societies as to isolate convicts in a desert. Transportation requires a rising society, tortured by its needs and hungry for labor supply. Only a society in process of formation permits reclassification, for necessity silences prejudice. When a new society emerges from the chaos and develops its own laws, it will reject transportation. Michaud concluded with an attempt to formulate a social philosophy of retributive justice from the rather brutal facts of economic developments. The function of transportation is to keep marching on and to make the criminal pay for the evils of his crime by blazing new paths.[43]

2. TRANSPORTATION IN OTHER COUNTRIES

Economic development of her colonies motivated French transportation for only a very short time. In the seventeenth and eighteenth centuries France made sporadic attempts along English lines to transplant portions of her criminal population. Authorized by royal decrees of January 8, 1701, March 12, 1719, and March 10, 1720, a few transports (now remembered chiefly because of Manon Lescaut) were shipped to New Orleans.[44] These efforts were soon abandoned for reasons with which we are already conversant from English experience, clearly expressed in the decree of 1722, abolishing transportation: "The colonies are at present peopled with a number of families who are much more fitted to carry on commerce with the natives of the country than these types of individuals who bring with them all the evils of their indolence and bad morals." [45] From this time on transportation followed the needs of French penal practice, and colonial policy played a minor role. Transportation was reintroduced as a result of the terrible conditions in the *bagni* of Toulon and Marseilles, where the worst criminals had been herded after the abolition of galley servitude. Those inmates who were leased to manufacturers and artisans had a tolerable existence, but the remainder, compelled to work in the arsenals and ports, lived miserably. Corruption was rife, the moral standard was extremely low, and the costs were high, not an unimportant consideration for the government. [46] It was therefore decided to reëstablish transportation in 1791, a project which proved impracticable because of the destruction of the fleet. Transportation to Guiana finally began in 1854.

The observations of Holtzendorff generally hold true for the Guiana colonies and they are accepted even by French administrative authorities. He wrote that under conditions of this sort one could not speak about a system and plan of employment, for only the doctors in the hospitals, not the convicts in the prisons, found regular work. [47] Deportation to this country, with a climate wholly unsuitable for Europeans, merely fulfilled the purpose of eliminating from the mother country people who were considered dangerous to society. It did that all the more effectively because a law of March 31, 1854, provided that, after the end of the sentence proper, every convict had to remain in the colony for an additional period equal to his penal term (*doublage*). This measure was successful in that recidivism among transported convicts (*forçats*) reached ninety percent before 1854, whereas the *doublage* system, which meant that they spent virtually all of their lives in the colony, drove it down to eleven percent. [48] But deportation to Guiana had no advantage beyond this eliminatory effect. There were no illusions about the colonizing value of convict labor in a colony where labor efficiency was practically zero and where there were no opportunities for work after emancipation.[49] Deportation was therefore a heavy financial burden on the state, and at the end of the nineteenth century the cost per convict was twice the cost in French penitentiaries.[50] Provisionally abolished in 1924, it was reintroduced in 1926 and finally abolished in 1937.[51]

The attempt which began in 1864 to transport criminals to New Caledonia is more interesting than the history of deportation to Guiana. The climate was much better, the land had great possibilities of development, and there was a crying need for labor power. The legend of the marvelous country spread through the French prisons so quickly that the inmates began to commit new crimes in order to be sent there. To combat this, a law was passed on December 25, 1880, providing that the new term of imprisonment was to be served in the prison from which the convict wanted to escape, not in the colonies.[52] The development of the penal settlements, however, did not take the line expected. The interests of the administration, of the large producers, and of the small freeholders were mutually antagonistic. The costs of administration and of the upkeep of the convicts were met by the mother country, so the officials showed no particular interest either in the development of the free settlers or in the future of the convicts. They reserved the largest part of the land for the administration, and only a small part of it was cultivated by convicts, who were either retained by the officials as servants or were exploited by the large companies at nominal wages, arousing the antagonism of the free settlers.[53] The pressure brought by the latter and the poor deterrent effect on crime were responsible for the end of transportation to New Caledonia in 1898.

For a country which does not possess colonies the question of transportation is obviously much more difficult. In the sixteenth and seventeenth centuries, the German authorities had handed criminals over to foreign countries for use in the galleys or in military service, and in the eighteenth century they were shipped to North America as slaves. Hamburg made particular use of this method, especially for foreign criminals.[54] At the beginning of the nineteenth century Russia made an agreement with Prussia to accept Prussian convicts in Siberia. But resistance in Russia was so strong and so many convicts succeeded in making their escape and returning home that the practice was quickly discontinued. Hamburg's efforts to come to an agreement with Australia in 1836 likewise remained fruitless.[55] In sum, deportation was no consideration in the nineteenth century for countries without colonies, since even the countries with colonies either were having their difficulties with the colonial population (England) or were unable to achieve any real reformatory effects (France), now that economic motives for penal colonization had disappeared.

VIII

THE FAILURE OF SOLITARY
CONFINEMENT

THE nineteenth century saw the widespread use of solitary confinement in Europe. In order to understand its history, we must first examine its use in the United States, where the peculiar conditions of the labor market constituted one reason for a relatively rapid change in penal policy.

1. SOLITARY CONFINEMENT IN THE UNITED STATES

Prison conditions in the United States at the beginning of the nineteenth century were very similar to those found by Howard in England in the last decades of the eighteenth. Financial considerations were predominant,[1] and it is therefore not astonishing that a system which promised to do away with financial abuses met with enthusiastic approval. The first, introduced with the help of the Quakers in Philadelphia in 1790, approximated the proposals of Mabillon in its leading ideas. Its essential feature was solitary confinement. The prisoners were isolated in single cells, which they never left until their time was up or until they died or went mad.[2]

The Quakers believed religion to be the only and sufficient basis of education, and they expected solitary confinement to have the effect of turning the sinner back to God. Prisoners were left to their own resources to such an extreme that they were not even allowed to work lest it divert them from self-contemplation.[3] The only occupation allowed was Bible-reading. Association with pious persons was considered helpful in the process of reform, and such persons were encouraged to visit the prisoners and to attempt to influence them. It was also argued that prisoners would thus run no danger of being corrupted by incorrigible criminals. Herding prisoners together does not destroy the original incentive to crime, but actually fosters it. Furthermore, it was a just system because real deprivation of liberty could be attained only through solitary confinement.[4] None of its exponents doubted for a moment that the results of such a regime could be anything but self-examination, self-knowledge, and character reform. An additional motive for sponsoring the system was the belief that the labor of prisoners would never be profitable.[5] The report of the Board of Inspectors of 1837 on the new prison system established in New Jersey in 1836 came to the conclusion that the Pennsylvania system was the only civilized one known.[6]

For all the enthusiasm of its advocates, however, this system of solitary confinement was soon abandoned in nearly every case, and replaced by the so-called Auburn system.[7] To understand this development, we must consider not only the psychological aspects, but also the state of the American labor market in the north. In the early nineteenth century there was a greater demand for workers in the United States than at any time during the mercantilist period in Europe. The importation of slaves had become much more difficult as a result of new regulations. The availability of free land and the rapid industrial development created in the labor market a vacuum which could not be filled by immigration. Anyone could find work, and wages were at least sufficient for the purchase of necessities. European visitors invariably concluded that American social conditions compared very favorably with conditions in their native countries.[8] Beaumont and Tocqueville said that France, a much richer country than the United States, had much more poverty and beggary on account of the more unequal distribution of riches. Whereas there was one pauper for every 16 inhabitants in France, in the state of New York there was only one in 107 including foreigners or one in 126 without foreigners.[9] The scarcity of labor is shown by the attention which was devoted to waifs and strays. What Adam Smith wrote about a thinly populated country colonized by a civilized nation applied: "The children, during the tender years of infancy, are well fed and properly taken care of, and when they are grown up, the value of their labour greatly overpays their maintenance." [10]

The shortage of workers was one cause of the "remarkable degree of law and order among the settlers." [11] "It must not be concealed that one great reason why crimes are so infrequent," wrote the attorney general of Maryland in 1832, "is the full employment the whole country offers to those who are willing to labor, while at the same time the ordinary rate of wages for a healthy man is sufficient to support him and the family. This is the point of which you will not lose sight in comparing the institutions of America with those of Europe." [12] Second offenses were comparatively rare. Convicts could easily find work after their release and the conditions (especially the high wages) fostered good conduct. Beaumont and Tocqueville drew a comparison with France where even those convicts who were resolved to lead an honest life were not infrequently forced back into crime by necessity.[13]

A shrewd German observer writing anonymously in 1802 stated this difference very clearly:

If in Philadelphia, where convicts are treated according to Howard's principles, a treatment which ought to be an example for other states, the ex-prisoners were not able to get their full value as laborers, if those states in which there exists a particularly strong spirit supported by the noble and patriotic aspirations of the Quakers, did not provide work for them on a large scale, and if the wages for such work and for any services rendered were not so attractive and so well worth working for; if indeed men were not more scarce there than they are here where a large population reduces a man's value towards zero, one would find the same decay of the system of punishment as in the European prisons.[14]

With such a background, one can readily understand why most administrators responsible for criminal justice thought it absurd to keep prisoners in solitary confinement and thus to allow their labor to go unused. The European mercantilists had similarly condemned the loss of valuable labor power by the destruction of criminals. When regular work was provided for all inmates of the state prisons of Pennsylvania in 1829, it proved to be very unprofitable. This method of restricting each prisoner to the labor which he could perform in his own cell might have been reformatory, but it could not have been remunerative.

The governor of New Jersey, where the Pennsylvania system had been introduced in 1836, concluded in his annual message for 1857 that no revenue had been derived from the state prison, that it was becoming a heavy charge upon the state, and that the existing system of discipline was inhuman and failed to answer its avowed purposes. Besides being more expensive than the old system of workhouses, it did not reform convicts. In the governor's opinion, therefore, the system should be changed.[15] The difficulties were increased by the industrial revolution. It should be remembered that one of the reasons for the breakdown of the older prison labor system at the end of the eighteenth century was the fact that the manufacture system could not compete with the new factories. Now that it was necessary to install machinery in the prison workshops if there was to be the slightest chance of competing with outside enterprises, the prison with separate cells had to carry out its industrial production under great handicaps.

Nearly every prison shifted to the Auburn system, which became practically synonymous with American penal administration.[16] This method of solitary confinement at night and collective labor in the workshops during the day permitted the organization of the prisoners for maximum industrial efficiency. With the gradual spread of machinery, it had a tremendous advantage over any cell system.[17] The prisons became busy factories once again and began to produce goods on a profitable basis. The Quaker theory of solitary confinement retained a certain measure of influence, however, in that the barrier of silence was introduced in order to prevent the mutual contamination of prisoners and to make them indulge in moral reflection.[18] Theorists insisted on the reformatory value of hard labor and on the other advantages of collective work as against solitary work in the cells. As a matter of fact, the prisoners were not merely forced to contemplate their own worthlessness, but were also provided with some small diversion, which gave them the external stimulus deemed necessary for mental health. In sum, we may accept Jagemann's conclusion that the term "penal

labor" virtually lost its meaning in America, since merely punitive labor like the treadmill was never used.[19]

Capitalists became accustomed to contract for the services of
such convict labor as they desired. At first the lease system allowed them to take complete charge of the prisoners during
working hours, but it was gradually supplanted by the so-called
"piece-price" system which left the supervision in the hands of
the authorities. The Civil War created an unprecedented need
for cheap clothing and rough footwear, which was satisfied by a
great increase in the use of prison labor.[20] Short- and long-term
criminals began to be separated. One reason why special prisons
were built for the latter must have been the fact that their labor
could be exploited much more profitably than that of short-term
offenders. Beaumont and Tocqueville produced statistics to
show that the new prison regime was established at small expense, was self-supporting, and was even a source of revenue.
They noted a steady reduction in prison costs after 1820 and a
surplus for the exchequer after 1830 as follows: Auburn $25 in
1830 and $1,800 in 1831; Wethersfield $1,000 in 1828, over
$3,200 in 1829, and nearly $8,000 in 1831; Baltimore $11,500
in 1828 and nearly $20,000 in 1829.[21]

Europeans believed the Auburn system to be far too lenient,
especially since prisoners were stimulated to work by the expectation of privileges and rewards, rather than through discipline.[22] It created the possibility of measuring good behavior
by a quantitative test, the amount of work performed. The practice of commutation was connected with this approach. A New
York statute of 1817, put into operation in the Auburn prison,
provided that all prisoners sentenced for five years or more could
earn a reduction of one-quarter of their sentence by good behavior. Such laws had great value for the administration. The
hope of commutation tended to reinforce discipline while serving as a substitute for money wages.[23]

The curtailment of convict labor in the last decades of the
nineteenth century was largely the result of opposition on the
part of the free workers. This opposition was always strong, but

it received a fresh stimulus from the gradual disappearance of the frontier. Wherever working-class organizations were powerful enough to influence state politics, they succeeded in obtaining complete abolition of all forms of prison labor (Pennsylvania in 1897, for example), causing much suffering to the prisoners, or at least in obtaining very considerable limitations, such as work without modern machinery, conventional rather than modern types of prison industry, or work for the government instead of for the free market.[24]

2. SOLITARY CONFINEMENT IN EUROPE

The Americans, as we have shown, did little experimenting with the system of solitary confinement. It was instituted in a few places and quickly abandoned because it was more profitable to turn the prisons into factories. The aims of criminal justice were satisfied merely by depriving law-breakers of their freedom and by making them work without appropriate pay, so that "the chief aim of a prison," as the Gluecks remark, seemed to be "to manufacture articles rather than remake human beings." [25] The prison authorities were not interested in the fate of the prisoners after their release. The report of a royal commission of 1863 stated that men branded by their prison records suffered an almost insuperable disadvantage in the severe competition for employment. Although some masters were willing to hire ex-convicts from motives of charity, it was necessary to conceal their previous condition from the other employees, who would refuse to work with them if they knew the truth. This feeling among the free working population, the commission held, was one which it was neither possible nor desirable to overcome.[26]

What European society with its industrial reserve army needed was a punishment which would strike fear even into the hearts of the starving. Beaumont and Tocqueville wrote that "in every place where one half of the community is cruelly oppressed by the other, we must expect to find in the law of the oppressor, a weapon always ready to strike nature which revolts all humanity that complains." [27] This idea of intimidation played an important part in the introduction of solitary confinement in

Europe. The feeling of complete dependence and helplessness which solitary confinement engenders was considered to be the worst torment one could inflict.[28]

The idea of possible intimidation was only one of the reasons for the introduction of solitary confinement. We have already dealt with the others, the ever-increasing number of prisoners and the impossibility of profitable exploitation of convict labor power. A small number of zealous reformers, like Stephen Grellet, Elisabeth Fry, Bedford, the two Gurneys, Allen Buxton, Theodor Fliedner, and Mathilde Wrede,[29] protested against the deterioration of prison conditions resulting from overcrowding and the absence of productive labor. Their well-meaning and necessary condemnation of the old methods gave rise to a number of experiments carried out on living subjects, which did away with some of the prevailing evils, but also led to new methods in comparison with which the barbarous treatment of the past seems almost merciful. The reformers saw their hopes realized in a strict system of solitary confinement, though they would have rejected any suggestion of a return to medieval forms of punishment. They did not want prisoners to be tortured; they wanted them to be reformed. Although they had not entirely given up the idea of prison as a deterrent force, their consciences would never have allowed them to accept a return to corporal punishment.

The great things expected of solitary confinement in the middle of the nineteenth century are well illustrated by Lieber's enthusiastic remarks:

We have to do with a cause in which millions and millions are interested, individually and collectively, bodily and morally, and though all the world should have penitentiaries on the Pennsylvania plan, and but one single prison on a different one should remain, and men should persuade the people not to change it, it would be worth our labor to answer the arguments and to endeavor to induce the people to change their penitentiary, as soon as circumstances may permit: for there are living men involved in this question; suffering men; more or less guilty men, some of whom may yet be rescued: generations of convicts yet unborn are in question, who, like most of their predecessors, shall begin with apparently trifling offences

when young and at a stage of life and criminality, when they yet
may be brought back to the paths of order, loyalty, industry, and
worth—generations that in turn shall become parents, and upon
whom the moral issue of their offspring will depend again.[30]

In defense of solitary confinement, the reformers argued that
intemperance and thoughtlessness are the causes of crime, and
that the prisons are full of people who have never seriously
thought about things. Now all is changed. Alone in his cell, the
criminal is assailed with recollections, his conscience troubles
him, a revulsion of feeling sets in, a struggle ensues between de-
praved habits and the stirrings of his better nature (which unfortunately brings some prisoners to the lunatic asylum), often
followed by insight, remorse, and a change of attitude.[31] Advocates of solitary confinement raised the further defense that it
works with automatic justice. As Füsslin stated it, the intimidating effect is shown by the fact that a man dreads solitude in
proportion to his moral depravity, so that the worst criminals
will fear solitary confinement most, whereas those who have not
sunk so far and who are more capable of being reformed will
actually look upon it as a favor.[32]

Solitary confinement was obviously advantageous to prison
governors and officials in maintaining proper discipline. Under
the old system they were faced with masses of unruly prisoners,
who were more and more inclined to revolt against the prison
officers as the needs of the time seemed to require increasingly
harsh treatment. The new system made it easy to govern a prison,
for the entire force of the authorities as well as the very archi-
tecture of the jail could be brought to bear on a single inmate.[33]
It must also be remembered that solitary confinement made
possible a calmer and more objective attitude toward criminals
without any relaxation of prison discipline. "The officials like
it," wrote Hepworth Dixon in the middle of the century. "It
gives them very little trouble, so, without pretending to understand its complicated effects, moral or mental, they almost all
swear by it." [34] Most of the official European investigators who
visited American prisons reported back in favor of the Pennsylvania system. The First International Prison Congress held in

Frankfurt in 1846 voted for it by a large majority, and after that nothing could prevent its triumphant progress through Germany, France, Belgium, and Holland.[35]

Where the system of solitary confinement was not adopted—and the reason was usually the cost of the necessary structural changes—an effort was made to obtain its advantages in a less elaborate fashion. Wagnitz had already advocated compulsory silence and the use of the privilege of conversation as a reward for good behavior.[36] This proposal now came into practice. In order to isolate prisoners who were still living together, absolute silence was imposed. Convicts were even obliged to remain sitting or standing in their places during their free time, Sundays and holidays.[37] In general, this system was looked upon as a mere substitute for solitary confinement, temporary if possible, for, as Beaumont and Tocqueville phrased it, "silence is easy for him who is alone." [38] In England, the conflict between the separate system and the silent system ended (at least theoretically) with a clear victory for the former when an investigating committee in 1863 came to the conclusion that "the system generally known as the Separate System must now be accepted as the foundation of prison discipline, and that its rigid maintenance is a vital principle to the efficiency of county and borough gaols." [39]

The results of the new method did not come up to expectations. The chief concern of administrators was to keep the prisoners isolated from one another. "Everything was done to render the separation real and complete; exercise was taken in separate yards, and masks were worn to prevent recognition." [40] For their part, the prisoners had but one thought as they sat in their cells, and that was how to establish contact with their fellow sufferers.[41] Prison labor was bound to be unproductive under such conditions, and it was largely abandoned. The idea of increasing the punishment played some part in this change, as we have already indicated. After 1848 the "crank," a kind of handmill, tended to displace all other forms of work in England; only in local prisons was productive labor retained in some degree until the centralization of prison supervision in 1877. Work on the "crank" could be made harder or easier by introducing sand or by adjusting a string.[42] It was provided with a device for registering the number of turns of the handle and that was its sole purpose. Its advocates quite frankly grounded their case upon its harshness and irksome severity.[43]

Bodily and mental health suffered extremely. A French prison doctor reported that nearly every prisoner lost weight steadily, whereas convicts generally gained weight in jails.[44] Eyesight suffered even among the younger men as a result of poor illumination and the lack of physical exercise.[45] The most destructive effects were on the nervous system. Taking the number of suicides as an index to the double torture of solitary confinement and the lack of work, the Webbs indicate that nothing is so eloquent as the extraordinary precautions to which the prison commissioners were driven in order to prevent attempts at suicide.[46]

Only a few people dared to object to the new system. "This absolute solitude," wrote Beaumont and Tocqueville, "if nothing interrupts it, is beyond the strength of men; it destroys the criminal without intermission and without pity, it does not reform, it kills." [47] During his visit to America, Dickens also went to see prisons where solitary confinement had been introduced:

In its intention, I am well convinced that it is kind, humane, and meant for reformation; but I am persuaded that those who devised this system of Prison Discipline, and those benevolent gentlemen who carry it into execution, do not know what it is that they are doing. I believe that very few men are capable of estimating the amount of torture and agony which this dreadful punishment, prolonged for years, inflicts upon the sufferers; and in guessing at it myself, and in reasoning from what I have seen written upon their faces, and what to my certain knowledge they feel within, I am only the more convinced that there is a depth of terrible endurance in it which none but the sufferers themselves can fathom, and which no man has a right to inflict upon his fellow-creature. I hold this slow and daily tampering with the mysteries of the brain, to be immeasurably worse than any torture of the body; and because its ghastly signs and tokens are not so palpable to the eye and sense of touch as scars upon the flesh; because its wounds are not upon the surface, and it extorts few cries that human ears can hear; therefore I the more denounce it, as a secret punishment which slumbering humanity is not roused up to stay.[48]

Experience has shown that solitary confinement was a failure. A method adapted to the unusual individual, whether he is a criminal or a noncriminal, is not suitable for the rehabilitation of average or below-average mass types. The enthusiasm of contemporary writers over the possibilities offered by solitary confinement for individual development can scarcely hide the absence of any attempt to change the course that the masses of criminals usually take. It may be true that this method of punishment led to the spiritual salvation of a few, but for most of the convicts it meant only illness, lunacy, and agony, and it rendered them still more helpless. The defenders of solitary confinement considered the damage inflicted on the majority of the convicts an inevitable consequence of the method, but in reality the harm far outweighs any possible benefits. Solitary confinement, without work or with purely punitive labor, is symptomatic of a mentality which, as a result of surplus population, abandons the attempt to find a rational policy of rehabilitation and conceals this fact with a moral ideology.[49]

IX

MODERN PRISON REFORM AND ITS LIMITS

1. RISING LIVING STANDARDS OF THE LOWER CLASSES AND THE EFFECTS ON CRIMINAL POLICY

THE condition of the lower classes in Europe improved considerably in the second half, and especially in the last quarter, of the nineteenth century. Europe now entered that period of prosperity which lasted until 1914, interrupted only by minor crises. The participation of the masses in the consumption of goods formerly inaccessible to them was the consequence partly of their increased income and partly of mass production.[1] Clapham notes that the rise in English wages in the eighties was not limited to the average wage earner in the towns, but benefited women and farm laborers as well.[2] Sée makes the same observation for France, where wages increased slowly until 1860 and much more rapidly thereafter.[3] In France, apart from the factors operative in Germany and England, that is, better organization of the working classes, technological progress, and mass production of consumption goods, another factor played a leading role in the improvement of lower-class conditions, namely, the lower birth rate and the consequent decrease in labor supply and increase in wages during the period of industrial expansion. In Germany, industrialization came later than in other western countries but living conditions improved nevertheless. Better transportation facilities automatically created an adjustment between standards of living in various parts of the same country. Unlike the situation in the seventeenth century, it was scarcely possible to find economic prosperity in one section and starvation in a neighboring region. Furthermore, governments began to alleviate poverty during periods of crisis. One important symptom of the improved standard of living is the decline of emigration at the very time when colonial expansion and the development of the American continent took place.

The influence of these economic developments on criminality soon became noticeable. Pike, the historian of English criminal law, remarked that prosperity and steady employment in the factories, aided perhaps by other factors, gradually softened that spirit of violence which formerly revealed itself upon the slightest provocation.[4] The criminal statistics of the period give the same impression. The number of offenses and convictions decreased everywhere, or at least remained stationary, as the following figures show. (It should be noted that they are not entirely comparable.)

TABLE 5. Decrease in Number of Convictions, Late Nineteenth and Early Twentieth Centuries

A. Germany: Convictions of Persons above the Age of Discretion, for Petty Larceny (per 100,000 Population)

PERIOD	NUMBER
1882–84	241
1885–89	206
1890–94	212
1895–99	187
1900–04	184
1905–09	181
1910–13	173

Source: R. Rabl, Strafzumessungspraxis und Kriminalitätsbewegung (Leipzig, 1936), p. 13.

B. England: Persons Tried before Assizes, Quarter Sessions, and Summary Courts for Offenses against Property without Violence (per 100,000 Population)

PERIOD	NUMBER
1876–80	200
1881–85	205
1886–90	180
1891–95	171
1896–99	146
1900–04	153
1905–09	158
1910–14	150

Source: Calculated from the annual Criminal Statistics, England and Wales.

The value of human labor power was again seen in a different light. It is true that population increased considerably in the nineteenth century and that the period of labor scarcity had disappeared forever; but the immense expansion of industrial production in the era of imperialism provided for a maximum absorption of labor power. The senseless imprisonment of individuals became undesirable and out of step with the times. Worms, a French economist, condemned both the damaging effect of laws against usury and the unreasonable methods of dealing with crime, in one and the same sentence, written in 1870. He stated that life and liberty came to be regarded as more valuable with the change to modern industrial production, and he drew the conclusion that to shorten the days of a citizen without urgent necessity or to prolong his senseless imprisonment without incontrovertible reason at a time when everyone is regarded, morally at least, as a responsible producer would constitute a loss of forces for society. Far from being useful, it is detrimental.[5] It has often been pointed out that the notion that it is undesirable to waste the social capital invested in members of society was one of the motivating forces in early social insurance programs. It also underlay the policy of crime prevention which the writers of the Enlightenment had earlier recommended as the best way to stop infringements upon property rights.[6]

The liberal progressive attitude which influenced Liszt and similar reformers in all parts of the world received its chief expression in the naturalistic philosophy of the second half of the nineteenth century. Ferri, for example, stated that after 1850 naturalistic philosophy, impelled by the new data from the experimental sciences, had "completely dissipated the moral and intellectual mists left by the Middle Ages," and that "the destruction of the old anthropomorphic illusions" had given rise to the fertile "vitality of the new experimental knowledge." [7] The reformers believed that man can influence man's development, just as he can dominate nature, and that crime can be combated by a proper social policy. The causal point of view, they thought, would show the inadequacy of prevailing methods of fighting crime, with their purely retributive character and their principle of strict equivalence between punishment and crime. Prins, the chief Belgian representative of the new school, said that the magistrates lose themselves in arithmetical operations, in complicated calculations, legal formulae, and academic distinctions, so that they must forget the social impact of their function. It is undeniable, he continued, that neither the French legislation of 1810 nor the Belgian of 1860 conceived of criminal law as a social science to be built up from the study of social facts.[8] And for these reformers, criminology was essentially a social science. Liszt, leader of the German reform school, defined crime as a necessary product on the one hand of the society in which the criminal lives and on the other of the criminal's character, partly inherited and partly developed by his experience.[9] Treatment of convicts, therefore, must not be primarily concerned with the deed of the offender, but must consider the deed as an indication of the offender's personality.

A comparison between the criminal procedure, which was improving steadily, and the unprogressive penal law led the new reformers to a negative judgment of the latter. Prins misunderstood the true relationship, however, when he explained the static character of substantive law on the basis of intellectual inertia and inadequacy.[10] In this theory, the negative repressive force receives a positive aspect. Punishment is to perform an educational function or be a lesson for the future, and it is incorporated into a broad program for raising the moral level of society. Although the criticism of the metaphysical character of punishment as retaliation in the classical doctrines seems to be justified, the shift in emphasis to the idealized aims of punishment leads us still further from social reality. In their attack on the classical position, modern theorists have stressed the barbarism and cultural backwardness which they considered to be the practical consequence of retaliatory doctrines. They have forgotten that in their own period the classical theorists had also come forward against the prevailing inhuman penal practice.[11] The new reformers thus create the illusion that a specific penal practice is bound up with a specific penal theory, and that it is sufficient to demolish the latter in order to set the former under way. The seductive character of every one-sided theory of punishment lies in the false hope that it makes possible a clear and fruitful praxis. We are actually turning things upside down, however, if we take at its face value the imaginary power of doctrine over reality, instead of understanding the theoretical innovation as the expression of a necessary or already accomplished change in social praxis.

Both the principle of proportion and the refined methods of criminal procedure were products of the bourgeois revolutions. Formalization of criminal justice offered many advantages in the central European countries where feudal-absolutist forces still retained much of their strength, as well as in the western countries where political power was long an object of struggle between different groups. The independence of the judiciary and the rationalization of criminal law were excellent weapons in the struggle against the remnants of feudalism and absolutist bureaucracy. The campaign waged by the Prussian judiciary all through the nineteenth century against government interference in cases of malfeasance, for example, was nothing more than one phase of this struggle.[12] The refinement of procedural methods was one of the most effective ways of protecting the acquisition and extension of economic power by means which were sometimes questionable even from the standpoint of the ruling classes. In the struggle against the lower classes, on the other hand, the independence of the judiciary, drawn solely from the upper classes, revealed itself to be not too great an obstacle in spite of formalism of method. In countries like England, informal patriarchal procedures were retained for petty offenders, that is to say, for lower-class crimes. The same result was achieved in other countries by the fact that a defendant without means was in no position to secure the assistance of an attorney. It is interesting to note in this connection that the institution of free legal aid never made enough headway in Germany, France, or England to allow one to speak of equality among the various strata of society in the exercise of legal rights.[13] Special courts or martial law were established for the quick and effective repression of organized attempts at social revolution, as after the defeat of the Paris Commune in 1871.[14]

The end of the nineteenth century marks the close of the period of antagonism between the last remnants of feudalism and the administrative bureaucracy on the one hand and the middle class on the other. As the latter strengthened their hold over the machinery of government and administration, it became less and less necessary to continue the process of formalizing criminal law as a guarantee of their social and economic position. The significance of an independent judiciary changed, too. The liberal attitude which we often find among judges in the first half of the nineteenth century gave way to strict conservatism after the reconciliation of the bourgeoisie with the bureaucratic and agrarian interests, and the ideology of independence gradually became a camouflage for the struggle against the lower classes. The orientation of criminal law was affected by these changes. "The improved relations between citizens and law," as Richard Schmidt calls this unification of the interests of the upper class,[15] undermined the political function of the system of legal guarantees which had arisen toward the end of the eighteenth century. It was no longer necessary to protect the bourgeoisie against the arbitrariness of the administration, now that the two were largely identical. The once political question of protecting the individual in criminal procedure had become a problem of mere legal technique.

This change in the political basis coincides with the development of a sociological approach to criminal law. Statistical inquiries into the relationship between crime rates and economic fluctuations revealed the degree to which crime is a purely social phenomenon. Furthermore, the problem of penal methods was no longer viewed as a problem of maintaining a just proportion between crime and punishment; it was examined from the viewpoint of the criminal's future, the expectation of rehabilitation, and the precautions which it was worth taking. Carried to its extreme, this approach would mean that in normal cases crime is evidence of the necessity of transferring the delinquent to a well-organized charitable institution. The ideal judge would be one who is fully conscious of society's guilt, acquits the poor defendant who pleads guilty of larceny, and gives him money for a new start.[16] The main representatives of sociological criminology did not go this far, however. They were content to place the main burden upon social policy and to advocate a thoroughgoing rationalization of criminal justice under the exclusive domination of theological viewpoints. Criminals who do not need correction and supervision should be kept out of prisons by an extensive use of probations and fines (administrative objections are met by pointing to the economic advantages to be derived from this procedure). The short-term sentence was condemned. "There is nothing more immoral and more absurd," wrote Liszt, "than the short-term sentences of imprisonment for apprentices in crime." [17] Criminals capable of reform should be morally reëducated with the utmost diligence. The idea of the guilt of society merges with the idea of giving the greatest possible number of productive forces back to society.[18] The reformation of convicts is thus regarded as a good investment, and not merely as a charitable whim. A convict should be banished from society for an indefinite period only when there is no prospect of rehabilitation. This idea of criminality as a social phenomenon which can be adjusted by appropriate measures received a characteristic formulation from Prins:

If crime broke out on chance occasions like a will-o'-the-wisp fluttering over the swamp at night, justice would only be able to strike back by chance. That is not the case. Crime tends to concentrate in a definite circle which expands or contracts under the influence of misery or prosperity. We do not grope in the dark and we can try to react with a greater chance of success.[19]

It is interesting to note that the reformers themselves endeavored to retain all the guarantees of procedure which had been built up since the end of the eighteenth century, as well as the exact definition of legal facts which had been developed through legislation and jurisprudence. The criminal reformers of our time have welcomed the proposal to separate the determination of guilt from the imposition of the sentence; the first is to be entrusted to a qualified judge, the second to a "social physician." Such a separation of functions is the logical outcome of the attempt to safeguard the interests of both the individual and society.[20] In spite of this attachment of the social-liberal reform school to the traditional guarantees of procedure, however, there is a definite connection between their theory and the decline of formalism in criminal law. If crime is primarily an index for more intimate knowledge of the delinquent's personality, the question of the crime which the delinquent has committed, or, if already convicted, whether he committed any crime at all in a given case, is forced into the background together with the question of those general political tendencies which sought to weaken the formalism of criminal law.

Richard Schmidt is quite right in attacking Radbruch's notion that liberalism regards punishment solely from the standpoint of society's security, and that merely repressive punishment belongs to conservatism.[21] Schmidt points out that the strict suppression of professional criminals of proletarian origin, the most absolutistic side of a penal system which centers about society's security, would be heartily welcomed in many militarists, agrarian, capitalist, and rural middle-class circles. More recent developments have fully confirmed his view. It is significant that the least liberal portions of the reform program, such as preventive detention and all other forms of rendering prisoners harmless, have been realized much more completely than other aspects like prison reform.

2. RESULTS AND LIMITS OF PRISON REFORM

Before we discuss the most recent trends, we must examine the development of punishment by imprisonment in the period of relative prosperity, the period when the reform school was at its height. We left it in the blind alley of solitary confinement. The new policy sponsored by the reformers was to keep as many delinquents as possible out of jail by a more extensive use of fines, which we will treat later, by a probation policy, and, above all, by seeking to ameliorate the social conditions responsible for crime.

The following table shows the shifts of the prison population in France between 1884 and 1932, and in England between 1880 and 1931.

TABLE 6. *Decline in Prison Population, Late Nineteenth Century and Twentieth Century*

A. France: Prison Population, 1884–1932

YEAR	MAISONS CENTRALES		MAISONS D'ARRÊT (AS OF DEC. 31)	
	MEN	WOMEN	MEN	WOMEN
1884	12,689	1,943	21,257	3,974
1887	11,547	1,635	21,394	3,573
1890	10,540	1,640	20,940	3,440
1891	10,054	1,439	20,336	3,338
1894	9,839	1,294	19,389	3,652
1897	8,434	1,008	15,636	2,790
1900	6,802	801	14,769	2,466
1902	5,906	673	13,941	2,152
1905	5,401	539	13,502	1,902
1909	5,540	507	13,304	1,885
1910	5,612	534	14,518	2,224
1913	6,413	726	14,123	2,219
1920	7,443	863	17,997	3,383
1921	6,247	1,086	13,920	2,911
1922	6,090	935	11,037	2,338
1925	5,529	885	12,278	2,095
1927	5,405	542	14,293	2,316
1929	4,992	573	12,537	2,038
1930	5,085	590	12,575	1,885
1931	4,662	546	11,695	1,756
1932	4,315	469	12,579	1,591

Source: Compiled from the annual *Statistique pénitentiaire.*

B. England: Persons Sent into Penal Servitude or Imprisoned

YEAR	NUMBER
1880	32,999
1890	24,628
1900	22,432
1905	28,257
1910	26,096
1911	23,758
1912	23,994
1913	21,463
1914	18,195
1915	11,802
1916	11,027
1917	11,930
1918	11,303
1919	12,732
1920	15,518
1921	15,756
1922	15,520
1923	14,788

TABLE 6 (*Continued*)

YEAR	NUMBER
1924	14,132
1925	13,580
1926	14,537
1927	14,446
1928	13,726
1929	13,526
1930	14,294
1931	13,838

Source: Fox, *Modern English Prison*, pp. 218–19.

The tendency to substitute other forms of punishment for imprisonment was accompanied by a decrease in the length and severity of prison sentences. That is clearly shown by the following table giving the distribution of sentences in Germany from 1882 to 1934. (Note the upswing in prison sentences beginning with the crisis in 1930.[22])

TABLE 7. *Distribution of German Sentences in Percents*

YEAR	DEATH SENTENCE	ZUCHT-HAUS	TOTAL PRISON SENTENCES	OVER ONE YEAR	THREE MONTHS TO ONE YEAR	LESS THAN THREE MONTHS	ARRESTS	FINES
1882	.03	4.3	72.0	1.6	9.6	60.8	.46	22.2
1886	.02	3.4	68.5	2.7	11.1	54.7	.36	26.5
1893	.01	2.7	61.6	3.0	11.0	47.6	.23	33.6
1900	.01	2.1	55.6	2.9	10.7	42.0	.11	39.7
1907	.01	1.4	47.8	2.3	8.9	36.6	.08	47.5
1913	.01	1.4	44.0	2.7	9.2	32.1	.05	52.0
1918	.01	1.7	60.1	3.4	11.7	45.0	.02	32.0
1921	.02	1.4	56.9	4.3	14.3	38.3	.02	39.3
1926	.02	1.2	32.5	2.3	10.5	19.7	.42	65.2
1928	.01	0.87	28.6	1.8	8.8	18.0	.49	69.2
1930	.01	0.78	31.8	1.9	9.5	20.3	.52	66.2
1931	.008	0.81	35.9	2.1	10.7	23.1	.45	62.1
1932	.009	1.12	41.5	2.5	12.9	26.0	.46	56.3
1933	.016	1.97	44.5	3.9	15.0	25.5	.51	52.6
1934	.025	3.22	41.7	4.6	14.6	22.4	.47	54.7

Source: Compiled from the *Kriminalstatistik für das deutsche Reich* and the *Statistisches Jahrbuch für das deutsche Reich*.

The general tendency toward leniency is quite obvious. The house of correction is replaced by the medium prison term and the latter by short-term imprisonment or fines. The trend would be even more evident if probation statistics were presented.

Rabl's studies have shown that this leniency was applied equally to all types of delinquency.[23]

The same manifestation in France is revealed by the following table, which presents a survey of the various methods of depriving a convict of his liberty from 1832 to 1933. The most severe punishments, *travaux forcés* and *réclusion,* decreased until the turn of the century, and the medium term of imprisonment also showed a decline in favor of the short term.

TABLE 8. *Distribution of French Prison Sentences in Percents*

YEAR	TRAVAUX FORCÉS AND RÉCLUSION	IMPRISONMENT FOR MORE THAN ONE YEAR	IMPRISONMENT FOR ONE YEAR OR LESS	
1832	5.7	14.3	80.0	
1836	4.0	16.9	79.1	
1842	3.7	14.9	81.4	
1848	2.6	10.7	86.7	
1855	2.5	14.0	83.5	
1857	2.3	12.9	48.8	
1865	1.7	9.0	89.3	
1873	1.8	8.4	89.8	
1880	1.3	6.0	92.7	
1884	1.2	5.4	93.5	
1892	1.1	3.7	OVER 95.2 THREE	
1900	0.9	3.3	THREE 95.8 MONTHS	
1905	0.9	3.8	MONTHS 95.2 OR LESS	
1912	0.8	3.8	17.5	77.0
1919	0.7	5.1	23.4	70.8
1921	1.0	5.3	24.1	69.6
1924	0.6	3.9	16.0	79.5
1927	0.4	3.4	24.3	71.9
1930	0.4	4.1	19.6	75.9
1932	0.4	3.6	18.9	77.1
1933	0.4	3.0	—	—

Source: Compiled from the *Compte général de l'administration de la justice. criminelle.*

After the turn of the century, this process came to an end. Further leniency is expressed in the liberal use of suspended sentences and in the increase of fines. (See Table 9.)

The trend toward greater leniency is most clearly revealed in Belgium. (See Table 10.)

Italy is an exception to this tendency. Between the years 1893 and 1933 we find a steady increase in the more severe forms of punishment, a decrease in the number of short-term sentences, and little change in the number of fines [24] (see Tables 11 and 12).

TABLE 9. *Fines and Suspended Sentences by the Tribunal Correctionnel in France (Percent of Total Sentences)* [a]

YEAR	FINES	SUSPENDED SENTENCES
1900	35.8	17
1905	39.1	20
1912	40.5	16
1921	52.5	17
1924	46.3	18
1927	46.1	16
1930	47.7	21
1931	48.6	22
1932	45.9	23
1933	47.5	23
1934	47.8	

Source: Compiled from the *Compte général* . . . .

[a] These figures do not include infractions of the regulations regarding tariffs, indirect taxes, forests, fisheries, tolls, etc.

The exceptional development of punishment in Italy coincides with the fact that the number of crimes does not show the same sharp downward trend as elsewhere in Europe.[25]

With the general improvement in living conditions, prison conditions also improved. The widespread substitution of prisons with an individual cell for each convict led to the construction of many new prisons and the abandonment of those regarded as unfit. Overcrowding with its moral and hygienic consequences was eliminated in part. Food was somewhat improved,

TABLE 10. *Distribution of Belgian Sentences (Tribunal Correctionnel) in Percents* [a]

YEAR	IMPRISONMENT			FINES	SUSPENDED SENTENCES
	OVER ONE YEAR	SIX MONTHS TO ONE YEAR	UNDER SIX MONTHS		
1905	2.4	2.2	47.4	48.0	35.0
1912	2.4	1.7	42.3	53.6	37.4
1919	10.2		35.3	54.5	32.1
1924	3.0		28.1	68.9	41.6
1927	4.1		34.7	61.2	38.8
1930	4.3		32.8	62.9	39.2
1933	33.5			66.5	42.5

Source: Compiled from *Statistique judiciaire de la Belgique* and *Annuaire statistique*.

[a] These figures do not include violations of forest regulations.

TABLE 11. *Distribution of Italian Sentences in Percents*

| YEAR | IMPRISONMENT | | | | FINES |
	OVER FIVE YEARS	ONE TO FIVE YEARS	SIX MONTHS TO ONE YEAR	UNDER SIX MONTHS	
1893	1.61	5.96	15.15	58.41	18.87
1902	1.00	5.57	5.12	66.48	21.83
1905	0.92	5.39	5.65	66.82	21.22
1908	0.80	4.97	5.32	68.09	20.82
1911	0.77	5.41	5.52	67.11	21.19
1917	0.79	4.98	5.10	68.43	20.76
1921	0.94	8.09	7.99	64.76	18.22
1922	1.12	7.32	7.70	62.74	21.12
1925	1.50	7.62	8.14	64.08	18.66
1928	0.97	5.89	6.13	63.95	23.06
1930	1.04	8.25	8.92	63.51	18.28
1931	1.16	7.64	68.71		22.49
1932	1.94	10.87	68.17		19.02
1933	2.02	12.63	65.08		20.27

Source: Compiled from the *Statistica guidiziaria penale.*

and attention was directed to problems of health. Chains and
other forms of physical restraint previously necessary for discipline were used more and more infrequently. The consequence
of all these improvements is readily apparent from the mortality
statistics. In England, for example, the prison death rate fell
from 1.08 percent in 1877 to 0.56 percent in 1898, and the suicide
rate from 1.76 percent in 1877 to 0.7 percent in 1896.[26]

It was in this social atmosphere that the literature of modern
prison reform arose. Its insistence on treating crime as a psycho-

TABLE 12. *Larcenies Reported to the Police in Italy (per 100,000 Population)*

YEAR	NUMBER
1887	305
1897	414
1910	447
1919	639
1921	648
1923	548
1927	469
1930	478
1932	550
1933	514
1934	505
1935	552

Source: Compiled from the *Statistica della criminalità.*

logical-medical problem, that is to say, on the social necessity of healing the prisoner if possible or of isolating him if no cure could be achieved,[27] spread to every section of the population. Thus, Hugo Haase, in explaining the demands of the German Social Democratic Party in the field of criminal law at its 1906 convention, took the position that the common practice of acquitting members of better families in cases of larceny by the introduction of medical evidence certifying kleptomania should be extended much more widely.[28] The *Reichsrechtliche Grundsätze über den Vollzug von Freiheitsstrafer,* an agreement between the various German states on June 7, 1923, regarding the treatment of delinquents, was perhaps the most notable example of the progessive spirit in criminal practice.

The criminologists of the modern reform school have retained the older notion that the standard of living within the prison must be below the minimum standard outside. Enrico Ferri, representative of a poor country whose lower classes scarcely participated in the general improvement in European economic conditions, expressed strong opposition at the end of the nineteenth century to "this upheaval of every principle of social justice which would have prisons more convenient and more comfortable than dwellings of poor and honest folk who may, so long as they remain honest, die there of acute or chronic starvation since society assures them food and lodging only when they commit culpable acts." [29] The problem became less acute at the turn of the century, because the progress of material culture and the general amelioration of lower-class life allowed for a certain improvement in prison conditions without destroying the line of demarcation from life outside. To this extent economic developments fitted in with the aims of the reformers, but we must not lose sight of the fact that their insistence on retaining the line of demarcation set narrow limits to the possibilities of reform and surrendered it to the mercy of every crisis in the market. Even in periods of prosperity large sections of the population lack the forces necessary in the struggle for survival, especially in the larger cities. Criminal statistics do not set this group apart, but we can get at the problem in another way. The rubric "foreigners" usually reveals a much higher crime rate than the average, and since the bulk of this group comes from the poorest elements of society, we have clear proof of the impact of an unfavorable economic position on criminality.[30]

There is a further relationship between material social conditions and the possibility of education in the prisons insofar as the awakening of the prisoner's better instincts assumes the prospect of a better material existence. There can be no psychological basis for improvement while the prisoner knows that society does not afford him the possibility of a normal and legal satisfaction of his needs. The most progressive methods in the world will be hard put to induce him to accept willingly the fate of the ordinary poor devil.

Prison labor remains a central problem despite the fact that it has lost its economic significance in countries with a highly developed industrial capitalism. In 1894, an English commission reported that a prison population presents no favorable features whatsoever for the development of industrial labor.[31] That is true a priori of the smaller prisons still used for short sentences, since the small number of inmates and the rapid turnover make any form of rational production an impossibility.[32] The same difficulty does not exist in larger prisons, but large-scale expenditure is necessary if their products are to compete with the products of private industry. The opposition is so strong both from the business world and from the trade unions that convict labor is generally limited to manufacturing goods for use in the prisons or in government departments.[33] Furthermore, now that the jailers are salaried officials, they have no private economic interest in convict labor, and these problems, so important in the seventeenth and eighteenth centuries, have been pushed far into the background. The state is satisfied with a partial return of its outlay, at least on the books, and the pedagogical side of prison labor has come strongly to the fore. A vicious circle is created, however. Most convicts are either unskilled workers or skilled artisans who become rusty because of the long period of inactivity. They must be taught a trade if they are to be given a weapon with which to fight their way through life honestly. That is rarely done, first because few institutions provide a sufficient division of labor. Convicts are often put to work in the fields, a solution particularly popular in Fascist countries as one of the coercive methods of raising production at a minimum expense.[34] Agricultural or other primitive work is no answer to the problem of reform, for that generally means that the convict leaves as he entered, without any training which might improve his chances in the competitive world. The expense involved, the difficulties of finding a market, and public opinion all contribute to prevent the introduction of an effective program of labor training.

Wages for convict labor are opposed on the same grounds as productive prison labor in general. Paying wages would mean placing such work more or less on the same level as free labor. In England, the work performed by prisoners used to be incorporated into the stage system, creating the possibility of shortening the judicial sentence. A report of the prison commissioner in 1929 indicated that this system merely operated as a negative check on misconduct and idleness, and concluded that some form of wage was necessary to induce the inmates to take the step from the minimum amount of work necessary to escape the black mark for idleness to the maximum possible productivity. A system of pay was then introduced.[35] In France the convict receives part of his earnings in money, but the amount is determined by his sentence and previous record, so that he actually receives between one-tenth and one-half of the sum assigned, an amount which is unduly low to begin with. A portion of the wages is placed at the prisoner's disposal for the purchase of additional supplies, as in other Continental countries. This feature has often been made a central point of the whole French prison supply system.

The continuity of tradition is clear. From Lepeletier St. Fargeau, the reporter on criminal law in the revolutionary assembly, to Mossé, author of the most recent official prison manual, every authority has accepted the principle that prison food should not be too substantial, that is to say, it should not exceed the amount absolutely indispensable for health. It is only natural, therefore, that the convict should be expected to spend some of his wages for additional supplies with which to replace the labor power he has expended.[36] In general, it seems correct to say that the impossible conditions of the earlier jails have been eliminated, insofar as food is concerned, but that a wide gap still separates prison fare from that of the lower strata of the free population.

The very nature of modern imprisonment creates an insoluble sex problem, except for a few countries like Mexico and the Soviet Union which allow prisoners to have visitors. Such a practice not only involves technical difficulties but also a transcendence of official morality and the institution of marriage, since married and unmarried convicts must be placed on the same footing. Furthermore, forced abstinence is held to be an essential part of the punishment.[37]

Sanitation and health conditions have a natural limit in the buildings themselves, many of them inherited from an earlier period.[38] Improvement in the care of the sick is somewhat difficult to evaluate. There can be no doubt about the technical progress which has been made in prison medical practice, but it is necessarily limited by the fact that the doctor must consider not only the objective condition of the patient but also the effect of his treatment on the other inmates and on institutional discipline.[39] Physical exercise and athletics have been introduced to conform with modern conceptions of the requirements of health. Here, too, a sharp distinction is drawn between conditions which are judged absolutely essential for the convict's health and activities which can afford him some positive pleasure.[40]

Modern theorists are far from united on the question of solitary confinement.[41] Prison administrators have gone their own way, however, building and rebuilding their institutions on the cellular plan, and today the majority of prisons are constructed in that form. The problem of solitary confinement is no longer a major point of discussion, for strict separation at night is almost universally accompanied by organized labor in the daytime, made necessary by the requirements of production.[42] The cellular system has been replaced as a criterion of progress by "a certain progressiveness in the methods of execution," as Belym has expressed it.[43] This progressiveness is reflected in the principle that "discipline should be maintained by constructive rather than merely repressive measures, by encouraging the prisoner to maintain a standard rather than by holding out physical punishments *in terrorem*." [44] That aim can be achieved by a planless method of favors, by a graduated system of privileges for good conduct (the so-called "stage system"), by reducing the term of imprisonment for good behavior, or by some combination of these methods. In one variation or another they can now be found everywhere. The most elaborate system has been developed in England, where the prisoner receives daily conduct marks upon which the length of his sentence depends. He can be released at any time after he has completed three-quarters of the term imposed by the judge. The stage system also works by allowing the convict certain commodities and amusements which have come to be regular factors in the daily life of the lower classes. We have already indicated that in many countries the level of prison subsistence is so calculated that additional food must be obtained by spending a portion of the wage, which can be taken away as a punishment. The gap between the living standard of the free lower classes and the goods available to the most favored convicts is greater than the gap between the highest and lower stages in the prison. The difficulty of introducing real distinctions within the prison walls in view of the tendency against raising the prisoner's level of existence to that of the outside world is clearly revealed in the discussions held at the 1935 *Congrès pénal et pénitentiaire international* (Berlin) on the differentiations which are necessary in order to distinguish between preventive measures and penalties restricting liberty.[45]

The chief advantage of the stage system is that it facilitates the maintenance of discipline. It has no reformatory value, since the standards required of the prisoner are those of submission to the external forms of prison discipline. When Macartney first entered Parkhurst Prison, the chief warder said to him: "Ten years is a long time. Still, men get longer. It's up to you whether you go out in seven and a half or do the full ten. There are two ways of doing lagging—rough or smooth." [46] There can be no doubt that the chief virtue produced by the so-called progressive system is conformism.[47]

The qualifications of the warden and his staff are determined by the aims of the progressive system.[48] As the head of a large bureaucratic apparatus, the warden must maintain a balance between the state, which demands fulfillment of its regulations at the smallest possible expense or at a profit if possible, the staff, which shares the character of every bureaucracy in that it tries to increase its power and influence, and the prisoners. In nearly every European country the lower officials are still recruited from retired noncommissioned officers of the army and navy who have a claim on the state. This procedure was justified before the war on the ground that the work was quite simple.[49] The post-war reformist phraseology makes it sound more advanced and more complicated,[50] but since the main characteristic of the progressive system is the right of the convicts to make certain material gains by voluntary submission to discipline and not the introduction of pedagogical methods of reform, the mechanical duties of the lower branches of the prison staff have been increased somewhat, while their basic character has not really changed. In countries where the reform ideology has become official the same method is used in selecting prison officials. The qualities now considered necessary in the administrator make the military caste all the more valuable. Conformism is a prime virtue in the army as well as in the prison. Curiously enough the official assumption of increased responsibility, false as it may be, has become a satisfactory ground for demanding higher pay.

In the field of punishment, the church acts as an adjunct of the bureaucracy. The chaplain's main charge in earlier times, and still today in the smaller prisons, was to obtain work and food for ex-prisoners, and the church thus became a sort of agency of prison administration from which the prisoners could obtain certain extras. This duty is usually performed more effectively than the function of reconciling the prisoner to the sentence which he has received. His "identification with the administration, the prisoners' traditional enemy," writes Sellin, "renders the chaplain's ministrations largely ineffective."[51]

When state intervention into the sphere of the individual increases, it becomes more and more necessary to have organs which will watch over the norms that regulate such interference. This question is especially important in the prison, for there life is subject to state control down to its last detail. Even the most carefully worked out system of complaints and appeals will find its effectiveness minimized by two factors. In the first place, the legality of every administrative order must be taken for granted, that is to say, the convict must obey no matter how unjust or meaningless the order may be. Then he may appeal, and when he does he comes up against a new difficulty, since there has never been any precise determination of what a prisoner may or may not do. Although the theory that prisoners have subjective rights and are entitled to legal protection may have received some recognition,[52] the execution of punishment is controlled in practice by purely administrative regulations, which can be arbitrarily interpreted and which are nothing more than instructions for the internal use of administrative bodies, something like the English standing orders.[53] The "free and ample opportunity of making complaints," of which Fox speaks,[54] is usually not sanctioned by clear legal norms. Apart from this imperfection, which is inherent in the right of appeal, there is the further drawback that the risk involved in much greater than the possible chance of success. The administration will support its officials, as a rule, so that the prisoner runs the danger of damaging his standing with them, of losing his right to appeal, and even of being punished for making unwarranted complaints.[55] The right of appeal thus amounts to a mere indirect check, insofar as the officials will try not to give grounds for complaint. Complaints may call forth unpleasant investigations despite the tendency of the authorities to support the official involved. Of course, even this consideration rests on the assumption that the higher authorities are interested in a proper administration of penal institutions, which may be true in some cases but not in others.

We have already spoken about remission of sentence as a method of obtaining better discipline. It has the further function of keeping the ex-convict within the law. A rational conception of the ex-convict as a person who is too weak to hold his own in a competitive society would lead to the conclusion that he must receive all possible assistance in the process of readjustment.[56] The president of a German prisoners' aid society who said that ex-convicts should receive preference in employment agencies was merely admitting the logical consequence of their greater helplessness.[57] But such preferential treatment is blocked in several directions. Employers do not like to hire former prisoners, both because of the risk and because the latter lack the necessary technical qualifications and the ability to work intensively.[58] Preferential treatment is only part of a broader problem, namely, the extent to which it is compatible with the principles of a competitive society to help reinstate the ex-convict into the labor process. This question is clearly reflected by Bertrand when he writes:

It is necessary to go as far along this path as one can without injuring or handicapping the citizens who obey the law. It is necessary to put the freed convict in as normal a position as possible towards an offer of employment. To do more for him than for his competitors would amount to forcing the latter into crime. It would be neither just nor prudent to support them to the detriment of the others.[59]

Bertrand's argument overlooks the fact that the establishment of a normal status requires special measures to overcome the specific disabilities of the ex-convict as a competitor on the labor market. In view of the common reluctance to employ ex-prisoners, the state would have to give them active assistance in concealing their prison records, and society, for reasons of security, strongly opposes such action. The only alternative is for the state to provide work. There is a contradiction between society's interest in the rehabilitation of the delinquent on the one hand, and its alleged interest in maintaining the deterrent function of imprisonment by not giving the prisoner special advantages. It is no wonder then that the numerous prison societies have not been very successful in their rehabilitation programs, in other words, in overcoming the disadvantages which the ex-convict must suffer in the competitive world.[60]

In this discussion we have tried to analyze the limits to the possibility of prison reform. In part, these limits are inherent in the very nature of official regulation and control of human life, and in part they are the result of the security requirements of a society which has not yet learned that the simplest guarantees are not always the most appropriate. Bureaucratization of the conditions of life and limitations upon personal freedom are inevitable features of imprisonment anyway, no matter how far one may succeed in reducing them. Our discussion of the problem of the ex-convict has revealed the inner contradiction which underlies every reform program to a greater or lesser degree. No reform program has been willing to abandon the principle that the living standard of the prisoner must be depressed in order to retain the deterrent effects of punishment. As a result, the very notion of progress finds its chief expression in a sharper differentiation within the various degrees of prison existence. Besides the insoluble contradiction between deterrence and rehabilitation, a reflection of the antagonistic tendencies in society itself, there is a further contradiction within the concept of rehabilitation in contemporary society. Rehabilitation means adaptation to an orderly life with regular work, and rests on the assumption that the mode of behavior learned in prison will enable the convict to readjust himself to the outside world after release. The realization on the part of the convicts that this assumption is largely fictive is one reason for the poor results of rehabilitation programs, as recidivism statistics show, and hence a reason why administrators quickly return to the deterrent approach. Dession has recently stated with full justice that "the criminal viewed as subject for treatment does not differ greatly in his processing needs from representatives of the other categories of social maladjustment and inequality." [61] An attempt to cure the symptoms is a dubious procedure, however, first because any method which fails to go beyond the symptoms to the roots of the disease can only have a restricted value, and then because within a more restricted sphere itself the inconsistency and the self-contradictory character of the methods used defy the ends.

3. THE WORLD WAR

The effects of the World War on crime have been thoroughly discussed, especially in the works of Exner and Liepmann on Germany and Austria.[62] The fluctuations in the crime rate show a distinct sensitivity to the general social conditions of the period. French and German larceny figures reveal a sharp decline in 1914 and 1915, and then a strong upward trend in 1916 and 1917. In 1918, however, the French figures indicate little change while the German continue to increase markedly, obviously connected with the turn which the war was taking.[63] The criminal statistics further reveal important changes in the proportions: the number of offenders among the women and youth increased, and shifts occurred among the various kinds of offense. The characteristic changes which developed in penal policy were not the result so much of different practice in the courts as of special laws which modified the policy of prosecution and punishment according to the needs of the war program. Table 13 indicates that the penal policy of the French *tribunaux correctionels* was not fundamentally different from pre-war practice.

TABLE 13. *Penal Policy of the French Tribunaux Correctionnels (in Percents)*

YEAR	CASES DISMISSED	IMPRISONMENT OVER ONE YEAR	IMPRISONMENT UNDER ONE YEAR	FINES
1913	9	2	48	41
1914	9	2	50	39
1915	12	2	48	38
1916	12	3	42	43
1917	13	3	40	44
1918	11	3	40	46
1919	12	3	42	43

Source: *Compte général*, 1919, p. XIX.

Special rules were issued in every country and military interests had a decisive influence. At the outbreak of the war, pending cases were dropped and convictions were set aside as a method of recruiting for the army. Convicts whose sentences had included, as a special dishonor, loss of the right to serve in the army often regained the right so that they could be sent to the front. Criminal policy toward those who stayed at home was dominated by the same approach. The universal lack of man power made it necessary to draw as many people as possible into the labor process, and the administration was busy in doing its part to this end. The Prussian ministry of justice, for example, issued decrees in 1916 and 1917 requesting the courts to take into consideration the possible usefulness of the convict in auxiliary war service before deciding to remit any sentence.[64] In France, *grâces* and *liberations conditionelles* increased from 4.6 percent to 9.6 percent of the annual total number of convicts between 1913 and 1917 as the result of a similar policy. The prison population declined sharply from an average of 29,-032 in 1913 to 18,576 in 1916, and then rose to 22,054 in 1918.[65]

The prisons themselves became important government factories, using the available labor power to a maximum degree. Thus, the English prison commissioners reported for the year ending March 31, 1919, that the "manufacture of War Stores has continued to employ every available inmate, and the result has been satisfactory, as in spite of the difficulties experienced in obtaining materials, the delivery of goods on order has been in nearly all cases within the limits of time required by the several Government Departments." [66]

In Germany one additional factor must be taken into consideration—hunger. It was even worse in the prisons than outside. In 1916, a prisoner wrote a very amusing letter to the court requesting a new trial on the ground that the judge intended such punishment as was customary before the war, and not the one which he was actually receiving, for his punishment had become more severe from lack of food.[67]

4. POST-WAR CONDITIONS

The steady progress of material culture in Europe ended with the World War. The post-war period was characterized by growing unemployment, declining real wages, and an increasing pauperization of the middle class, though not at the same rate in every country. By and large, the effects were less sharply felt in western Europe and Scandinavia than in central and eastern Europe. Apart from frauds and sexual offenses, which increased, the total number of crimes in the former group of countries tended to drop or, at worst, to remain at pre-war levels until the crisis of 1929.

TABLE 14. *Post-War Crime Rates*

A. England: Indictable Offenses (per 100,000 Population)

YEARS	NUMBER
1910–14	175.1
1915–19	171.5
1920–24	154.3
1925–29	162.9
1930–32	169.8

Source: Compiled from *Criminal Statistics, England and Wales.*

B. France: Persons Tried before Cours d'Assises and Tribunaux Correctionnels (per 100,000 Population)

YEAR	NUMBER
1913	545
1920	598
1923	481
1926	554
1929	544
1932	534

Source: O. Kirchheimer in *Revue de science criminelle et droit penal comparé,* I (1936), 365.

C. Sweden: Crimes per 100,000 Population

PERIOD	NUMBER
1911–15	171.8
1916–20	149.8
1921–25	141.2
1926–29	148.8
1930	161.5
1931	175.8
1932	180.4

Source: Compiled from the *Brottsligheten.*

The situation was completely different in countries like Poland, Hungary, and Bulgaria, where the economic condition of the lower classes was bad throughout the post-war period. In Poland, the number of larcenies increased by 60 percent between 1923 and 1931, while the population increased but 15 percent; in the same period, embezzlements increased by 200 percent, frauds by 170 percent, and assaults by 180 percent.[68] The population of Hungary increased by 10 percent from 1923 to 1931, the number of larcenies by 30 percent, assaults by 160 percent, and frauds by 500 percent.[69] The Bulgarian figures from 1920 to 1931 are: population increase 20 percent, larceny 45 percent, fraud 400 percent, and forgery 270 percent.[70] In the early post-war period, German conditions were quite comparable to these of Poland, Hungary, and Bulgaria, as a result of the war and the inflation. The period of stabilization after 1923 brought a sharp decline in crime which lasted until the depression.

TABLE 15. *Germany: Offenses against Property (per 100,000 Population)*

YEAR	NUMBER
1911–13	522
1920	881
1921	899
1922	893
1923	1,220
1924	901
1925	571
1928	493
1931	542
1932	596

Source: A. Amend, *Die Kriminalität Deutschlands 1919–1932* (Leipzig, 1937), p. 62.

The pre-war tendencies toward a general mitigation of methods and the introduction of the so-called progressive system continued to operate in the field of penal practice. It is easy to see why there should have been no difficulties with the continuation of the humanitarian trends in the countries with relatively favorable economic conditions. The criminal statistics, which showed a static condition at worst, were no cause for unrest or worry. The pressure for a more rational and more humane praxis was particularly strong in England and Belgium. In France, the tendency toward amelioration was particularly strong in dealing with war veterans, but at the same time the penal system was administered according to purely bureaucratic viewpoints, and the senseless system of transportation and the scandalous conditions in the reformatories were allowed to continue.[71]

At first sight it is difficult to see why the reform school had so much success in Germany, where the economic conditions were unstable and where the crime rate rose after the war. The fact that the number of crimes increased immediately after the war despite increasing severity of punishment may have been an object lesson in this connection. The observation of the close relationship between crime and social and economic conditions taught those concerned with the problem that it is futile to fight crime by introducing harsher punishments. An immediate expression of this observation appeared in the new legislation with regard to fines and suspended sentences,[72] designed to reduce the prison population to a minimum. Apart from the purely practical consideration that the rehabilitation of the criminal saves the state money, the theory of the responsibility of society for crime and a belief in the possibility of human progress and in the duty of society as a whole in this task were in full accord with the spirit of the political parties dominant in Weimar Germany. The *Reichsrechtliche Grundsätze über den Vollzug von Freiheitsstrafer* of June 7, 1923, as we have already indicated, placed the problem of rehabilitation in the center of the penal system, at least in theory. The progressive tendency was further accentuated by the sharp reduction of the prison population and the increase in available funds that accompanied the period of stabilization. Table 16 shows the increased per capita ex-

TABLE 16. *Prussian Prison Population and Expenditures*

YEAR	AVERAGE NUMBER OF PRISONERS	BUDGET PROVISION FOR CARE OF PRISONERS (REICHSMARKS)	PER CAPITA (REICHSMARKS)
1924	60,000	10,800,000	180
1925	70,000	14,700,000	210
1926	60,000	12,600,000	210
1927	48,000	11,040,000	230
1928	36,000	9,180,000	255

Source: Wackermann in *Strafvollzug in Preussen*, p. 43.

penditure for prisoners and the decline in the prison population after the inflationary crisis.

In general, post-war developments followed the paths marked
out at the end of the nineteenth century. The reform theories
were officially accepted everywhere, but the fact remains that
prison conditions in economically backward countries were
pretty bad. Official Polish statistics, for example, admit that
the prisons were filled to 89.6 percent of their maximum capacity
in 1923, 100 percent in 1931, and 142 percent in 1934–36.[73]
Overcrowded prisons, bad conditions among the lower classes
generally, and the inefficiency of the administrative apparatus
characterize the prison conditions of these countries. No effort
has been made, however, to explain these poor conditions as
the consciously desired product of an ideology. On the contrary,
the effort is made to prove that western European reform doctrines are accepted in these countries too.[74]

X

THE FINE IN RECENT PENAL PRACTICE

I N European penal systems about the middle of the nineteenth century there were important changes, marked, as we have seen, by the disappearance of transportation as a significant punishment. Deportation was continued in France down to the beginning of 1937 as a way of eliminating more serious offenders, and the small number of convicts involved reveals its unimportance. Imprisonment remained the central point of the whole system, but it received increasing competition from the fine, which is today a close rival insofar as frequency of application is concerned.

The tables which we have presented in the previous chapter give a clear picture of the progress of the fine. The following figures show that this phenomenon is not merely the result of new crimes, like violations of purely police measures regulating

TABLE 17. *Increasing Use of the Fine in Germany*

A. *Distribution of Punishments for Larceny*

YEAR	CONVICTIONS PER 100,000 POPULATION ABOVE THE AGE OF DISCRETION	PERCENT IMPRISONED			PERCENT FINED
		ONE YEAR OR OVER	THREE MONTHS TO ONE YEAR	UNDER THREE MONTHS	
1882–84	241	0.6	4.8	90.0	—
1885–89	206	1.0	6.3	88.1	—
1890–94	212	1.0	6.6	85.6	—
1895–99	187	1.0	7.1	83.2	—
1900–04	184	0.9	6.9	81.6	—
1905–09	181	0.5	4.8	82.1	—
1910–13	173	0.5	4.9	83.2	—
1920–21	386	1.1	8.5	79.9	—
1922–24	447	1.1	9.2	31.2	54.6
1925–29	139	0.6	8.1	38.8	49.0
1930	134	0.4	6.0	38.1	51.4
1931	134	0.3	6.0	39.2	50.9
1932	149	0.4	5.9	41.8	49.2

Source: Rabl, *op. cit.*, p. 20.

TABLE 17 (*Continued*)

B. Distribution of Punishments for Fraud

YEAR	CONVICTIONS PER 100,000 POPULATION ABOVE THE AGE OF DISCRETION	PERCENT IMPRISONED			PERCENT FINED
		ONE YEAR OR OVER	THREE MONTHS TO ONE YEAR	UNDER THREE MONTHS	
1882–84	36	2.3	9.3	76.1	11.0
1885–89	40	2.6	8.8	72.1	14.1
1890–94	51	2.3	9.1	68.8	18.1
1895–99	54	2.1	9.2	64.8	22.1
1900–04	54	1.9	8.6	60.8	26.6
1905–09	52	1.3	6.6	54.4	34.7
1910–13	53	1.4	6.7	49.2	40.7
1920–24	62	2.4	12.3	36.8	47.5
1925–29	94	1.5	11.4	39.0	47.7
1930	97	1.0	8.9	39.3	50.5
1931	101	1.0	8.3	40.3	50.2
1932	101	1.2	9.4	41.7	47.5

Source: Rabl, *op. cit.,* p. 27.

traffic, but is also the consequence of a general policy of substituting the fine for imprisonment.[1]

We have already seen that the Enlightenment doctrine of proportion gave the fine added impetus as the specific upper-class punishment. Beccaria approved it in principle, but doubted that it could be used extensively in view of the poverty among large sections of the population.[2] That was precisely the reason why a broad system of fines was impossible in the mercantilist period.[3] Bentham advocated its widest possible use, with arguments which reappeared in innumerable variations during the first half of the century. The fine has the merit of perfect frugality, he said, because it not only avoids superfluous pain but produces pleasure on the part of the damaged person. Furthermore, it usually permits a minute application of the principle of proportion.[4] To the objection that the fine operates plutocratically, Montesquieu had already replied with the suggestion that it be graduated.[5] Nevertheless, the poverty of the lower classes remained a successful obstacle to its introduction on a broad basis before the middle of the nineteenth century. It was necessary to establish an equation between the money of the upper classes and the time of the lower classes; what loss of time by the latter is equivalent to a given sum of money? Legislation took cognizance of the problem as early as the end of the eighteenth century. The *Allgemeines Landrecht* was the first to set up precise equations.[6] Subsequent developments were more closely connected with the *Landrecht* than with the French revolutionary legislation, for both the *Code pénal* of September 25 and October 6, 1791, and the *Code rural* of September 28, 1791, starting from a fictive equality, established a rigid system of fines calculated according to the normal working day and inflicted mechanically.[7] The *Code pénal* of 1810 followed the same approach whenever its severity necessitated a decrease in the use of fines.

In general, therefore, the application of fines in the first half of the nineteenth century was infrequent because the necessity of commuting the punishment into imprisonment would have unduly complicated criminal procedure. As a theoretical justification, the argument was raised that widespread use of fines would have a bad economic effect by interfering with the circulation of money and reducing the national wealth.[8] The decline in unemployment and the rising living standard in the second half of the century, however, introduced a fundamental change. Many of the earlier difficulties lying in the way of a fine system lost their force. The increasing emphasis on material goods provided an argument for the extended application of fines in place of short-term imprisonment. Money had become the measure of all things, and it was only right that the state, which extends positive privileges in the form of monetary grants, should also introduce the negative privilege of taking wealth away in punishment for delinquency. Bonneville, a French *procureur* in the middle of the century, argued that virtue and wealth, vice and poverty, constitute antithetical pairs of concepts. Since virtue is rewarded by wealth, vice should entail impoverishment.[9]

The moral defense of the fine system was accompanied by economic arguments. A society, wrote Ihering, "which sacrifices the life or labor time of its members to the aims of punishment without compelling necessity acts against its own interest as much as the property owner who harms his animal by mistreatment." [10] The fine costs the state nothing while procuring the maximum penal effect. The economic system retains its labor power, the convict's family is not thrown upon public charity, and society, as represented by the state, receives damages for the wrong done to it instead of having to pay the costs of punishment.[11]

Certain difficulties still stood in the way of a full rationalization of the penal system through the introduction of fines. The main problem was the precise calculation of the size of the fine according to the condition of the delinquent and the amount of damage caused by his crime. The fine must not exceed his capacity to pay, but it must exceed the benefits he has derived from his illegal act. No solution was found in the nineteenth century which would not violate one or the other requirement too seriously. As a result, the prisons were filled with people who were unable to pay the fines inflicted upon them. As late as 1913, 49.6 percent of all males and 68.2 percent of all females received in English prisons were there in default of fines.[12] From a purely theoretical standpoint, these people were imprisoned for debt, not as punishment, since they went to jail only because they could not meet a financial obligation and since the state was willing to release them the moment they did pay.[13] The fact is not altered, however, that the prisons were being filled with people who were sentenced to pay a fine precisely because they were not considered ripe for imprisonment.

If one carries the theory of substitute procedure to its logical conclusion, as in the French system of *contrainte de corps* which regards imprisonment as a deprivation of liberty for an indeterminate period in order to force a monetary payment, one comes upon other interesting and insoluble problems.[14] Opponents of the *contrainte de corps* have repeatedly pointed out that those who were clearly unable to pay were placed on an equal footing with those who fraudulently refused to pay.[15] The system must assume that those who are fined are capable of paying, and it thus justifies imprisonment for nonpayment. The French bureaucracy was well aware of the necessity for this presumption. In the discussion leading up to a law of July 22, 1867, setting a maximum period of two years for *contrainte de corps,* the logical proposal was made in the legislature to exempt anyone who could prove inability to pay. The administration fought the proposal with the valid argument that the poor would then be unpunishable. To avoid that unfortunate result, a compromise was reached and convicts of proven insolvency were imprisoned for a maximum of one year.[16] Today the fiction that *contrainte de corps* is a method of forcing payment of a debt to the state has been abandoned in practice. A law of December 30, 1928, established a six-month maximum and provided for a graduation of the period of imprisonment according to the amount of the fine.

A Swedish statute of 1937 indicates the precise limits within which it is possible to relax the system of commuting fines into imprisonment under the prevailing social relationships. This progressive statute requires a second examination of the case before commutation, and it opens up the possibility of remission of sentence where the delinquent is unable to pay the fine. Commutation is mandatory, however, if the prisoner is refractory or negligent, or if it is considered necessary for his reform. Lest there be any doubt about the intent of the legislature in this respect, the official commentator says: "It [the retention of commutation] has its basis in the danger of insecurity which might arise if fines inflicted upon paupers could not be commuted even in cases of recidivism." [17] We see, therefore, that carefully drawn legislation and administrative practice may reduce the injustices inherent in the operation of the fine system as it affects the lower classes, but this cannot solve the fundamental problem.

The installment principle has been introduced in recent years in order to avoid crowding the prisons with people who cannot pay their fines. It has had the desired effect of keeping as many people as possible out of the jails. Thus, 10,542 people were received in English prisons in 1935 for nonpayment of fines, but in 1936, as a result of the Money Payments (Justices Procedure) Act (25 & 26 Geo. 5, c. 46), the number dropped to about 7,400.[18] The installment system became equally common in Germany after the laws of October 20, 1923, and February 6, 1924, which allowed a general substitution of fines for sentences of imprisonment under three months. Smooth operation of such a system is strongly conditioned by the market. Efforts to reduce commutation to a minimum by installment payments, and thus to make the fine system applicable to people in very reduced circumstances, can succeed only when the strata affected receive an income no matter how small. This is clearly revealed by the correlation between total convictions and imprisonment in default of fines in Germany from 1925 to 1931.

TABLE 18. *Germany: Commitment to Prison for Nonpayment of Fines*

YEAR	TOTAL CONVICTIONS FOR VIOLATING REICHSGESETZE	TOTAL SENTENCES TO FINES (PER- CENT OF TOTAL CONVICTIONS)	FINES PAID IN FULL	PERCENT OF FINES LEVIED	IMPRISON- MENT IN DEFAULT OF FINE	PERCENT OF FINES LEVIED
1926 a	598,460	65.6	316,022	72.2	40,186	9.2
1927	612,215	66.7	347,743	76.8	38,641	8.5
1928	588,492	69.8	353,530	77.6	37,360	8.1
1929	595,656	68.4	341,825	76.5	44,085	9.8
1930	596,127	66.2	316,463	71.9	53,027	12.5
1931	564,903	67.8	240,296	63.2	59,076	15.4

Source: Compiled from *Statistik des deutschen Reichs*, CDXXIX, *Kriminal- statistik für das Jahr 1930* (Berlin, 1933), 44–46.

a Without Thuringian figures after April 1st.

From 1926 to 1928, the height of the boom, the percentage of fines levied and of fines paid increased, whereas the percentage of imprisonments for default dropped. The reverse process began in 1929 with the beginning of the crisis and it continued through the crisis years. We see an inverse proportion between imprisonment for nonpayment of fines and the number of fines levied. The latter decreases in a period of severe unemployment because of the reduced possibilities of collecting the fine, while the number of defaults goes up rapidly.[19]

The extent to which a fine system can be developed and the character of the offenses to which it is to be applied in any given country are not merely problems of legislation and judicial custom. They are decisively influenced by the whole social situation and by the conditions of the various social strata. Table 19 gives the most recent figures on the number of sentences to fines in various countries.

TABLE 19. *Fines (Percent of All Punishments)*

NATURE OF CRIME	FRANCE (1933)	BELGIUM (1930)	SWEDEN (1934)	GERMANY (1933)	ITALY (1928)	POLAND (1934)	BULGARIA (1935)
Man-slaughter	52.3	38.4	94.4	31.6	—	—	—
Intentional assault	68.9	74.6	91.6	60.2	25.4	23.7	11.8
Unintentional assault	87.4	91.1	94.4	95.7	51.2		
Resisting arrest or assaulting an officer	40.0	80.7	63.9	48.4	22.7	16.9	16.4
Illegal entry	52.4	42.9	81.3	57.7	—	—	45.8
Malicious damage	63.1	79.3	97.9	62.2	51.2	—	64.3
Larceny	15.5	24.4	25.1	29.3	0.01	1.3	0.03
Receiving stolen goods	20.4	22.5	30.5	36.9	—	21.9	—
Fraud	10.5	10.7	46.9	34.2	—	—	—
Violation of seals	32.2	29.9	98.0	78.4	—	—	—
Adultery	99.5	83.0	70.9	58.1	—	—	—
Indecency	12.9	31.1	45.7	34.3	—	—	—
Abortion	0.1	—	1.0	24.5	—	—	—
All crimes	49.36 [a]	57.64 [b]	67.35 [c]	45.18 [d]	16.72 [e]	16.85 [f]	8.07 [g]

Sources: France, *Compte générale de l'administration de la justice civile et commercielle et de la justice criminelle pendant l'année 1933* (Paris, 1937); Belgium, *Statistique judiciaire de la Belgique 1930* (Brussels, 1933); Sweden, *Brottsligheten år 1934* (Stockholm, 1937); Germany, *Kriminalstatistik des deutschen Reiches für 1933* (Berlin, 1936); Italy, *Statistica della criminalità 1928* (Rome, 1935); Poland, *Concise Statistical Year Book of Poland 1936* (Warsaw, 1936); Bulgaria, *Statistique criminelle 1935* (Sofia, 1936).

Absence of figures indicates either: (1) no fine provided by law, (2) no fines recorded in criminal statistics, (3) no comparable figures exist.

[a] As inflicted by the *tribunal correctionnel.*
[b] *Ibid.*
[c] Penal code, without nuisances and drunkenness.
[d] *Reichsstrafgesetzbuch* only.
[e] Penal and commercial codes.
[f] Without the group labeled "Other infractions."
[g] Penal code and special laws.

There are many gaps in this table and the categories are not always identical, but one thing stands out clearly. The poorer the population of a country, the less frequent is the use of fines for the offenses characteristic of the great mass of the people.

The figures for Italy, Poland, and Bulgaria are unmistakable. The fact that the German statistics for 1933 differ sharply from those of this group of countries is clear evidence that the frequency of fines is not primarily the result of legislative or judicial measures or theories, but is rather an accurate reflection of the prevailing social and economic conditions. In countries where broad strata of the population still live outside the sphere of capitalist relationships and do not command money or commodities, the fine tends to be a punishment for specific crimes of the middle and upper classes, as in the Middle Ages.

The fine system (especially after installment payments became common) helped empty the prisons and reduced the costs and work of administration, which would otherwise have increased greatly with the rise in the number of administration offenses. In general, the fine system contributed to the rationalization of criminal administration. The process of rationalization was particularly strong in two types of offenses:

1.—*Cases in which the state need have no concern for the delinquent.* The violations of police regulations have increased steadily with the growing complexity of human existence. The state's sole interest in such offenses is to compel obedience by levying sufficiently large fines. Whether the delinquent's interest or pleasure in trespassing the norms is sufficiently restricted or not depends entirely on the efficiency with which the authorities can control observance of the norms and prosecute violations. Failure to prosecute with sufficient vigor automatically leads to wholesale violations, for these merely technical offenses are not accompanied by any feeling of guilt or wrongdoing.

2.—*Violation of labor laws by employers.* In European judicial practice, these offenses are handled in the same way as violations of police regulations. The statistics of every country show that there is a remarkable unanimity in restricting the punishment to fines. In England, for example, 97 percent of all those convicted in 1928 for violating labor laws were fined, and 95 percent in 1934; no one was imprisoned for more than three months.[20] Of the 6,461 convicted in Germany in 1933 for violating the regulations about hours of labor, two were sentenced to prison for less than three months and the rest were fined. Of the 378 convicted for repeated violations of the same regulations, one was sentenced to a regular prison term and one to a minor form of imprisonment called *Haft*.[21]

This widespread coupling of labor law violations with violations of police regulations is a matter for serious consideration because such offenses, much more than crimes against property, allow for a calculable profit. Since the practice is to levy light fines without regard for the profit derived from the transgression, the efficacy of the labor laws is undermined. The general principle that the punishment must be sufficient to negate the profits of crime is not applied. The reward is greater than the risk, or, as an English factory inspector cited by Marx phrased it:

The profit to be gained by it [overworking in violation of the Act] appears to be, to many, a greater temptation than they can resist; they calculate upon the chance of not being found out; and when they see the small amount of penalty and costs, which those who have been convicted have to pay, they find that if they should be detected there will still be a considerable balance of gain.[22]

The ineffectuality of such criminal practice is clear from the French statistics. Recidivism is amazingly frequent. The *Tribunal de police,* where first offenses against the labor laws are tried, condemned 2,307 offenders in 1922 and 3,341 in 1932, while the *Tribunal correctionnel,* the court which deals with second offenses occurring within a year as well as with a few special cases, convicted 296 in 1922 and 2,652 in 1932, all sentenced to fines.[23]

It may be assumed that the authorities would like to insure legal conduct with respect to the labor laws. In another group of delicts including begging and prostitution, however, which are punished by fines in some countries, the state does not even have the intention of putting an end to a situation held to be undesirable. All that is sought is a measure of supervision and observance of certain formal rules in the practice of one's occupation. Eighty-nine percent of all prostitutes convicted in England in 1928 and 1934 were sentenced to fines, and of all convicted for violating the vagrancy acts in 1928 and 1934, 67 percent and 60 percent respectively.[24] Such punishment is obviously not designed to improve the groups involved or to take them out of their trades. If it were so designed, fines would not be levied on people who are reproached for the manner in which they earn their living, since the money with which the fines are paid must necessarily come from the very occupations condemned.[25] The only conclusion, then, is that the state levies fines because it dislikes the activity but is not seriously prepared to put a stop to it. The state rests content with fines because it is not interested in the social strata involved or in their rehabilitation. In the long run, the punishment is an uneconomic way of avoiding administrative and financial difficulties.

An extensive commercialization of the penal system has developed with the progress of the fine. The tendency which arose at the end of the eighteenth century to consider the administration of criminal justice as a debit item in the budget was not destroyed by this process of commercialization, but it was weakened somewhat.[26] The process found its most complete expression in the purely police delicts, as we have already seen. The fine system is thus tantamount to a licensing system, but unlike the usual administrative practice which requires the license before permission is given, here the fee is paid after the act, and then only if the act is apprehended. That is equally true of violations of labor law by employers, which in practice have been put on the same level as violations of police regulations.

Unlike imprisonment, the fine need not have the negative effect of penetrating one's whole life. It has a distinct class character, despite all efforts to the contrary, because its effect on different social strata is most divergent. The penal aspect has virtually disappeared in the case of wealthier offenders who can pay the fine without feeling it or who can shift it, especially where violations of police regulations or labor laws, to which no social stigma is attached, are involved. The chief effect of the punishment in more severe offenses lies in the social stigma and the police record. For the majority of the people, however, this rationalized form of administering criminal justice does have serious effects, since it necessitates major restrictions and deprivations on the part of the offender and his family.[27] If the offender owns no property, but receives a small, steady income, the fine is a serious burden, and it has a real penal character if he cannot shift it. The situation is even worse in the frequent cases in which the offense is either wholly or partly the consequence of acute poverty. The impossibility of a sensible policy of fines for this last category has often been discussed. We have already dealt with one aspect of the problem, the commutation of fines into imprisonment. A favorite proposal, often placed on the statute books, is to eliminate imprisonment in default of fines by allowing the offender to work the debt off.[28] This solution has rarely been carried out in practice, and for good reason. The infliction of fines on poor offenders presupposes that the state is not forced to concern itself with the delinquent and his social situation. The state assumes no obligations toward him, as it does to a limited extent toward the convict and his family while he is in prison. If the state must obtain work for the offender, however, the administration would be obliged to procure a wage which would be sufficient to maintain him and his family and still permit the payment of the fine. The apparatus for the administration of criminal justice is not adjusted to such positive activity, nor is it expected to be so adjusted under the prevailing conceptions. We can safely conclude, therefore, that the application of fines has its natural limits in the material conditions of the lower strata of the population.

XI

NEW TRENDS IN PENAL POLICY UNDER FASCISM

MODERN reform theory, as we have seen, has not destroyed the notion that the policy of repression is a satisfactory way to combat crime. The general conclusion drawn by the official English Home Office publication on criminal statistics for the year 1928 (published in 1930) is very symptomatic:

If one summarizing conclusion had to be hazarded, perhaps it would be that the community's efforts to deal with offenders leniently and yet with discrimination, under various enactments and practices which were devised by the older generation, have succeeded *with that generation* for, among that generation, serious crime and petty offences alike have, in general, decreased; but that whether the same methods hold good, and will continue to hold good, *with the new generation* is another matter.[1]

It is easy to see why such reflections have taken on greater meaning with the outbreak of the crisis and the accompanying increase in crime.

TABLE 20. *Increase in Crimes against Property, 1928–32*

YEAR	ENGLAND		GERMANY	
	LARCENY	BREAKING AND ENTERING	LARCENY	ROBBERY
1928	37,530	2,846	86,347	683
1929	36,217	2,748	91,109	811
1930	38,244	3,360	97,596	1,028
1931	40,024	3,783	99,355	1,197
1932	42,511	4,894	112,568	1,471

Source: *Criminal Statistics, England and Wales 1934*, p. XI; Amend, *op. cit.*, pp. 62 and 65.

The effects of the increase in crime on penal policy should be most noticeable in Germany, the country in which the crisis was most severe, and in which wage cuts and unemployment created the sharpest decline in the living standard of broad sections of the population. During the crisis, German prisons were filled to capacity for the first time in many years. The administration was hard put to accommodate this influx, especially since many obsolete institutions were abandoned during the boom years when the number of crimes and commitments had been comparatively low. The crisis also made it more and more difficult to provide the convicts with work. Prison conditions automatically deteriorated as a result of these two factors, without any conscious efforts on the part of the administration. Dziembowski, a Prussian prison official, wrote at the beginning of 1932:

With very few exceptions, the idle prisoners today feel that in the idleness forced upon them by economic necessity they are the victims of a measure to intensify suffering. . . . . We feel to a greater and greater degree that we in the prisons are losing touch with the convicts. They beg for work, the need for which becomes more urgent every day. . . . . As a result of the present idleness, most of the prisoners are not sufficiently tired to need the usual period of rest. They lie in the darkness for hours without sleep, and they are readily susceptible to evil thoughts under such conditions. The convicts are certainly not the only people who have to retire early in order to economize on light, but the similarity between their conditions and those of the outside world ends there.[2]

The reform program had struck many snags even before the onset of the crisis, despite its partial acceptance in various laws and administrative regulations. By 1931, two years before the political change, the failure of reform was more or less unanimously recognized. Finke, a high Prussian official, expressed this fact clearly, behind all the characteristic ambiguities of his phraseology, when he wrote:

Every innovation requires a maturation period during which it is exposed to all the negative forces of development . . . . we are no longer in the middle stage of evolution, however, but are approaching its end, which is a fiasco. Post-war authorities have shown great zeal in the interest of institutions of charity and education, and attempts were made ten years ago to turn penal administration into a new path, to characterize it as an educational institution. These undertakings have failed in their purpose. Loud voices arise in the committee rooms of prison guards and higher officials, declaiming the impossibility of penal education and asserting that the old theory of deterrence is the only correct one.[3]

Statements like this are sufficient to refute the charge that Weimar Germany was a criminal's paradise, a view which was occasionally expressed before the political change of 1933, and much more frequently thereafter.[4]

The late nineteenth-century reformers, whose ideas influenced post-war German practice, always insisted on maintaining the full guarantees of legal procedure along with progressive penal reform. The group now in power is not interested in either. Procedure and substantive law that are too precisely fixed would impede the development of the new power relationships. The retention of exact, calculable norms of criminal law could provide the political opposition with a point of departure, for it would allow the judicial bureaucracy, which had won considerable political independence in the Weimar period, to exercise a certain measure of control. This power has been taken away, from the very outset, by a whole series of special laws and by the general doctrine that politically relevant acts are not subject to judicial review.[5] Despite its formal acceptance of the principle of judicial independence, the new German regime has effectively accomplished the coördination of the judiciary by making it impossible for the judge to fall back upon the statute as a defense. Formerly he was able to call upon the law, which could be changed only by new legislation. But a statute which can be altered every day without formal procedure is in fact nothing more than an administrative order, and a judicial decision that is unsatisfactory to those who hold the administrative power is nothing more than an indication of further administrative regulations which are needed. The shift from the general law of earlier capitalism to the administrative command of monopoly capitalism thus destroys the influence of judicial decisions over the future relationships between individuals or between the state and the individual.

The separation of law from morality, an axiom in the period of competitive capitalism, has been replaced by a moral conviction derived immediately from the "racial conscience" *Volks-*

gewissen), one of the most frequently used disguises in the new technique of domination.[6] The "racial conscience" has been introduced into the criminal law through the elevation of concepts like "welfare of the people" and "healthy national sentiment" to official normative standards.[7] This process has helped considerably in restricting the judge's freedom of decision. The judge is expected to follow the wishes of the politically dominant group in interpreting these concepts. The ascendancy of the prosecution, always latent in German criminal procedure, has been strengthened by legislation at the expense of the judge and the defense attorney, especially of the latter. The following remarks of Freisler show the extent to which the defense is handicapped (the comment is all the more interesting because the author's intention was to plead for greater freedom of action for the defense attorney):

If I have accepted a case which I have a right to accept as a German lawyer in general, and, further, in consideration of my special ties which follow from my membership in certain organizations, and if I have conducted the defense vigorously and properly as the defendant's representative and have acted within the frame of the community interests which I am obliged to protect, then no judicial or administrative authority can challenge my responsibility.[8]

The struggle in the field of substantive law is directed against "the isolation of 'general' concepts, like guilt, accessory, attempt, from the concrete crimes," condemned as artificial and meaningless abstractions torn out of the concrete relationships of life,[9] and against a too precise formulation of specific criminal acts.[10] This represents a double attack on the power of the judge to fall back upon his subordination to formal law. The significance of the reintroduction of the principle of analogy and the abandonment of the principle of *nulla poena sine lege* lies just here. They provide the administration with a method of forcing the refractory judge to arrive at the desired interpretation of the statute. As a last resort, any objectionable interpretation can be blocked by a law of the leader (*Führergesetz*), retroactive if necessary.

The Italian criminal law theory has held fast to traditional liberal doctrines until very recently, and it was even reflected in the penal code of 1930. The practical significance of this theoretical continuity must not be overestimated, however, for, as Hall points out, the "setting up of special tribunals to hear political offences in disregard of constitutional law, and the very broad definition of crimes along with the turning over of the chief interests of the state to administrative boards, no doubt facilitated retention of traditional laws in the ordinary run of offences." [11] Most recently, Italian theorists have begun to imitate the Germans, although they vigorously deny this relationship and insist on their own originality and national tradition.[12] The "nonlogical" character of penal theory now comes to the fore.[13] The law of procedure loses its function as a guarantee of the rights of the individual and takes on the character of "a legal instrument for the realization of the punitive aims of the state." [14]

In sum, all the guarantees for which liberalism had struggled since the end of the eighteenth century have been destroyed. They have become unnecessary for the steadily contracting circle of the ruling strata, since the demarcation between permissible and impermissible social practices in the Fascist countries is determined from case to case by direct agreement with the bureaucracy. The rest of the middle class must accept the fact that a reduction in legal guarantees is the necessary consequence of the retention of their social position.

The deterioration of both substantive and adjective criminal law has been accompanied by a change in penal policy. The official justification for the shift away from the leniency of the Weimar period is clearly expressed in the following statement of Rietzsch, a Prussian official, in 1933:

It is not surprising that complaints about the increase in crime have been frequent in public and in the press during the last few years, and that the police have been dissatisfied with the lack of coöperation on the part of the judicial administration. Indeed, the figures quoted leave no doubt but that criminal administration and court procedure must adopt new methods if crime is to be effectively prevented. The very foundations of the criminal policy of the last epoch have given way.[15]

We need not discuss the obvious fallacies in this argument. Even subjectively, it fails to present the real ground for changing the whole policy of sentences and punishments. The new criminal practice is not motivated primarily by criminological viewpoints, but by a specific social educational function. A significant feature of present-day German social and economic policy is the avowed necessity to keep down the living standard of the lower strata. In order to facilitate the acceptance of this program by the masses, considerable effort is spent in cultivating a moral distinction between those who are poor but honest and the strata which have become criminal. The masses are offered the misfortune of some in place of a thoroughgoing improvement in their material existence and the happiness of all. This process of ideology construction has played a basic role in all the critical periods of the modern era, such as the French Revolution, as Horkheimer has shown.[16]

Contemporary writers are not very successful in disguising the ideological function when they replace rational arguments by references to mass consciousness, the dignity of the state, and the metaphysical impossibility of deducing punishment.[17] It comes out the more clearly the weaker the intellectual apparatus for the enunciation of the new principles. *Polizeigeneral* Daluege, for example, wrote in the *Hakenkreuzbanner Mannheim* for November 5, 1936: "The state cannot draw the line of demarcation *too sharply* between the honorable portion of the population and the asocial enemy of the people, if it wishes to prevent moral savagery." [18] Against the background of a caricatured version of the humane Weimar methods,[19] the National Socialists have projected a new system, in which the elements of a biological race-and-predestination doctrine are mixed with the retaliatory principles of classical German penal theory. The guarantees of substantive law and procedure, in the name of which the classical theorists fought against the reformers, have been completely destroyed, however.

The most striking aspect of the new penal system is the return of capital punishment. It is frequently applied against political opponents by the so-called People's Court, an administrative organ, and it is becoming more and more common in ordinary criminal practice as well,[20] although little effort is made to provide a theoretical justification. One theoretician has even said: "The necessity of retaining it in the National Socialist state requires no defense. The death penalty is the expression of the domination of the whole over the individual. . . . ." [21] The argument is occasionally raised that capital punishment is justified by its deterrent effects, but the criminal statistics are not very conclusive.

TABLE 21. *Convictions for Murder in Germany per 100,000 Population above the Age of Discretion* a

YEAR	FIRST-DEGREE (MORD)	SECOND-DEGREE (TOTSCHLAG)	TOTAL
1928	0.18	0.64	0.82
1932	0.20	1.10	1.30
1933	0.32	1.02	1.34
1934 b	0.63	0.69	1.32
1936	0.29	0.45	0.74

Source: Compiled from the *Statistisches Jahrbuch für das deutsche Reich.*

a The shift in the proportion between first-degree murder (*Mord*) and second-degree (*Totschlag*) represents a change in court practice, not in the crime rate itself.

b The 1934 figures do not include those who were executed on the basis of the law of July 3, 1934, establishing "measures of state emergency."

A second noteworthy tendency appears in the treatment of certain delicts which are immediately comprehensible from the social position of the offender and which do not indicate any particular opposition to the state. They are isolated from their social base and labeled treason against the community, a violation of the compulsory allegiance to the regime. Even labor contracts are conceived as a special kind of allegiance, and a breach of contract is a felony, a "decomposition of the racial will to work (*völkische Arbeitswille*)." It is alleged that this conception goes back to ideas rooted in old German law, but that is only a method of arguing away the social basis of mass criminality.[22]

The reorganization and suppression of the *Gerichtshilfe* is an analogous phenomenon. In the Weimar period the *Gerichtshilfe* was an essential factor in the rationalization of penal practice: it provided the court with information about the delinquent's social milieu and personal history, which could then be taken into consideration in determining the sentence.[23] In 1937 a committee for criminal procedural reform set up by the *Akademie für deutsches Recht* decided that *Gerichtshilfe* is not necessary in every case, and that where it might be desirable, as in metropolitan areas, it is to be considered merely auxiliary to the activity of the prosecution and not independent social work.[24] This view represents more than just an attempt by the judicial bureaucracy to poach on the preserves of the social service bureaucracy. A decree of October 7, 1937, shows that the complete subordination of the reorganized *Gerichtshilfe* to the prosecution serves to insulate the courtroom as far as possible against those social influences which do not fit the new criminal policy.[25] It is a way of avoiding any discussion of the collective responsibility of society which would result from a sociological conception of crime. The latter is admittedly incompatible with the totalitarian theory.[26] A standard of responsibility set up in its place shows that the social relationships do not permit the calculation of culpability according to the capacity of the ordinary citizen. From the incontrovertible thesis that the demands which can be made on the will power of the individual cannot be measured by the psychic potentiality of the delinquent, Siegert, for example, draws the startling conclusion that the average citizen lowers the average. "This danger is overcome," he continues, "when we measure the psychic potentiality of the actor against the strong-willed *Volksgenosse*. The demands which we make upon the latter in view of his psychic potentiality must also be made upon the activity of the delinquent." [27] The reason given for replacing the average individual by the superior citizen as the standard is that the "other *Volksgenossen* will have to say to themselves that such a rigid standard will also be applied to their behavior if they ever become culpable." This change in standards is expected to bring about a "reshaping of the will power of vacillating personalities." [28] When we place this new juristic phraseology in its social setting, we see that it is theoretically akin to the reorganization of the *Gerichtshilfe* and similar measures designed to eliminate sociological considerations from criminal procedure. The demands on the individual increase as the social conditions become worse. The normal standard of psychological capacity no longer suffices. The individual is not measured by the potentialities of his average neighbor, but by some ideal picture which has been constructed.[29] This conception cannot be maintained in practice, however, as both the German and Italian amnesty laws of recent times show. They provide for mass pardon of criminals to a degree which is unknown in democratic countries, and which is absolutely incompatible with the theory that increased demands must be made upon every citizen.[30]

A tendency is clearly perceptible in Germany to increase both the severity and the length of imprisonment. The judge is subjected to strong pressure from above to intensify punishments on the ground that the authority of the state must be defended.[31] The number of acquittals has been declining steadily.

TABLE 22. *Percentage of Acquittals in Germany in All Cases*

YEAR	PERCENT
1925	13.80
1930	14.04
1932	15.05
1933	12.87
1934	12.64
1936	10.50

Source: Compiled from the *Statistisches Jahrbuch für das deutsche Reich.*

The figures of Table 22 reflect the change in the official attitude toward defendants and particularly the decreasing possibility of an efficient defense.

Table 23 shows that the characteristic development in recent German penal practice, the decline in fines and the increase in the number and length of prison sentences, began before Hitler came to power in 1933. Increasing severity of punishment, therefore, is in the first instance a change in criminal policy conditioned by economic crisis. The political events of 1933 merely accentuated the process, particularly in the greater use of the death penalty and penal servitude, and in the increasing proportion of long-term imprisonments. The history of the fine is especially

TABLE 23. *Distribution of Punishments in Germany per 100,000 Convictions* [a]

			PENAL SERVITUDE (ZUCHTHAUS)		IMPRISONMENT						
YEAR	DEATH	LIFE	TEM-PO-RARY	THREE YEARS OR MORE (PERCENT OF TEM-PORARY)	TOTAL	THREE MONTHS (PER-CENT)	THREE MONTHS TO ONE YEAR (PER-CENT)	OVER ONE YEAR (PER-CENT)	FEST-UNGS-HAFT	HAFT	FINE
1930	7.2	0.8	785	— [b]	31,788	64.0	30.0	6.0	18.5	523	66,202
1931	8.7	1.4	813	23.4	35,981	63.9	29.9	6.2	15.9	459	62,100
1932	9.2	1.4	1,123	24.7	41,540	62.5	31.0	6.5	34.0	466	56,320
1933	16.0	3.9	1,971	26.9	44,516	57.3	33.7	9.0	7.7	517	52,607
1934	25.5	3.9	3,197	29.1	41,549	53.8	35.2	11.0	0.0	478	54,408
1936	17.0	2.0	2,955	26.9	41,585	47.0	41.2	11.8	1.0	443	54,309

Source: Compiled from *Statistik des deutschen Reichs*, Vols. CDXXIX and DVII, *Kriminalstatistik* 1933 and 1934 respectively; *Statistisches Jahrbuch für das deutsche Reich.*

[a] These figures do not include people interned in concentration camps.

[b] No figures were published prior to 1931.

interesting. National Socialist theoreticians have little liking for this method of punishment. Rietzsch writes:

Today the fine seems to us to be an unsympathetic, unworthy method of punishment, a stop-gap. In the future, it will be . . . . inflicted much more sparingly than before . . . . above all, the fine must lose its wholly plutocratic character. The principle of equal suffering for poor and rich must be carried through; where the poor man can redeem himself only by a heavy sacrifice, the rich man must not buy himself off lightly.[32]

Harsh reality, however, compels recognition of the fine as the mass punishment of our period, and after this bow to the anti-capitalist ideology nothing remains but the old demand of the reformers that the fine be worked off by labor. The state has the moral right to take more severe measures only if the condemned man refuses to work the fine off.[33] How can the latter be accomplished in a period of unemployment? After many evasions and circumlocutions, the official theorists come to the conclusion which we have already found in the French parliamentary debates of 1867—the punishment is not to be executed.[34] But the actual statistics show that the history of the fine is closely bound up with the conditions of the market, despite the theories of its capitalist character and of the necessity of working it off. The drop from 69 percent in 1928 to 52.6 percent in 1933 and the upward swing in 1934, the very year in which the avowed National Socialist policy against this method of punishment should have gone into effect, indicate how the market—in this case an improvement in the labor market—weakens and neutralizes penal tendencies moving in another direction.

The reintroduction of extensive property confiscations into the system of criminal law, a practice which was held to a minimum under liberalism, is tied up less with "Aryan legal thought" [35] than with the transition from the system of competition to monopoly capitalism. Protection of the property of the individual capitalist must yield before the task of protecting the monopolist groups which control the state, both against outsiders and against any possible outbreak from within the monopoly group itself.[36]

If the prolongation of punishments is not feasible, increased severity can still be achieved by making prison conditions worse and by introducing harsher punishments. The innovators found themselves blocked, however, for they discovered that the tendency in the past had been for different forms of imprisonment to become the same. They therefore sought new forms like *Kerker,* which was to be clearly differentiated from the milder *Zuchthaus,* and they tried to reëstablish the rapidly disappearing difference between the latter and the prison.[37] One official soon pointed out that the problem of making punishment more severe is complicated by the fact that sufficient leeway must remain so that disciplinary cases could receive additional punishment within the prison.[38] Even if some ingenious method could be devised to overcome this difficulty, however, the problem of extensive differentiation would not be solved. Official statistics reveal that the per capita cost of prison administration in 1931 was 1,228 reichsmarks, whereas in 1934 it was only 725 reichsmarks.[39] Under such conditions, the possibility of appreciably differentiating among the prisoners becomes highly questionable, for the living standard has been so reduced that the old bromide of maintaining the prisoner's health and labor power has lost much of its meaning.[40] The fact that the lowest limit has nearly been reached, making further differentiation practically impossible, has received quasi-official recognition. The *Denkschrift* of the *Akademie für deutsches Recht* says: "Since the diet of prisoners at the present time is generally no more than the amount required [for health], it is necessary in practice to abandon any notion of giving substantially less or simpler food to the inmates of *Zuchthäuser*." [41] The new regime has constructed an ideology around this process of deterioration. The position taken by the German and Italian representatives at the Berlin Prison Congress of 1935 was nothing more than the old principle that the living standard in the prisons must not be above the lowest level of that of the free population.[42]

Next to the declining prison standards, a product of the general deterioration of living conditions, the chief mark of the new policy is the overpopulation of the prisons. Partly the result of the economic decline, as in every country, the overpopulation in Germany was further stimulated by the prolongation of prison

TABLE 24. *Number of Persons Received in Prisons*
A. Italy a

YEAR	CARCERI GIUDIZIARIE		STABILIMENTI DIE PENA	MISURI DI SICUREZZA
	TOTAL	PER 10,000 POPULATION	TOTAL	TOTAL
1912	208,809	57	4,092	—
1922	230,223	59	5,403	—
1925	227,756	58	3,782	—
1926	243,239	61	4,139	—
1928	262,445	65	4,777	—
1930	233,305	57	3,887	—
1932	287,441	69	4,913	2,232
1933	260,152	62	5,841	2,548
1934	296,416	69	4,391	2,786
1935	259,643	60	3,641	2,642

Source: Compiled from the *Annuario statistico* and the *Statistica degli Istituti di prevenzione di pena e dei riformatori, 1928–1933* (Rome, 1936).

a The Italian figures do not include administrative punishments like deportation. The picture would still look worse if it were not for the amnesty law of 1932, which we have already discussed.

TABLE 24 (*Continued*)

B. *France*

YEAR	MAISON D'ARRÊT		MAISON CENTRALE	DÉPÔT ON THE ISLAND RÉ FOR CONVICTS AWAIT-ING DEPORTATION
	TOTAL	PER 10,000 POPULATION	TOTAL	TOTAL
1912	230,549	59	4,118	883
1919	127,472	34	6,512	172
1923	137,729	34	3,637	701
1928	142,856	35	3,580	447
1930	137,094	33	2,911	236
1931	136,698	32	2,967	791
1932	131,069	31	2,505	216

Source: Compiled from the *Statistique pénitentiaire.*

terms and by the more sparing use of paroles and other forms of early release.[43]

Even Italian observers cannot deny the considerable increase in prison commitments during the last few years. When de Castro, however, takes the year 1926 as his point of departure and calculates the rise in commitments to be about six percent from 1926 to 1933,[44] he is understating the real increase because 1926 is precisely the year when the sharp rise began. The survey of world prison population prepared for the League of Nations by the Howard League in 1936 gives the 1935 German figure as 156.9 per 100,000 population, excluding prisoners in concentration camps.[45]

Italy also compares unfavorably with France when we examine the capacity of the prisons as compared with the size of the prison population.

This overpopulation, so chronic in Italy that even Italian authors must admit it,[46] reached a point where the rules about isolation at night could not be followed. The same situation prevails in Germany. No official figures are published, but the fact is clearly established by the intensified court practice, and it is not denied in official publications.[47]

Overpopulation is accompanied by an inability to find enough productive labor for the prisoners. The crisis had limited prison

TABLE 25. *Prison Capacity and Population*

	FRANCE: MAISON D'ARRÊT			ITALY: CARCERI GIUDIZIARIE		
		AVERAGE			AVERAGE	
		DAILY	MAXIMUM		DAILY	MAXIMUM
		POPULATION	DAILY		POPULATION	DAILY
		(PERCENT OF	(PERCENT OF		(PERCENT OF	(PERCENT OF
YEAR	CAPACITY	CAPACITY)	CAPACITY)	CAPACITY	CAPACITY)	CAPACITY)
1929	26,900	42.7	70.7	34,592	104.9	123.8
1930	29,992	46.9	66.9	34,595	89.9	108.8
1931	31,547	44.3	64.1	35,477	90.2	109.1
1932	30,179	45.0	63.0	35,593	98.6	117.5
1933	— —	— —	— —	35,472	81.3	100.2

Source: Calculated from the *Statistique pénitentiaire* and the *Statistica peniteziaria.*

work even in the countries with fewer convicts,[48] and the situation was much worse in the countries with overfilled prisons, as Table 26 shows.[49]

This table shows a sharp decline in unemployment for lack of work in Italy in 1933, a decline which official reports claim to have accelerated in 1934 and 1935;[50] but this increase is very doubtful for several reasons. Insofar as some of the loss is absorbed under the heading "Other Reasons," we cannot speak of a decline in prison unemployment at all. That part of the drop which is due to the use of convict labor for draining malarial swamps as part of a land reclamation program must also be excluded from classification as employment in the present sense.[51] Such forced labor has become customary in Germany, too.[52] It

TABLE 26. *Employment of Prison Labor in Percents*

| | ITALY: STABILIMENTI DI PENA | | | | FRANCE: MAISON CENTRALE | |
| | EMPLOYED | | UNEMPLOYED | | EMPLOYED | |
YEAR	PRISON SERVICES	OTHER WORK	LACK OF WORK	OTHER REASONS	MEN	WOMEN
1928	10	53	11	26	79	86
1929	9	52	15	24	85	92
1930	11	52	13	24	88	90
1931	11	49	21	19	82	88
1932	11	46	28	15	80	87
1933	14	58	6	22	—	—

Sources: *Statistica degli Istituti di prevenzione* . . . . , p. 26, and the *Statistique pénitentiaire.*

has nothing to do, even approximately, with the rule that "as far as possible the work should be instructive and of a nature which may enable prisoners to earn their livelihood after liberation." [53] In Germany, the scarcity of labor and raw materials has recently given a certain impetus to the employment of convicts in working up waste materials, which might have some meaning from the standpoint of a scarcity economy, but which can hardly be considered vocational training for the prisoner.[54] It is evident that the problem of rehabilitation has been shelved, together with efforts to prepare the convict, at least physically, to enter the struggle for existence after his release.

We have seen that the difficulties with the progressive system lay in the fact that it could amount to nothing more than a practical device for obtaining better discipline. National Socialist literature on penology reveals a desire to place severe limitations on the system of favors granted to prisoners as well as a tendency to increase the requirements for promotion from one stage to the next. The decline of the system of favors, strongly weakened to begin with in its material extent, becomes even more apparent when it is examined together with the severe restrictions which are placed on the right of complaint. Germany has gone far beyond Italy in this respect. The theory still prevails in Italy that the convict has subjective rights and that penal administration must follow a strict set of rules. Recent legislation has attempted to limit the discretionary powers of penal administration by the introduction of a system of supervisory judges, whose duties are to be carefully separated from the work of the regular prison officials.[55] How far this theory is carried out in practice is a doubtful point, for there is no public opinion to control it, either in the organized form of parliamentary control or in the unorganized form of private societies and press.[56] In this connection it is worth noting that Ugo Conti, the Italian representative to the Berlin Prison Congress of 1935, shifted the emphasis from the legal aspects of the separation between ordinary officials and supervisory judges to the purely technical problems of jurisdiction.[57]

In Germany, on the other hand, an effort has been made to

remove the legal guarantees which are inherent in the theory of the subjective rights of the convicts. The function of law in penal administration has changed from guarantee of the convict's rights to assurance that the officials will not neglect the repressive character of punishment.[58] Paragraphs 147 to 153 of the May 14, 1934, regulations on imprisonment severely limit the right of appeal both in content and in form.[59] It is further weakened by the fact that complaints are not heard by a rival bureaucracy, such as the judicial bureaucracy in Italy, but by higher prison officials. That means that complaints are useless, unless one is willing to accept the argument of a representative of the German ministry of justice that "distrust of the onesidedness of a decision made through administrative channels is baseless, that, on the contrary, expert knowledge and a sense of responsibility guarantee a proper investigation and decision." [60]

In the field of juvenile delinquency there has been no sharp departure from generally accepted principles. Proposals to place adolescents on the same level with adults have found no response in court procedure (apart from military criminal law) and very little in the field of punishment.[61] The proposal to institute a severe short-term imprisonment for juveniles (called *Jugendarrest*) has not met with any more success.[62] The increasing severity and brutality of penal treatment of adults has had the effect of widening the gap between ordinary penal methods and the treatment of juvenile delinquents, for prevailing opinion has clung to educational principles in the latter case. The section on juvenile delinquency in the regulations of the *Reichsjustizministerium* of January 22, 1937, reveals the immanent contradiction between the ideology of the racial community (*Volksgemeinschaft*) and the needs of modern capitalist society. Paragraph 25 provides that workshops must have the character of apprentice schools, that hand work is to be preferred, and that machines for mass production are not to be used. It thus reveals the dual character of the regime, which is afraid to admit that the education of the lower classes at the present time is education for their incorporation into the capitalist system of production.

XII

PENAL POLICY AND CRIME RATE

IN THE course of our inquiry, we have frequently encoun-
tered the view that penal policy is a sort of sluice gate which
can be used to regulate the flow of crime. The introduction of new
methods or degrees of punishment, especially in recent times, has
often been accompanied by the argument that an increase in
crime is the result of excessive leniency, and vice versa, that the
crime rate can be driven downward by intensifying punishment.
No serious effort is made, however, to prove this relationship by
precise investigation. Discussion is usually limited to general
remarks about the connection between social and political unrest, the weakening in the authority of the state, and the frequency of crime. There can be no doubt that a cracking social
order tends to give rise to increased crime, and political and
social stability to a decrease. Criminology is not concerned,
however, with the efficacy of methods of suppressing social and
political opponents in general. It operates in terms of the normal
organs of police and justice in a state in which most men obey
the laws.

It does not seem superfluous, therefore, to examine the statistical material in order to study the extent, if any, to which penal
policy affects the crime rate. We shall limit ourselves to English,
French, German, and Italian figures. Our concern is only with
the possible deterrent effects of punishment on potential criminals, and not with its effects on actual delinquents. Table 27
provides comparative figures for criminality and methods of
punishment in England for the years 1911 and 1928.

Before proceeding to analyze these figures, we must indicate
the reasons for choosing them. The official English statistics for
1928 take as their point of departure for this problem the number. of crimes known to the police, not the number of prosecu-
tions. The results show a large number of decreases in specific

TABLE 27. *Crime Rate and Method of Disposal in England* a

OFFENSE	YEAR	CHANGE OF CRIME RATE b 1911-28 (PERCENT)	OUT OF 100 PROSECUTIONS					OUT OF 100 CONVICTIONS			OUT OF 100 SENTENCED TO IMPRISONMENT					
			CHARGE WITH-DRAWN OR DIS-MISSED	CHARGE PROVED, ORDER MADE WITH-OUT CONVICTION	TOTAL CON-VICTIONS	TOTAL IM-PRISON-MENTS		RE-FORMA-TORY SCHOOL	WHIP-PING	FINES	OVER SIX MONTHS	SIX MONTHS AND OVER THREE	THREE MONTHS AND OVER TWO	TWO MONTHS AND OVER ONE	ONE MONTH AND OVER 14 DAYS	14 DAYS AND UNDER
Simple larceny and minor larcenies	1911	-3.8	12.0	33.0	55.0	56.0		3.5	6.0	33.0	0.1	5.0	19.9	20.0	36.0	19.0
	1928		10.0	47.0	43.0	36.0		2.0	0.5	58.0	—	26.0	25.3	16.2	25.2	7.3
Larceny from the person	1911	-63.8	22.0	27.0	51.0	80.0		4.0	5.0	11.0	—	9.6	37.4	21.7	23.3	8.0
	1928		21.0	30.0	49.0	76.0		2.0	1.0	21.0	—	43.0	33.0	11.0	12.0	1.0
Larceny by a servant	1911	-29.4	6.0	46.0	48.0	64.0		3.5	0.3	32.0	—	12.0	22.5	25.5	32.0	8.0
	1928		4.0	60.0	36.0	50.0		2.0	—	47.0	—	32.0	31.5	19.5	15.0	2.0
Embezzle-ment	1911	-31.2	10.0	38.0	52.0	74.0		3.0	1.0	21.0	0.2	5.4	22.6	33.9	32.3	5.6
	1928		8.0	54.0	38.0	70.0		2.0	—	24.0	—	24.0	33.0	25.0	16.0	2.0

Offense	Year														
Obtaining by false pretenses	1911	15.0	24.0	61.0	72.0	2.0	0.5	24.0	0.2	9.7	30.5	21.0	28.2	10.4	+0.7
	1928	11.0	27.0	62.0	71.0	0.3	—	24.0	—	37.0	27.0	15.0	17.5	3.5	
Receiving stolen goods	1911	22.5	19.5	58.0	43.0	0.3	1.0	55.0	0.5	8.0	26.0	22.0	37.0	6.5	+9.5
	1928	19.5	30.5	50.0	33.9	0.3	0.1	64.7	—	34.0	29.0	15.0	19.0	3.0	
Indecent assaults on females under 16	1911	16.1	10.2	73.7	80.0	2.0	3.5	14.5	0.3	37.5	29.3	19.6	12.0	1.3	+41.9
	1928	17.0	27.0	56.0	69.0	3.0	4.0	23.0	—	46.0	30.0	12.5	11.0	0.5	
Summary of indictable offenses	1911	12.0	32.0	56.0	57.0	3.5	6.0	32.0	0.1	6.5	22.0	21.0	34.4	16.0	−9.5
	1928	10.5	46.0	43.5	42.0	2.5	0.5	52.0	—	30.5	27.0	16.5	21.0	5.0	

Source: Calculated from *Criminal Statistics, England and Wales*, 1911 and 1928.

a The figures under the heading "Convictions" do not total 100 percent because only the major methods of disposal are included. Police cells, recognizances, and the rubric "otherwise disposed of" have been omitted, for they have no numerical significance. In calculating the crime rate, all proceedings for indictable offenses were included (Assizes, Quarter Sessions, and Summary Jurisdiction). For all other figures, however, only Summary Jurisdiction was considered because no similarly detailed statistics are available for Quarter Sessions and Assizes. The latter would not change the picture in any event because so few cases are tried in those courts.

b Adjusted to the rise of population.

crimes despite the lenient penal policy, but also a certain number of increases. Consequently, the editor of the report did not state any unequivocal conclusions about the relationship between a lenient penal policy and the crime rate, although he is inclined to deny all connection.[1] Sellin has recently given an elaborate defense of the use of police figures as the starting point for a discussion of this problem.[2] We have preferred the court figures for several reasons. Some of the factors which may contribute to an increase in the number of crimes known to the police without indicating a real increase in criminality have already been noted in the 1928 volume of English statistics. They include increased police efficiency, "increased willingness on the part of the police to record as 'crimes' incidents that become known to them, are reported to them, which probably indicate crimes" but are never clearly proved to be so, increased willingness of people to report certain crimes (especially sexual offenses), and the increased popularity of insurance.[3] The most important argument for not using police figures, however, is that few police statistics carefully differentiate among the cases in which crimes reported to the police are not prosecuted. Since the number of crimes not prosecuted is much greater than the number prosecuted, and since the reasons for failure to prosecute vary greatly, the police records (or the records of complaints to the prosecutor's office in Continental countries) could be used as a starting point only if the conditions laid down by Sellin (that by "crimes known to the police we mean, of course, that residue of crimes reported which, upon investigation, will prove well founded") could be fulfilled.[4] An examination of police records and denunciation statistics shows that this condition is not fulfilled, in Europe at any rate. English criminal statistics for 1934, for example, give the number of indictable offenses known to the police as 227,285, whereas the number of persons proceeded against was only 72,206.[5] The Italian figures are even more significant, for they are basically concerned with offenders and not with offenses. In 1933, 3,012 out of every 100,000 persons (514 for larceny alone) were enrolled on the registers of the prosecuting authorities, whereas the corresponding number actually tried was 1,793 (120 for larceny).[6] Only the French statistics gave detailed information (until 1931) about the reasons for filing cases, so that we can differentiate between denunciations which the authorities considered to be wholly false or incapable of substantiation on the one hand, and denunciations which were considered valid but for some reason were not prosecuted on the other hand.

When we examine the table, we see a decline in convictions for larceny and embezzlement and an increase in the number of orders made without conviction. In these categories of crime there is a general decline in the use of imprisonment and a tendency to shift from sentences of two months or under to somewhat longer terms. The use of fines jumps sharply. In sum, a more lenient penal policy—apart from the increase in medium prison sentences—goes hand in hand with an appreciable drop in the crime rate. The tendency in the case of obtaining by false pretense is different. There is a sharp shift from short- to medium-term sentences without an increase in the number of fines or a decrease in convictions. The more severe penal policy shows no effect on the crime rate, which remained stationary. In the case of indecent assaults and receiving stolen goods, finally, the tendency toward a more lenient policy is accompanied by a sharp rise in the crime rate. The figures for all indictable offenses tried before summary courts reveal the trend already visible in offenses against property. A 9.5 percent decrease in the rate of crimes is accompanied by a milder penal program, with the exception of the shift from short- to medium-term prison sentences. A comparison of the various figures leads to the conclusion that the lenient policy did not have a negative effect on criminality. On the contrary, a consistent policy of reducing the number of convictions in favor of probationary sentences, of more frequent infliction of fines, and of medium (rather than short) prison terms coincided with a noticeable drop in the general crime rate.

When we study Table 28 for the individual types of crime, we observe the following:

Larceny.—From 1900 to 1910 there is a slight drop in the rate of crime, with a largely unchanged penal policy; or, more precisely,

TABLE 28. *Crime Rate and Method of Disposal in France* [a]

OFFENSES AND YEAR	CRIMES PER 10,000 POPULA- TION	SUSPENDED SEN- TENCE	FINE (PERCENT OF ALL CONVIC- TIONS)	IMPRISONMENT (PERCENT)			
				OVER ONE YEAR	THREE MONTHS TO YEAR	UNDER THREE MONTHS	UNDER SIX DAYS
Larceny							
1900	10.24	23.2	8.92	4.54		80.01	
1910	9.62	24.0	7.40	4.79	21.19	52.56	4.01
1922	13.74	25.4	14.64	5.36	29.72	40.75	2.03
1932	11.94	28.0	13.97	3.63	23.01	50.21	1.61
Fraud							
1900	0.71	13.9	6.04	10.50		82.23	
1910	0.76	15.9	18.51	13.34	26.48	38.08	1.66
1922	0.82	13.7	7.00	9.11	41.09	39.15	1.34
1932	1.01	21.2	7.36	13.09	35.23	42.21	0.73
Embezzlement							
1900	1.03	21.2	8.96	3.75		85.94	
1910	1.47	21.7	10.75	4.93	32.34	46.45	2.04
1922	1.47	19.8	6.28	6.69	36.03	47.68	0.78
1932	1.81	24.5	13.59	7.39	32.16	43.26	1.20
Outrages against public officials							
1900	3.30	19.5	33.05	0.5		66.38	
1910	3.52	21.2	37.42	0.27	2.47	50.39	9.09
1922	2.26	25.7	41.88	0.22	5.18	42.34	9.74
1932	1.59	28.7	47.69	0.03	1.69	44.58	5.47
Vagrancy							
1900	2.86	4.8	0.26	0.10		98.07	
1910	2.76	4.8	0.88	0.08	6.25	78.49	8.40
1922	2.28	4.7	0.90	0.23	9.70	72.71	6.50
1932	2.91	5.6	0.51	0.03	2.62	84.17	3.65
Intentional assault							
1900	8.76	26.6	49.73	0.50		48.95	
1910	8.61	30.3	50.29	1.34	7.27	35.82	4.05
1922	8.50	28.8	56.79	0.88	8.32	29.88	3.14
1932	8.70	31.8	66.86	0.71	4.18	24.78	2.36
Indecency							
1900	0.70	22.9	15.64	3.39		78.72	
1910	0.55	25.9	13.20	2.06	20.18	54.47	3.85
1922	0.57	19.0	10.59	2.87	25.64	53.02	3.69
1932	0.79	32.0	15.62	2.12	20.29	52.00	2.30

Source: Calculated from the *Compte général* . . .

[a] Total crime figures include children under eighteen who are returned to the care of their parents or of a third party, or are sent to a *Colonie pénitentiaire*. Such cases are omitted from the percentages, however, which do not total 100 for that reason. Since Alsace-Lorraine was not included in the French statistics from 1900 to 1922, those figures have also been omitted for 1932.

an insignificant increase in heavier punishments and suspended sentences. By 1922 there was a sharp increase in crime despite a parallel increase in more severe prison sentences and a shift from lighter prison sentences to fines. The period from 1922 to 1932 is marked by a drop in larcenies with a milder penal policy, illustrated by the shift from longer to short terms of imprisonment and by a decline in short-term sentences in favor of fines and suspended sentences.

Fraud.—There is an uninterrupted increase in crime, but an uneven penal policy. After a tremendous jump in the use of fines from 1900 to 1910, this penalty dropped back to its original level by 1922. The rise in imprisonments for less than one year between 1910 and 1922 is followed by a partial retrogression in the next period, whereas long-term imprisonments return to the 1910 level after a drop in 1922. Suspended sentences were increasing on the whole, especially in the period after 1922.

Embezzlement.—Crime increases until 1922 despite a shift from suspended sentences, fines, and short-term imprisonment to medium- and long-term sentences. Between 1922 and 1932 the penal policy was reversed, but crime has continued to increase.

Outrages against public officials.—A declining crime rate during the entire period is accompanied by a steady increase in the use of suspended sentences and fines.

Vagrancy.—The rate of crime dropped until 1922, but returned in 1932 to the 1900 level. There is a slight increase in paroles all through the period, and an uninterrupted decrease in sentences under six days. Long-term prison sentences and fines are always negligible. From 1922 to 1932 there is a marked shift from prison terms of three months to one year to sentences for less than three months.

Intentional assault.—An unchanging crime rate is accompanied by a distinctly lenient trend in the penal policy, expressed in the more frequent application of suspended sentences and fines while all degrees of imprisonment tend to decline.

Indecency.—Between 1900 and 1910, there is an appreciable fall in the rate of crime, an increase in suspended sentences, and a shift from long-term imprisonments and fines to medium-term sentences. The period from 1910 to 1922 reveals a very slight increase in crime and a more severe penal policy. The increase in crime is still going on in 1932, but the penal policy has become more lenient again.

In conclusion, the French figures also provide no basis for assuming that the policy of punishment affects criminality. With certain crimes which show a decline or no movement at all, there is an unmistakable trend toward leniency of punishment, specifically toward a decreasing use of long-term sentences and a shift from short terms to suspended sentences and fines. An attempt was made to stop the increase of frauds and embezzlements with heavier punishments, but it was not carried through with any great consistency or thoroughness. The statistics do not permit the conclusion that this attempt—if one can really speak of an attempt in view of the absence of a uniform penal policy—was crowned with success.

The recent careful study of Rabl has convincingly proven that German penal policy has had no influence on the crime rate, either before or after the war.[7] Table 17, taken from Rabl, presents the figures for larceny, socially perhaps the most revealing of all crimes. They lead to the same conclusions which we have already indicated for France and England. There is a decline in the rate of larceny from the beginning of the century to the outbreak of the war, accompanied by a shift from longer to short-term imprisonment. The post-war inflation led to a tremendous jump in the number of crimes, and an effort was made to meet the crisis with a measurable increase in the severity of punishment in 1920 and 1921. The crime rate continued to rise in the years 1922–24, however, with no further increase in penal severity. The period of stabilization brought a drop in crime below the pre-war level, and the penal policy showed a pronounced tendency toward amelioration. The crisis led to a new crime wave in 1932, and a slightly greater severity of punishment as well. The conclusion is unmistakable. Once again we see that the rate of crime is unaffected by the penal policy but is closely dependent upon economic developments.

The German fraud figures (Table 17) provide another excellent example of the uselessness of shifting penal policies as a weapon against socially determined variations in the crime rate. Two attempts were made to halt the steady increase in the number of frauds, one at the end of the nineteenth century and one between 1920 and 1924. In neither period was the increased severity of punishments effective in the slightest degree, as the crime figures for the succeeding years show beyond the shadow of a doubt.

The Italian experiences with this problem have a special interest, because in that country, unlike England, France, and Germany, there was no general policy of penal leniency, but rather the opposite.

When we examine Table 29 for the individual types of crime, we see the following:

Simple larceny.—Simple larcenies declined until 1922, and then rose sharply before 1928, whereas the penal policy shows a steady trend toward increasing severity.

Larceny with aggravating circumstances.—From 1906 to 1910, a decline in the crime rate is accompanied by a certain amelioration in punishments, expressed in the increase in suspended sentences and the decrease in long-term prison sentences. By 1922 we find the reverse process in both crime and punishment, whereas in 1928 we see more frequent suspended sentences, a slight increase in short-term sentences, and a slight drop in crime.

Fraud.—Between 1906 and 1910 the crime rate falls despite a clear trend toward leniency in punishment. Subsequent years saw the reverse process.

Violence, resistance, and insults against authorities.—The 1910 figures reveal increasing crime and decreasing severity of punishment. In both 1922 and 1928 we find a further appreciable drop in the number of offenses despite a shift from imprisonment to fines and suspended sentences.

Personal injury with aggravating circumstances.—The 1922 and 1928 figures show a clear drop in crime and a more severe penal policy.

Private violence and threats.—Decreasing criminality is ac-

TABLE 29. *Crime Rate and Method of Disposal in Italy a*

			DISTRIBUTION OF PUNISHMENTS IN PERCENTS				
		SUSPENDED SENTENCE	IMPRISONMENT				
OFFENSE AND YEAR	CRIMES PER 10,000 POPU- LATION	(PER- CENT OF ALL SEN- TENCES)	MORE THAN THREE YEARS	SIX MONTHS TO THREE YEARS	ONE TO SIX MONTHS	ONE MONTH OR LESS	FINES
Simple larceny							
1906	93.34	42.04	0.01	1.00	9.14	89.67	0.18
1910	66.31	45.09	0.00	1.22	11.10	87.37	0.31
1922	57.54	34.79	0.04	2.91	18.45	87.35	0.25
1928	69.69	42.58	0.05	2.93	18.36	87.52	0.14
Larceny with aggravating circumstances							
1906	33.84	36.09	3.23	40.54	51.89	4.25	—
1910	30.43	42.57	2.25	40.46	54.23	3.06	—
1922	38.23	33.29	4.15	48.38	45.52	1.95	—
1928	36.25	37.29	3.40	42.95	50.87	2.78	—
Fraud							
1906	8.82	19.57	0.73	18.38	45.40	35.49	—
1910	7.56	24.62	0.31	15.46	45.69	38.54	—
1922	9.15	16.17	0.88	18.99	43.97	36.16	—
1928	11.92	15.70	1.97	22.27	44.88	30.88	—
Violence, resistance, and insults against authorities							
1906	36.15	22.37	0.15	2.37	31.98	56.88	8.61
1910	39.44	28.37	0.01	1.35	29.18	59.62	9.82
1922	31.80	21.73	0.11	3.08	27.72	53.71	15.38
1928	23.21	30.87	0.04	2.21	28.75	46.28	22.72
Personal injury with aggravating circumstances							
1906	22.25	45.71	1.55	34.55	61.36	2.53	—
1910	22.76	52.98	1.59	34.14	62.37	1.86	—
1922	12.31	43.05	1.92	38.14	57.99	1.95	—
1928	12.55	35.91	2.24	45.65	50.19	1.92	—
Private violence and threats							
1906	22.54	44.15	0.08	2.25	46.73	22.85	28.09
1910	23.28	55.99	0.06	2.44	52.89	20.54	24.07
1922	17.41	32.13	0.61	3.61	53.96	21.74	20.07
1928	13.39	47.52	0.55	4.27	52.80	22.67	19.71
Offenses against sexual liberty							
1906	2.89	14.15	23.86	60.75	14.56	0.83	—
1910	3.02	16.57	21.17	60.85	17.15	0.30	—
1922	1.53	17.72	27.38	56.22	17.25	0.85	—
1928	2.95	20.97	27.18	54.61	17.97	0.42	—

Source: Calculated from the *Statistica della criminalità.*

a No statistics are available for the distribution of punishments after 1928.

companied by intensified punishments in the form of a shift to long-term imprisonment.

Offenses against sexual liberty.—There is a slight increase in crime from 1906 to 1910, accompanied by an uneven penal practice. The number of suspended sentences rises. The penal policy remains inconsistent to 1922, but the rate of crime falls noticeably. Then the number of offenses take a sharp upward turn, and still the penal policy does not change.

In general, the Italian figures reveal the relative unimportance of fines. There is a distinct tendency to increase medium- and long-term prison sentences, whereas the use of suspended sentence shows no significant extension beyond the 1910 level.[8] The trend toward leniency noted in other countries, especially the increasing preference for fines and paroles, is missing. Medium- and long-term sentences tend to rise, as elsewhere, but this phenomenon has a completely different character in Italy because it is not accompanied by a wide extension of fines and suspended sentences, as in England and France. The repressive penal policy has not been followed by a significant decline in the crime rate. Larcenies and frauds, for example, have tended to increase. Although aggravated larcenies have dropped, this fact is no proof of the value of a repressive policy because the very years 1922 to 1928 in which the fall took place saw a lenient policy of punishment. The offenses against morality present no consistent picture. The assault category alone could be attested as mild support for a policy of repression, for there is a certain coincidence between intensified punishment and a decline in the crime rate, but here, too, the argument breaks down when we observe that the numerically most significant group of crimes in this category, violence, resistance, and insults against authorities, declines at the same time that the punishments become milder. In sum, a relatively more severe penal policy has had no more effect on crime than a relatively lenient policy.

A word of caution against the recent German and Italian figures is necessary in this connection. They seem to reveal a sharp and steady drop in the crime rate during a period of more severe penal practice. Official German statistics give the following crime rate per 100,000 population above the age of discretion: 1932, 1,125; 1933, 973; 1934, 761; 1936, 737 (the lowest figure ever attained since official criminal statistics for all of Germany were first published in 1880). These data are from the *Statistisches Jahrbuch für das deutsche Reich.*

These figures do not really indicate a declining crime rate, and thus indirectly the success of the repressive policy, for they do not take into consideration the amnesties which have become more and more frequent since 1933 for all kinds of petty offenders, and for adherents of the political regime regardless of the gravity of their offenses. Since all pending cases within certain categories are quashed as a result of the amnesty decrees, the statistics do not give an accurate picture of the development of crime. The seriousness of this omission can be seen from the following figures. The total number of offenders convicted for violation of *Reichsgesetze* in 1933 was 383,315. As a result of the amnesty law of April 23d, 1936 (*RG. Bl.* I, 378), 254,675 cases involving minor crimes and 3,532 cases involving acts committed "in the heat of the struggle for the National Socialist movement" were quashed.[9] Not all of these cases would have come to trial even without the amnesty law, and still fewer would have ended in a conviction, of course, but the fallacy in the statistical picture is obvious. No precise calculations can be made, however.

A similar situation exists in Italy. The official number of people convicted for delicts in recent years is as follows: 1931, 281,157; 1932, 273,430; 1933, 209,959; 1934, 250,651; 1935, 252,-255 (figures from the *Annuario statistico* for 1935, p. 275). The startling drop in 1933 is ample proof that the operation of the amnesty law of November 5, 1932, destroys the actual picture of the crime rate.

Our investigation has thus substantiated on a still broader basis the conclusions which Ferri had reached at the end of the nineteenth century on the basis of Italian experiences,[10] that the policy of punishment and its variations have no effective influence on the rate of crime. Changes in penal praxis cannot seriously interfere with the operation of the social causes for delinquency. If the effects of the policy of punishment could be isolated, that is to say, if they could be examined in a period of complete social and political stability, then it might be possible to discover a certain measure of influence. This very necessity for isolation, however, itself reveals the social irrelevance of methods of punishment as a factor in determining the rate of crime.[11] Tarde made an effort to save the theory of the possible influence of punishment on crime within circumscribed limits, although he was convinced of the essential social causation of crime. He sought to differentiate between *criminalité de luxe*, inspired by the artificial desire for libertinage and good living, from a more or less necessary criminality, inspired by hunger, revenge, and love. The first group, he thought, could be checked by increasing repression, but he was thoroughly skeptical about similar success with the second category.[12] The difficulties with this approach are evident. The distinction between necessary and luxury crimes is a pure value judgment, and the answers would vary according to the professional viewpoints of the judge, the prosecutor, the defense attorney, and the medical advisor, and according to the social position of the defendant. Furthermore, the differentiation is possible only among motives, not among the criminal acts themselves.

XIII

CONCLUSION

IN OUR discussion of Fascist and National Socialist penal policies we have analyzed the efforts to introduce a more severe policy of punishment for social educational reasons and the limits beyond which this program could not go. It was restricted in the first place by the economic crisis, which automatically led to an intensification of punishment, and then blocked by the rationalization which modern industrial society requires, because a full execution of the Fascist penal program entailed tremendous waste. As a result, the program found its most complete realization in the greatly enlarged field of political offenses. The needs of the politically dominant group in its struggle to maintain power overcame all other considerations and led to an unprecedented degree of repression in this one sphere. It was carried out only in part by the traditional prison authorities. The larger share fell to special administrative and party organs, who went far beyond the worst possible prison administration in the matter of cruelty and general maltreatment of convicts.

An interesting dualism is revealed in the other fields of criminal law. The great mass of minor offenses against the existing social order is growing steadily with the growing economic difficulties and the increase in bureaucratic regulations, but it is not followed by a corresponding intensification of the repressive program. The system of fines, the epitome of rationalized capitalist penal law, is at its height, despite the ideological attacks against it. Periodic amnesty laws discharge a mass of petty offenders in unprecedented numbers. It is noteworthy, however, that many minor offenses (whole categories or merely individual cases) are singled out as injurious to the welfare of the nation and classed with the more serious crimes. They are treated with greater severity than before, and we have already seen the ideological significance of this policy.

The existing social system with its need for rationalization not only restricts the extension of a repressive penal policy but also sets narrow limits to the reform program. The penal system of any given society is not an isolated phenomenon subject only to its own special laws. It is an integral part of the whole social system, and shares its aspirations and its defects. The crime rate can really be influenced only if society is in a position to offer its members a certain measure of security and to guarantee a reasonable standard of living. The shift from a repressive penal policy to a progressive program can then be raised out of the sphere of humanitarianism to constructive social activity. So long as the social consciousness is not in a position to comprehend and act upon the necessary connection between a progressive penal program and progress in general, any project for penal reform can have but doubtful success, and failures will be attributed to the inherent wickedness of human nature rather than to the social system. The inevitable consequence is a return to the pessimistic doctrine that man's evil nature can be tamed only by depressing the prison standard below that of the lowest free classes. The futility of severe punishment and cruel treatment may be proven a thousand times, but so long as society is unable to solve its social problems, repression, the easy way out, will always be accepted. It provides the illusion of security by covering the symptoms of social disease with a system of legal and moral value judgments. There is a paradox in the fact that the progress of human knowledge has made the problem of penal treatment more comprehensible and more soluble than ever, while the question of a fundamental revision in the policy of punishment seems to be further away today than ever before because of its functional dependence on the given social order.

NOTES

NOTES

CHAPTER I

1. Georg von Mayr, *Die Gleichmässigkeit im Gesellschaftsleben* (München, 1877); *Statistik und Gesellschaftslehre,* Vol. III, *Moralstatistik mit Einschluss der Kriminalstatistik* (Tübingen, 1917). On Quetelet's work see R. Wassermann, *Die Entwicklungsphasen der kriminalstatistischen Forschung* (Leipzig, 1927), pp. 10–40.
2. L. Günther, *Die Idee der Widervergeltung in der Geschichte und Philosophie des Strafrechts* (3 vols.; Erlangen, 1889–95). Books like R. His, *Das Strafrecht des deutschen Mittelalters* (2 vols.; Leipzig and Weimar, 1920–35), which give an extraordinary exposition of the various criminal laws and regulations, but always within the categories accepted at the time of writing, are virtually useless for an examination of the relationship between systems of punishment and social order. See the pertinent criticism of E. Schmidt in his review of His in the *Zeitschrift für die gesamte Strafrechtswissenschaft,* LV (1936), 429–32.
3. See, for example, the typical study of E. Durkheim, "Deux lois de l'évolution pénale," *L'Année sociologique,* IV (1899–1900), 65–95.
4. R. von Ihering, *Der Zweck im Recht* (2d ed.; Leipzig, 1884), I, 492, says that anyone who places the social goods on one side and punishments on the other has the value-scale of society.

CHAPTER II

1. See the interesting remarks of Gustav Radbruch in "Stand und Strafrecht," *Schweizer Zeitschrift für Strafrecht,* III (1934–35), 17–30, especially p. 19.
2. See J. Kulischer, *Allgemeine Wirtschaftsgeschichte des Mittelalters und der Neuzeit* (München, 1928), I, 128–35; G. Schmoller, *Grundriss der allgemeinen Volkswirtschaftslehre* (Leipzig, 1904), II, 513; Max Weber, *General Economic History,* tr. by F. H. Knight (New York, 1927), pp. 132–33.
3. W. S. Holdsworth, *A History of English Law* (3d ed.; London, 1922–24), II, 36.
4. P. Vinogradoff, "Wergeld und Stand," *Collected Papers* (Oxford, 1928), II, 84–152.
5. Radbruch, *op. cit.;* C. R. Köstlin, *Geschichte des deutschen Strafrechts im Umriss* (Tübingen, 1859), p. 113.
6. Art. 4 of the *coutumier de Sion* of the year 1338, quoted in J. Graven, *Essai sur l'évolution du droit pénal valaisan* (Lausanne, 1927), pp. 266–67.
7. J. Goebel, Jr., *Felony and Misdemeanor,* I (New York, 1937), 237.
8. Holdsworth, *op. cit.,* III, 242. The same picture is revealed in a complaint mentioned in the Recess of Courten, dated Dec. 14, 1543, where it is protested that the governors impose excessive fines and legal costs on their subjects. This is easily comprehensible in view of the practice of dividing revenue under these two heads between judges and justiciaries; see Graven, *op. cit.,* pp. 208–13.
9. A. Doren, *Italienische Wirtschaftsgeschichte,* I (Jena, 1934), 577, writes in this connection: "The system of fines is already at an advanced state of evolution in the direction of its present position in the administration of criminal law. In essence we are already far removed from the composition system of German

laws. Fiscal considerations are clearly perceptible in the town and guild statutes." For the same development in England see J. C. Fox, *The History of Contempt of Court, the Form of Trial and the Mode of Punishment* (Oxford, 1927), p. 138; for France, R. Garraud, *Traité théorique et pratique du droit pénal français* (2d ed.; Paris, 1898), I, 111. Most recently, Goebel, *op. cit.,* pp. 133, 222, 227n., 228, and 236, has emphasized the exclusively fiscal character of seignorial justice.

10. R. H. Tawney, *Religion and the Rise of Capitalism* (London, 1926), p. 86. In Florence in 1380, 17,000 out of a total population of about 90,000 were dependent on charity; see G. Dahm, *Das Strafrecht Italiens im ausgehenden Mittelalter* (Berlin, 1931), p. 23.

11. G. von Below, *Probleme der Wirtschaftsgeschichte* (Tübingen, 1920), p. 443.

12. F. G. Knapp, *Die Bauernbefreiung und der Ursprung der Landarbeiter in den älteren Theilen Preussens* (Leipzig, 1887), I, 43–44.

13. More, *Utopia with the "Dialogue of Comfort"* (London, 1928), p. 23.

14. W. Andreas, *Deutschland vor der Reformation* (Stuttgart, 1932), pp. 370–71.

15. G. Steinhausen, *Geschichte der deutschen Kultur* (3d rev. ed.; Leipzig, 1929), p. 312.

16. Andreas, *op. cit.,* p. 289.

17. E. Frohneberg, *Bevölkerungslehre und Bevölkerungspolitik des Merkantilismus* (Frankfurt, 1930), p. 17.

18. J. Strieder, *Zur Genesis des modernen Kapitalismus* (2d ed.; München, 1935), p. VIII.

19. Tawney, *op. cit.,* p. 86. Doren, *op. cit.,* I, 660, takes a very similar view of the conditions prevailing in the Italian towns of this period. It is worth noting that he, too, describes the guilds as a cover and instrument for the policy of the employers. He writes that the proletariat was strangled by its inability to obtain raw materials and working instruments, by the law, and by the regulations of the guilds which admitted workers to membership with no rights whatever; the proletariat was held captive by the state, definitely a class state which acted as protector for the interests united in the large capitalist guilds; it was held down by legal restrictions on the right of association and thus prevented from improving its condition by lawful means. F. Rörig, "Die europäische Stadt," *Propyläen Weltgeschichte,* IV (Berlin, 1932), 324–26, writes similarly of the Flemish towns.

20. T. Somerlad, "Zur Geschichte der Preise," *Handwörterbuch der Staatswissenschaften,* VI (4th ed.; Jena, 1925), 1037–55.

21. Schmoller, *op. cit.,* II, 295. According to Lamprecht's calculation, the average wage of a carpenter in the years 1277–84 was 3.43 g. silver; this rose in 1344–45 to 6.84 g.; then the fall set in and by 1465 it had sunk to 3.20 g., and in 1497 stood at 2.50 g.; see Somerlad, *op. cit.,* p. 1042.

22. E. Bielschowsky, *Die sozialen und ökonomischen Grundlagen des modernen gewerblichen Schlichtungswesens und seine Bedeutung für die Lösung der sozialen Frage* (Berlin, 1921), p. 30.

23. J. Huizinga, *The Waning of the Middle Ages,* tr. by F. Hopman (London, 1927), p. 21.

24. Radbruch, *op. cit.,* p. 21.

25. Gandinus, *Tractatus de maleficiis,* ed. by Hermann Kantorowicz in *Albertus Gandinus und das Strafrecht der Scholastik* (Berlin and Leipzig, 1926), II, 347–48; cf. Dahm, *op. cit.,* pp. 23–28; H. Gwinner, *Der Einfluss des Standes im gemeinen Strafrecht* (Breslau-Neukirch, 1934), pp. 18–21.

26. *Clagspiegel,* ed. by Sebastian Brant (Strassburg, 1538), folio 131. R. von Hippel, *Deutsches Strafrecht* (Berlin, 1925), I, 128–29, confirms this process

which is well known to all historians of criminal law. He writes that the injured party could come to an agreement with the offender, even in the case of an offense punishable by law, by requiring him to make compensation without bringing the matter before a court. Even a person who had been sentenced to punishment by the public authorities could compensate the injured party and so avoid punishment.

27. As regards the different interpretations see R. E. John, *Landzwang und widerrechtliche Drohung* (Göttingen, 1852); Gwinner, *op. cit.*, pp. 160–63. The value attributed to the right of carrying on a feud is shown by the fact that persons not possessing such a right would transfer their claims to a nobleman, charging him with their enforcement; see Gwinner, *op. cit.*, p. 161*n*. The right of carrying on a feud is rather a class privilege than an estate privilege, since it was available to all who were capable of exercising it, that is to say, all the wealthy.

28. C. L. von Bar, *A History of Continental Criminal Law*, tr. by T. S. Bell (Boston, 1916), pp. 110–11.

29. *Commentaires sur les Ordinnances de Blois établies aux États généraux convoquéz en la ville de Blois par Henry de Valois III, MDLXXIX* (3d ed.; Lyon, 1584), pp. 313–18.

30. S. Pregnant, *La Condition juridique du bourgeois de Lille en droit criminel au XIVième siècle* (Lille, 1929), p. 182. See also C. Beyerle, *Von der Gnade im deutschen Recht* (Göttingen, 1910).

31. A thoroughgoing rationalization, as well as restrictions on the exercise of the royal prerogative of mercy, was recommended by Junius Brutus, for example, in his *Defence of Liberty against Tyrants*, ed. by Harold J. Laski (London, 1924), pp. 153–54.

32. C. von Schwerin, *Grundzüge der deutschen Rechtsgeschichte* (München, 1934), p. 195, rightly remarks in this connection: "Medieval criminal law received its special character not by a fundamental alteration of the system of punishment, but rather by the change in its application. The composition of Frankish time was to a large degree replaced by corporal punishment. This, together with the increasing importance attributed to the deterrent factor in punishment and with the general increase in its cruelty, led to a degree of savagery and brutality, toward the end of the Middle Ages, hitherto unknown in criminal law." On the increasing severity of punishment, see K. Metzger, *Die Verbrechen und ihre Straffolgen im basler Recht des späten Mittelalters* (Basel, 1931), Part I, p. 53.

33. On the different interpretations, see G. Radbruch, *Die peinliche Gerichtsordnung Kaiser Karls V. von. 1532* (Leipzig, n.d.); Gwinner, *op. cit.*, pp. 40–43.

34. See pages 66; 103–4; 226, *n* 65.

35. Gwinner, *op. cit.*, p. 35*n*, also admits that class differentiation was a general practice although estate differentiation did not exist everywhere. There is no doubt that the latter usually resulted in an additional privilege for the upper classes, but in a few special cases it worked out in favor of the lower classes. Further reference is made below to this point, on pages 30 and 66.

36. R. Schmidt, *Die Aufgaben der Strafrechtspflege* (Leipzig, 1895), pp. 182–83.

37. *Ibid.*, p. 227.

38. *Ibid.*, pp. 183–84. This development can easily be traced in the variations of punishment for larceny and robbery between the thirteenth and the sixteenth century. Whereas in Sion (in Switzerland), larceny accompanied by violence was punished in 1239 with a fine of 60 livres and reparation of the damage, and simple larceny was punished in 1269 with a smaller fine and reparation of damage, Articles 158 and 159 of Charles V's *Peinliche Gerichts-*

ordnung of the sixteenth century inflicted capital punishment for robbery regardless of the amount of the stolen property, and for simple larceny it inflicted carcan, fustigation, and banishment; see Graven, *op. cit.*, p. 528.

39. Dahm, *op. cit.*, p. 301.
40. R. Schmidt, *Die Strafrechtsreform in ihrer staatsrechtlichen und politischen Bedeutung* (Leipzig, 1912), pp. 185–86.
41. In the seventeenth century authors report this cruel and useless practice with every sign of horror; see Christian Henelius, *Tractatus politicus de Aerario* (Berlin, 1670), p. 325.
42. T. Hampe, *Crime and Punishment in Germany as illustrated by the Nuremberg Malefactors Books*, tr. by M. Letts (London, 1929), p. 139.
43. J. Nagler, *Die Strafe* (Leipzig, 1918), pp. 135–37.
44. Hippel, *op. cit.*, I, 157, quoting Rau.
45. *Ibid.*, I, 135.
46. H. von Hentig, *Punishment: Its Origin, Purpose and Psychology* (London, 1937), Chap. II, "The Evolution of Punishment," pp. 17–116.
47. H. Knapp, *Das alte nürnberger Kriminalrecht* (Berlin, 1896), p. 82. When Metzger, *op. cit.*, p. 101, finds exile more painful for citizens than for alien vagabonds and prostitutes, he overlooks the fact that there are poor citizens and rich citizens.
48. Hentig, *op. cit.*, p. 131.
49. Steinhausen, *op. cit.*, p. 416; J. Hansen, *Zauberwahn, Inquisition und Hexenprozess im Mittelalter und die Entstehung der grossen Hexenverfolgung* (München, 1900), p. 506.
50. See the examples in J. Marcus, *Étude médico-légale du meurtre rituel* (Paris, 1900), pp. 15–18.
51. Huizinga, *op. cit.*, p. 15.
52. Nagler, *op. cit.*, p. 131n.
53. See the enumeration of punishments used in eighteenth-century France in D. Joussé, *Traité de la justice criminelle en France* (Paris, 1771), I, 39; K. F. Rosshirt, *Geschichte und System des deutschen Strafrechts* (Stuttgart, 1838), II, 13.
54. Quoted from F. von Holtzendorff, *Das Verbrechen des Mordes und die Todesstrafe* (Berlin, 1875), p. 211.
55. More, *op. cit.*, p. 26.
56. Huizinga, *op. cit.*, p. 16.
57. His, *op. cit.*, I, 12 and 70; Nagler, *op. cit.*, pp. 130–31.
58. M. Liepmann, "Der Strafvollzug als Erziehungsaufgabe," *Reform des Strafvollzuges*, ed. by L. Frede and M. Grünhut (Berlin and Leipzig, 1927), p. 5.
59. Hippel, *op. cit.*, p. 158.
60. See Max Horkheimer, "Egoismus und Freiheitsbewegung, Zur Anthropologie des bürgerlichen Zeitalters," *Zeitschrift für Sozialforschung*, V (1936), 161–234.

CHAPTER III

1. The best discussion of labor problems under mercantilism is E. F. Heckscher, *Mercantilism*, tr. by M. Shapiro (London, 1935), II, 145–72.
2. Adam Smith, *An Enquiry into the Nature and Causes of the Wealth of Nations* (London, 1793), II, 460, said that the discovery and colonization of America helped augment the industry of countries like Spain, Portugal, France, and England which established direct trade relations with it; and, secondly, of countries like Austria, Flanders, and some provinces of Germany which had no direct trade but sent their goods to America by way of other countries.
3. E. Levasseur, *La Population française* (Paris, 1889–92), I, 188–93, estimates

that the population of France at the time of Henry III did not amount to more than fourteen million, whereas before the outbreak of the Hundred Years' War it had already reached twenty to twenty-two million. For England see Kulischer, *op. cit.*, I, 130–31.

4. S. Kawerau, *et al.*, *Synoptische Tabellen für den geschichtlichen Arbeitsunterricht vom Ausgange des Mittelalters bis zur Gegenwart* (Berlin, 1921–22), p. 8.

5. Quoted from M. J. Elsas, *Umriss einer Geschichte der Preise und Löhne in Deutschland vom ausgehenden Mittelalter bis zum Beginn des 19. Jahrhunderts* (Leiden, 1936), I, 78. For Strassburg see I. Jastrow, *Die Volkszahl deutscher Städte zu Ende des Mittelalters und zu Beginn der Neuzeit* (Berlin, 1886), I, 67. The same information can be derived from the birth registers of Leipzig, which show a decline of about fifteen percent in the period between 1552–61 and 1613–18; *ibid.*, I, 143n.

6. Elsas, *op. cit.*, I, 82.

7. The statement from De La Court appears in O. Pringsheim, *Beiträge zur wirtschaftlichen Entwicklungsgeschichte der vereinigten Niederlande im 17. und 18. Jahrhundert* (Leipzig, 1890), p. 48.

8. See K. Hinze, *Die Arbeiterfrage zu Beginn des modernen Kapitalismus in Brandenburg-Preussen* (Berlin, 1927).

9. B. Erdmannsdörfer, *Deutsche Geschichte vom westfälischen Frieden bis zum Regierungsantritt Friedrichs des Grossen* (Berlin, 1892), I, 106, quotes a farmer of the Black Forest, writing in 1653, who complains that only the mob has any joy or courage left under the prevailing conditions. He demands that this favorably placed rabble should be required to pay a maidservant or manservant tax, though he is quite aware of the dangers inherent in such a measure and recounts how the authorities of a certain town had been forced to impose a very small levy on servants, whereupon the latter threatened to band together and seek work elsewhere, forcing an abandonment of the attempt.

E. S. Furniss, *The Position of the Laborer in a System of Nationalism* (Boston, 1920), p. 209, says that all historians were agreed that the economic position of the English laborer during the seventeenth century was not only comfortable but showed a tendency to improve. The situation in France was somewhat different because state intervention in favor of employers suspended the operation of economic factors making for a rise in the living standard of the lower classes; see H. Sée, *Französische Wirtschaftsgeschichte* (Jena, 1930), I, 266.

10. H. Hauser, Preface to his *Recherches et documents sur l'histoire des prix en France de 1500 à 1800* (Paris, 1936), p. 67.

11. This point is stressed by W. Sombart, *Der moderne Kapitalismus* (2d ed.; Münschen, 1917), I, 2, 800. The following description by J. P. Süssmilch, *Die göttliche Ordnung in den Veränderungen des menschlichen Geschlechts, aus der Geburt, dem Tode, und der Fortpflanzung erwiesen . . . .* (3d ed.; Berlin, 1765), I, 534, clearly reveals the local character of economic catastrophes at this time: "Famine is an even worse enemy than plague. Its prevention is therefore still more necessary. Large towns require particularly careful attention, for the common people seldom look into the future, they think little of times of need and live so much in the present that they do not save, and thus often find themselves suddenly in great danger of losing health or life. There may not even be a general harvest; the price of their daily bread need only be doubled and there is danger of wages losing the necessary ratio to the price of the bare necessities of life. If nothing is saved when things are cheap, there is no help for them. A town in which there

are many flourishing factories can be filled with an army of beggars under such circumstances; I have known examples of this myself, and can only think of the results with horror. . . . In cases where markets for goods have been closed, owing to war or other causes, the crowds of beggars crying for bread in the back streets become so great that one hardly knows how to escape them."

12. E. Lipson, *Economic History of England* (London, 1931), II, 64–65, rightly stresses this point for England. The same situation is described for France by L. Lallemand, *Histoire de la charité*, Vol. IV, *Temps modernes* (Paris, 1910), I, 177.

13. See the discussion of this question in Bielschowsky, *op. cit.*, p. 33.

14. See Paul Mantoux, *The Industrial Revolution in England in the Eighteenth Century*, tr. by Marjorie Vernon (London, 1929), p. 350.

15. Süssmilch, *op. cit.*, I, 407. The same sentiments were expressed by I. H. G. von Justi, *Die Grundfesten zu der Macht und Glückseligkeit der Staaten* (Königsberg, 1760), I, 175; and *Gesammelte politische und Finanzschriften über wichtige Gegenstände der Staatskunst, der Kriegswirtschaften und des Kameral —und Finanzwesens* (Kopenhagen, 1761), I, 199. Sonnenfels recommended that every mother should be presented with ten Reichstaler on leaving a lying-in hospital. Theodor Lau complained that opposition of the God-fearing clergy prevented the legalizing of polygamy, the sovereign means of making a country more populous; see L. Elster, "Bevölkerungslehre und Bevölkerungspolitik," *Handwörterbuch der Staatswissenschaften*, II (4th ed.; Berlin, 1924), 748.

16. Süssmilch, *op. cit.*, I, xi ff.; cf. I, 396.

17. K. Pribram, *Die Entstehung der individualistischen Sozialphilosophie* (Leipzig, 1912), p. 41.

18. F. Willenbücher, *Die strafrechtsphilosophischen Anschauungen Friedrichs des Grossen* (Breslau, 1904), p. 46. See also E. Schmidt, *Staat und Recht in Theorie und Praxis Friedrichs des Grossen* (Leipzig, 1936), p. 34n.

19. Voltaire, *Œuvres*, ed. by A. J. Q. Beuchot, LIV (Paris, 1831), 401.

20. *Allgemeines Landrecht für die preussischen Staaten* (Berlin, 1832), Part II, Title 1, paragraphs 1015–1119. Nearly one hundred paragraphs (887–984) deal with infanticide, devoted chiefly to preventive measures.

21. F. Meinecke, *Die Idee der Staatsräson* (München and Berlin, 1924), p. 357.

22. R. Fürst von Montecuccoli, *Ausgewählte Schriften*, ed. by Direktion d. k. u. k. —Kriegsarchivs, Vol. II, *Militärische Schriften*, Part II (Wien, 1899), 469, suggested that "orphans, bastards, beggars, and paupers who were looked after in infirmaries should be brought up in military schools after the fashion of the Janizaries."

23. H. Delbrück, *Geschichte der Kriegskunst im Rahmen der politischen Geschichte*, IV, *Neuzeit* (Berlin, 1920), 282–83.

24. *Ibid.*, p. 285.

25. F. Kapp, *Der Soldatenhandel deutscher Fürsten nach Amerika* (2d ed.; Berlin, 1874), p. 31.

26. L. O. Pike, *History of Crime in England* (London, 1876), II, 372–73.

27. Kapp, *op. cit.*, p. 96. Frederick William I ordered that disobedient townsmen and peasants who did not make good should be put into the army. Frederick II particularly liked to see writers of seditious or other harmful literature do their penance in the army; see Delbrück, *op. cit.*, pp. 283 and 289.

28. See the remarks of H. B. Wagnitz, *Historische Nachrichten und Bemerkungen über die merkwürdigsten Zuchthäuser in Deutschland* (Halle, 1791), I, 213 ff. It was considered creditable on the part of Goethe's duke, Karl August, when in 1796 he surrendered only petty offenders to a Prussian military com-

mission and the so-called "voluntary" character of this "change of residence" was preserved; see F. W. Lucht, *Die Strafrechtspflege in Sachsen-Weimar-Eisenach unter Karl August* (Berlin and Leipzig, 1929), p. 58.

29. F. C. B. Avé-Lallemant, *Das deutsche Gaunerthum in seiner socialpolitischen, literarischen und linguistischen Ausbildung zu seinem heutigen Bestande* (Leipzig, 1858), I, 85.

30. Gwinner, *op. cit.*, pp. 177–78.

31. Pike, *op. cit.*, II, 373. Generally, a soldier convicted of a capital crime could not be executed without the King's decision. A. F. Lueder, *Kritische Geschichte der Statistik* (Göttingen, 1817), p. 425, refers to the gangs of ruffians whom the combined influence of vice, crime, and the right to pardon had brought under the banner, men whom only the gallows would mourn, whether they died on the field of honor or in their beds.

32. Sée, *op. cit.*, I, 243.

33. Mantoux, *op. cit.*, pp. 29–32. In Brandenburg-Prussia, it was chiefly the textile industry which received state aid. The government provided everything from building sites and labor power to working capital; see the royal orders collected in *Acta Borussica*, ed. by Schmoller and Hintze, I (Berlin, 1892), especially an order of Aug. 21, 1754 (No. 359) in which the Crown announces the repayment of the remainder of a debt owed by a certain Mr. Schnitzer, silk manufacturer, with the expectation that he would respond by applying himself to the conduct of his business with increased zeal. In Austria, Becher obtained a concession and general subsidies for his *Manufakturhaus* on the Tabor (Vienna); see H. Hatschek, *Das Manufakturhaus auf dem Tabor in Wien* (Leipzig, 1889).

34. E. Levasseur, *Histoire des classes ouvrières et de l'industrie en France avant 1789* (2d ed.; Paris, 1901), II, 789; see also Sombart, *op. cit.*, I, 2, 810.

Agriculture, it is worth noting, also suffered from a scarcity of men on the large estates. Wages in Prussia, for example, were so high that the landowners struggled to avoid hiring free laborers by intensifying the exploitation of their tenants. The latter sought to flee to the towns and the owning class replied by establishing serfdom; see Knapp, *Bauernbefreiung*, I, 67 and 70; H. Sieveking, *Grundzüge der neuren Wirtschaftsgeschichte vom 17. Jahrhundert bis zur Gegenwart* (4th ed.; Leipzig, 1925), p. 35. At first, the master merely had first choice when the peasant's child was ready to enter service, but service eventually became compulsory and the period was determined by the master; see Sieveking, *Wirtschaftsgeschichte* (Berlin, 1935), pp. 105–6. The Prussian *Allgemeines Landrecht* (Part II, Title 7, paragraph 185) allowed the lord to take peasant children from their parents and make them servants at his court. Similar English conditions are described by Lipson, *op. cit.*, II, 391.

35. Sée, *op. cit.*, I, 243. Cf. the *Allgemeines Landrecht*, Part II, Title 20, paragraph 148, which provides a punishment of four to eight years' imprisonment or *Festungshaft* for anyone who incites or helps heads of factories, employees, or workmen to emigrate.

36. M. Sering, *Geschichte der preussisch-deutschen Eisenzölle von 1818 bis zur Gegenwart* (Leipzig, 1882), p. 2.

37. Quoted in M. Adler, *Fabrik und Zuchthaus* (Leipzig, 1924), p. 62. Süssmilch, *op. cit.*, I, 406, arguing in the same vein, noted that a higher value was placed on men in countries where slavery had existed in the past or still existed than in Europe.

38. Justi, *Grundfesten*, I, 240.

39. Mandeville, *The Fable of the Bees*, ed. by F. B. Kaye (Oxford, 1906), I, 192.

Similar statements can be found in Süssmilch, *op. cit.*, I, 132. It is the thesis developed at length by Witt, Petty, Temple, and others that a certain increase in the price of necessities was not undesirable as a stimulus to work.

40. Thus, in order to counteract the effects of Blue Monday, which had become a tradition all over Europe, the factory regulations of the Royal Manufactories of St. Maur–Des Fossées provided that workers must be in town between nine and ten on Sundays and holidays so that they would be at the workshops on time the following morning; see Levasseur, *Classes ouvrières*, II, 425.

41. Pringsheim, *op. cit.*, p. 49; E. Baasch, *Holländische Wirtschaftsgeschichte* (Jena, 1927), p. 155.

42. Sée, *op. cit.*, I, 264.

43. When charges of this kind were brought before the Grand Jury in England in 1639, the judge stressed the point that working-class associations were unlawful because they served to deceive the people by setting excessive prices upon the works or commodities; see Lipson, *op. cit.*, III, 388. For France, see Levasseur, *Classes ouvrières*, II, 508–11; Sée, *op. cit.*, I, 269 and 363.

44. See the remarks of Sombart, *op. cit.*, I, 2, 831.

45. See the contract between the Crown of Middelburg and the Protestants of French origin for the employment of orphans, as quoted in Pringsheim, *op. cit.*, p. 55. For seventeenth-century Holland, see Baasch, *op. cit.*, p. 155. See also the order of Frederick II to General Meyerinck (Oct. 27, 1748; *Acta Borussica*, Vol. I, Nr. 147), in which he instructed the General to place at the disposal of a certain Moses Ries, manufacturer of damask and silk, orphan apprentices, whom the orphanage would continue to look after.

46. A. Ganz, *Das ökonomische Motiv in der preussischen Pädagogik des achtzehnten Jahrhunderts* (Halle, 1930).

47. The peace congress of Rastatt (1714) decided that the noblest and most worthy memorial they could erect would be a spinning school for the poor children of the district; see Kulischer, *op. cit.*, II, 187.

48. *Ibid.*, II, 449. See also C. Brinkmann, *Versuch einer Gesellschaftswissenchaft* (München, 1919), p. 79; Sombart, *op. cit.*, I, 2, 804.

49. In the *Robotpatent* of 1738 for Bohemia and Moravia, for instance, it is explicitly provided that subjects are under obligation to spin for their rulers or to pay a tax in default; see Adler, *op. cit.*, p. 76.

50. *Loc. cit.* For Prussia, see Hinze, *op. cit.*, pp. 173 ff.

51. Many painters after Giotti gave similar expression to this conception of poverty. Cf. Dante, *The Divine Comedy, Paradise*, XI.

52. Weber, *The Protestant Ethic and the Spirit of Capitalism*, tr. by Talcott Parsons (London, 1930), p. 177.

53. B. Groethuysen, *Die Entstehung der bürgerlichen Welt-und Lebensanschauung in Frankreich* (Halle, 1930), II, 40.

54. See the brilliant analysis of Groethuysen, *op. cit.*

55. Ch. Paultre, *De la repression de la mendicité et du vagabondage en France sous l'ancien régime* (Paris, 1906), p. 26, clearly describes conditions in France: "The beggar was not considered a delinquent during the fourteenth and the first two thirds of the fifteenth centuries. What disturbed the central municipal authorities was the large number of unemployed who dared to offer their labor only on certain conditions and at certain rates of remuneration. It was chiefly a rise in wages that was feared, and this fear led the authorities to force the beggar to work, thus utilizing this idle section of the population in public workshops. These beggars working under compulsion were paid at a very low rate, and in this way it was hoped to encourage paupers to move into slightly better paid private employment and thus to prevent a general

rise in wage levels." The ordonnances mentioned are quoted by Paultre, p. 63.

56. For England, see the critique of the Statute of Laborers in F. M. Eden, *The State of the Poor: or, an History of the Labouring Classes in England, from the Conquest to the Present Period* (London, 1797), I, 43. Eden regarded this statute as useless.

57. Levasseur, *Population française*, I, 189.

58. Paultre, *op. cit.*, p. 26.

59. Holdsworth, *op. cit.*, IV, 390.

60. For England, see M. Leonhard, *The Early History of Poor Relief* (Cambridge, 1900), p. 62. For France, see C. Bloch, *L'Assistance & l'état en France à la veille de la Révolution* (Paris, 1908), pp. 40–46.

61. Weber, *Protestant Ethic*, p. 80.

62. See Groethuysen, *op. cit.*, Chap. IV, "Christliche und bürgerliche Lebensauffassung."

63. Luther, "An Open Letter to the Christian Nobility," *Works*, tr. ed. by C. M. Jacobs (Philadelphia, 1915–32), II, 135.

64. J. B. Kraus, *Scholastik, Puritanismus und Kapitalismus* (München, 1930), pp. 260–61.

65. Weber, *Protestant Ethic*, pp. 170–71.

66. *Ibid.*, p. 177.

67. *Ibid.*, p. 281n.

68. *Ibid.*, p. 163.

69. See the discussion in E. Troeltsch, *The Social Teaching of the Christian Churches*, tr. by O. Wyon New York, 1931), II, 554–60. See also Weber, *Wirtschaft und Gesellschaft* (2d ed.; Tübingen, 1925), I, 337; and Kraus, *op. cit.*, p. 284.

70. The whole problem is well treated in L. Feuchtwanger, "Geschichte der sozialen Politik und des Armenwesens im Zeitalter der Reformation," *Schmollers Jahrbuch*, XXXII, 3–4 (1908), 167–204; XXXIII, 1–2 (1909), 190–228. On the transition from church to town administration of poor relief, see W. V. Marx, *The Development of Charity in Medieval Louvain* (Yonkers, N.Y., 1937), pp. 83–99.

71. G. Wizel, *Von der Busse, Beicht und Bann* (1534), quoted in I. Döllinger, *Die Reformation, ihre Entwicklung und ihre Wirkungen im Umfange des Lutherischen Bekenntnisses* (Regensburg, 1848), I, 46–47 and 76–77.

72. On the subject of the Nürnberg and Ypres poor regulations, see Cardinal Ehrle, "Die Armenordnungen von Nürnberg und Ypern," *Historisches Jahrbuch*, IX (1888), 450–79. His conclusions seem to be correct: "Luther's fierce attack against good works and the charitable institutions and foundations often engaged in them and against begging gave a new impetus to the passing of regulations relating to mendicity, though only in the sense that it added to forces already existing and functioning, thereby increasing their effectiveness." See also the conclusions of Lallemand, *op. cit.*, IV, 1, 619, though he is somewhat biased and inclined to overestimate the bad influences of the Reformation. On the relation between the Catholic humanist Vives and the Protestant authors of the Strassburg statutes, see Feuchtwanger, *op. cit.*, XXXII, 198–200.

73. Holdsworth, *op. cit.*, IV, 394.

74. Bloch, *op. cit.*, p. 43.

75. Lallemand, *op. cit.*, IV, 1, 184–85.

76. The pamphlet is reprinted in Eden, *op. cit.*, I, 165–70, along with other pamphlets of the same type.

77. See the remarks of Sombart, *op. cit.*, I, 1, 817. A. V. Judges, *The Elizabethan Underworld* (London, 1930), p. xxx, correctly emphasizes the fact that the

early labor laws looked upon unemployment as "a kind of vice, practised only by those who challenged the prevailing order of society." On the prohibition of alms, see Pike, *op. cit.*, II, 67; Kraus, *op. cit.*, p. 127.

78. The decree is quoted in Lallemand, *op. cit.*, IV, 1, 152.

79. The decree is quoted in E. Hertz, *Voltaire und die französische Strafrechtspflege* (Stuttgart, 1887), p. 31.

80. Holdsworth, *op. cit.*, IV, 397.

81. A. J. Copeland, *Bridewell Royal Hospital, Past and Present* (London, 1888); F. Doleisch von Dolsperg, *Die Entstehung der Freiheitsstrafe unter besonderer Berücksichtigung des Auftretens der modernen Freiheitsstrafe in England* (Breslau, 1928); A. Van der Slice, "Elizabethan Houses of Correction," *Journal of the American Institute of Criminal Law and Criminology*, XXVII (1936–37), 44–67.

82. Lipson, *op. cit.*, III, 424–25.

83. Valuable information about the development of the Amsterdam houses of correction will be found in R. von Hippel, "Beiträge zur Geschichte der Freiheitsstrafe," *Zeitschrift für die gesamte Strafrechtswissenschaft*, XVIII (1898), 419–94, 608–66. A. Hallema has more recently brought new materials to light; a list of his numerous articles on the subject will be found in his *In en om de Gevangenis, Van vroeger Dagen in Nederland en Nederlandsch-Indie* ('s Gravenhage, 1936), pp. 174–76.

84. This is indicated by the following foundation dates: Bremen 1609, Lübeck 1613, Hamburg 1622, Danzig 1636, Lüneburg 1675, Bern 1614, Basel 1616, Freiburg i.A. 1617. The documents relating to the foundation of the *Zuchthaus* in Spandau make explicit reference to the example of the Netherlands; see Eberhard Schmidt, *Entwicklung und Vollzug der Freiheitsstrafe in Brandenburg-Preussen bis zum Ausgang des 18. Jahrhunderts* (Berlin, 1915), p. 65, who quotes the decree of June 30, 1693, which established the *Zuchthaus*. Several towns in northern Germany procured copies of the Amsterdam institution's regulations; see Hippel, *Beiträge*, pp. 648–49. English pamphlets of the seventeenth century also recommend the example of the Netherlands; see Eden, *op. cit.*, I, 169. The architect of the Hamburg *Spinnhaus* was sent to Amsterdam to study the building plans there; see A. Ebeling, *Beiträge zur Geschichte der Freiheitsstrafe* (Breslau, 1935), pp. 64–65. As for the report of a Hungarian schoolmaster on his visit to the Dutch institution, see below, p. 48.

85. Hippel, "Beiträge," pp. 446–47.

86. See Hallema, *op. cit.*, p. 83, and Lipson, *op. cit.*, III, 425.

87. Hippel, "Beiträge," p. 632.

88. Paultre, *op. cit.*, pp. 231–54; Lallemand, *op. cit.*, IV, 1, 266; C. Joret, *Le Père Guevarre et les bureaux de charité au XVIIe siècle* (Toulouse, 1889).

89. Hippel, "Beiträge," p. 460.

90. J. Howard, *The State of the Prisons in England and Wales* (4th ed.; London, 1792), p. 45.

91. Bloch, *op. cit.*, p. 91.

92. Doleisch von Dolsperg, *op. cit.*, p. 61.

93. E. Schmidt, *Entwicklung*, pp. 31–32. See also E. Rosenfeld, "Zur Geschichte der ältesten Zuchthäuser," *Zeitschrift für die gesamte Strafrechtswissenchaft*, XXVI (1906), 1–12.

94. Schmidt, *Entwicklung*, p. 20.

95. *Ibid.*, p. 9.

96. See Hallema, *op. cit.*, p. 39, for Rotterdam, and more particularly his data on Delft, pp. 60–68. The same complaints were raised against the French *Hôpitaux généraux;* see Paultre, *op. cit.*, p. 463.

97. We hear that unskilled workers at Winchester were to be detained for at least five years, three years for learning, two for repaying board and tuition; Lipson, *op. cit.*, III, 425. The poor children of Bordeaux who learned a certain stitch *(point de France)* were required to spend four years in training and two years in working to repay costs. Attempts to escape were very frequent; see E. H. Guittard, "Un grand atelier de charité sous Louis XIV," *Mémoires et documents pour servir à l'histoire du commerce et de l'industrie en France*, ed. by J. Hayem, IV (Paris, 1916), 138–39. The Berlin establishments' lease of 1718 provides that children under twelve years of age must remain for at least three years, since a minimum of eighteen months was required for their training; see Rosenfeld, *op. cit.*, p. 9.

98. A. C. Riedel, *Beschreibung des im Fürstentum Bayreuth zu Sanct Georgen am See errichteten Zucht- und Arbeits-Hauses* (Bayreuth, 1750), pp. 64–67.

99. Schmidt, *Entwicklung*, p. 37. See also ordinances of Frederick William I, Jan. 26 and May 18, 1738, printed in Mylius, *Corporis constitutionum marchicorum continuatio prima* (1744).

100. The difficulty was not overcome by measures like Article 55 of the French edict of 1656, quoted by Paultre, *op. cit.*, p. 181, which required the guilds to furnish instructors for the houses of correction.

101. For Bremen, see Hippel, "Beiträge," p. 613n.; for Troyes, see Lallemand, *op. cit.*, IV, 1, 543.

102. E. Rosenfeld, "Zur Entstehung der Entlassenenfürsorge," *Zeitschrift für die gesamte Strafrechtswissenschaft*, XXV (1905), 153–90.

103. See the 1782 "Mémoire tendant à perfectionner les fabriques de France et à faciliter les nouveaux établissements," *Revue d'histoire économique et sociale*, VII (1914), 81.

104. Doleisch von Dolsperg, *op. cit.*, p. 51.

105. Knapp, *Nürnberger Kriminalrecht*, p. 75.

106. Quoted in Paultre, *op. cit.*, p. 231.

107. Quoted in Hippel, "Beiträge," p. 476.

108. *Ibid.*, p. 474. A still larger portion of compulsory spiritual nourishment was assigned to the occupants of the ducal *Zuchthaus* of *Württemberg* as Ludwigsburg; see O. Weissenrieder, "Alte Hausordnungen," *Blätter für Gefängniskunde*, LXVII (1936), 50–73, where the Ludwigsburg regulations of August 28, 1736, are reprinted. For further details see G. Saam, *Quellenstudien zur Geschichte des deutschen Zuchthauswesens bis zur Mitte des 19. Jahrhunderts* (Berlin and Leipzig, 1936), pp. 36–38. The curriculum of the English houses shows the same features. See the discussion of the regulation of St. Edmonds at Bury, set out by the Justices of Peace in 1589, in Van der Slice, *op. cit.*, pp. 33–34.

109. Paultre, *op. cit.*, p. 232.

110. *Ibid.*, p. 181. On payment of salaries as a method of furthering productivity, see the regulation of the Hamburg *Zuchthaus* in Ebeling, *op. cit.*, p. 85.

111. Guittard, *op. cit.*, p. 142. This attitude toward religious practices seems to have remained unchanged in French prison policy through the centuries. In 1822, when the director of missions of the diocese of Troyes proposed to the prefect of Aube a forty-day mission among the prisoners, the lessees of the establishment demanded compensation at the rate of fifteen centimes per head. The minister of the interior estimated the cost of such a mission for the whole of France at 10,356 francs a day and proposed the reduction of its duration to twenty days. Whereupon the ecclesiastical authorities decided to give up the project, "not being able to hope for a sincere conversion after such a short trial period as twenty days."—Barthès, "L'Organisation des maisons centrales avant 1830," *Revue pénitentiaire*, XXX (1906), 897.

112. The document is quoted in Hippel, "Beiträge," p. 640n. On the joint endowment of the Delft institution, see Hallema, *op. cit.*, pp. 56–59.
113. E. Gothein, *Wirtschaftsgeschichte des Schwarzwalds und der angrenzenden Landschaften* (Strassburg, 1892), p. 700.
114. The letter is quoted in Lallemand, *op. cit.*, IV, 1, 268.
115. Lipson, *op. cit.*, III, 489.
116. Hippel, "Beiträge," pp. 612, 625n, 635n.
117. See the edition of this ordonnance quoted above, p. 213, *n* 29, the remarks of Bloch, *op. cit.*, p. 42, and Ebeling, *op. cit.*, pp. 56–57.
118. La Bruyère answers someone desiring to get rich quickly by recommending three methods: the way of the miser, of the patron of a political group, and of the administrator of an *Hôpital;* quoted in M. Marion, *Dictionnaire des institutions de la France en XVIIe et XVIIIe siècle* (Paris, 1923), p. 277.
119. E. Schmidt, *op. cit.*, p. 31.
120. Hippel, "Beiträge," p. 469.
121. Hallema, *op. cit.*, p. 58.
122. Hippel, "Beiträge," p. 612. Hamburg made use of lotteries for both the construction and operation of a house of correction; see Ebeling, *op. cit.*, pp. 23–30, 57.
123. Lallemand, *op. cit.*, IV, 1, 375.
124. Hallema, *op. cit.*, pp. 45–51.
125. Lallemand, *op. cit.*, IV, 1, 372.
126. R. Vámbéry, "Das amsterdamer Tuchthuis in ungarischer Beleuchtung," *Zeitschrift für die gesamte Strafrechtswissenschaft,* XXXVII (1916), 108.
127. Quotations from Bornitius and Döpler will be found in Hippel, "Beiträge," pp. 469–70.
128. Henelius, *op. cit.*, p. 324. His remark, pp. 335–336, that it is more profitable to set up houses of correction in populous and busy centers than in smaller towns, is also interesting in this connection.
129. M. Bitter, *Das Zucht- und Arbeitshaus sowie das Kriminalinstitut des Reichsgrafen L. Schenck von Castell zu Oberdischingen im Kreis Schwaben von 1789 bis 1808* (Murnau, 1930).
130. See the conclusions of L. Frede, "Gefängnisgeschichte," *Handwörterbuch der Kriminologie,* I (Berlin, 1933), 540.
131. Wagnitz, *op. cit.*, I, 44; II, 93.
132. J. Füsslin, *Die neuesten Verunglimpfungen der Einzelhaft durch Entstellung der Erfolge des bruchsaler Zellengefängnisses* (Heidelberg, 1861), p. 5.
133. Hippel, "Beiträge," p. 470. The same tendency is found in the various publications of E. Schmidt and L. Frede.
134. N. Halder, "Die Strafvollzugspraxis in der helvetischen Zentralauchtanstalt Baden," *Schweizerische Zeitschrift für Strafrecht,* LI (1937), 94, quoting a report of January 31, 1803.
135. Hallema, *op. cit.*, p. 62. See, further, the arguments used in connection with the foundation of a house of correction in Maastricht; Hallema, pp. 109–12.
136. If the English workhouses of the seventeenth and eighteenth centuries were financial failures because of technical organizational reasons and because English industry was more advanced than the Continental, as is conclusively proven by S. and B. Webb, *English Local Government: English Poor Law History,* I (London, 1927), 233–40, that does not mean that they were not established with a view to deriving profits.
137. J. Döpler, *Theatrum poenarum, suppliciorum et executionum criminalium; oder Schau-Platz derer Leibes- und Lebens-Straffen, welche . . . . auch noch*

Heut zu Tage in allen vier Welt-Theilen üblich sind (Sondershausen, 1693), I, 704.

138. Kulischer, *op. cit.*, II, 150.

139. *Historie van de wonderlijcke Mirakelen, die in menichte ghebeurt zijn ende noch dagelijcx gebeuren binnen de vermaerde Coop-stadt Aemstel-redam: in een plaets ghenaempt het Tucht-huys, ghelegen op de Heylighe-wegh. Hier achter is noch by ghevoeght een wonderlijck Mirakel van S. Justitia* (Amsterdam, 1612). On the origin of this pamphlet, see Hallema, *op. cit.*, pp. 18–32.

140. Joret, *op. cit.*, p. 18.

141. See P. C. Gordon Walker, "Capitalism and the Reformation," *Economic History Review*, VIII (1937), 18, who correctly emphasizes the point that Protestant society had no monopoly of the advance of capitalism.

CHAPTER IV

1. More, *op. cit.*, p. 81.

2. For the rowers (numbering about 5,600 on the ships under the command of Don Juan d'Austria, see L. Stroobant, *Notes sur le système pénal des villes flamandes du 15e au 17e siècles* (Malines, 1897), pp. 52–53; and the remarks of P. Frauenstädt, "Zur Geschichte der Galeerenstrafe in Deutschland," *Zeitschrift für die gesamte Strafrechtswissenschaft*, XVI (1896), 519–46.

3. Detailed information on these decrees is to be found in J. Damhouder, *Praxis rerum criminalium* (Editio ultima; Antwerp, 1570), pp. 476 ff.; all of Chapter CLI of this widely used sixteenth-century textbook is very useful as a source of information. The increasing importance of galley servitude as a form of punishment in this period is shown by the fact that the earlier editions of Damhouder contained nothing on the subject. He later decided, at the instigation of his friends and disciples, to add a whole chapter on this matter.

4. Joussé, *op. cit.*, I, 47 ff.

5. Frauenstädt, *op. cit.*, pp. 525–30.

6. Knapp, *Nürnberger Kriminalrecht*, pp. 79–81.

7. Frauenstädt, *op. cit.*, p. 527. In France, where transportation was undertaken by the authorities themselves and where the chained prisoners were made to go on foot from the place of assembly to Marseilles, where they were then put on the ships, the number of deaths was very high. In 1662, 44 out of one group of 96 died on the way; see the report made to Colbert from Lyon on June 16, 1662, in *Correspondance administrative sous le règne de Louis XIV*, ed. by G. B. Depping (Paris, 1850–55), II, 893.

8. G. Hafner and E. Zürcher, *Schweizerische Gefängniskunde* (Bern, 1925), p. 5; see also E. Osenbrüggen, *Das alamannische Strafrecht im deutschen Mittelalter* (Schaffhausen, 1860), p. 97.

9. Frauenstädt, *op. cit.*, p. 536.

10. *Correspondance administrative*, II, 940.

11. *Ibid.*, p. 891.

12. *Ibid.*, p. 890. The practice of sending religious opponents to the galleys was also used in other countries; see Damhouder, *op. cit.*, p. 478; Hafner and Zürcher, *op. cit.*, p. 5.

13. The French decree is quoted in G. Bohne, *Die Freiheitsstrafe in den italie-nischen Stadtrechten des 12–16. Jahrhunderts*, II, *Der Vollzug der Freiheits-strafe* (Leipzig, 1925), 306; similar decrees of Charles V and Philip II with a minimum of six years are cited in Damhouder, *op. cit.*, p. 464.

14. Bohne, *op. cit.*, II, 324.
15. Heckscher, *op. cit.*, II, 298–300.
16. The declarations of January 8, 1701, March 12, 1719, and March 10, 1720, quoted in Paultre, *op. cit.*, p. 319, authorized the courts to send vagabonds into the colonies instead of shipping them to the galleys.
17. Frauenstädt, *op. cit.*, pp. 538–39.
18. Düvival *jeune*, "Galérien," *Encyclopédie ou dictionnaire raisonné des sciences, des arts et des métiers*, VII (Neufchâtel, 1757), 445.
19. Bohne, *op. cit.*, II, 318.
20. Hippel, "Beiträge," pp. 434–35. See also the discussion between Bohne and Eberhardt Schmidt in the *Zeitschrift für die gesamte Strafrechtswissenschaft*, XLV (1925), 36–45, 152–77.
21. *Correspondance administrative*, II, 941. Damhouder expresses the policy quite frankly when he writes (*op. cit.*, p. 465): "nullo modo autem infirmos, debiles, mutilos, mancos, decrepitos, insanos, freneticos, aut similes, cuique ob etatem, aut corporis infirmitatem atque vicium aliquod nauticis laboribus usui esse ac sufficere non possint est ad condemnandum aut vincula nautica. Quo circa tales inutiles condemnandi sunt, non ad relegationem nauticam sed alia poena secundum delictorum; rationem et secundum id quod jus postulat et requirit et juxta leges scriptas aut juxta locorum consuetudinis aut Principum edicta, sive capitaliter, ut more sequatur, sive citra mortem." Cf. the decree of Margaret of Parma, cited above, p. 53.
22. The decree is quoted in Joussé, *op. cit.*, I, 50. The French historian of criminal law, Albert Du Boys, in his *Histoire du droit criminel de la France depuis le XVIme jusqu'au XIXme siècle* (Paris, 1874), II, 41, remarks that the government of Louis XIV had such need of oarsmen that it did not shrink from any method of obtaining the required number. On the death penalty for attempts to escape and on the fugitive galley slaves themselves and those who assisted them, see Damhouder, *op. cit.*, p. 466.
23. Marion, *op. cit.*, p. 252.
24. For details on the living conditions on board the galleys, wretched beyond belief, see Damhouder, *op. cit.*, pp. 478–79.
25. On the early history of transportation, see H. E. Barnes, "Transportation of Criminals," *Encyclopaedia of the Social Sciences*, XV (New York, 1935), 90–93.
26. The subsequent history and the abolition of transportation as a form of punishment is discussed at some length below, pp. 114–26.
27. Adam Smith, *op. cit.*, p. 359.
28. J. D. Butler, "British Convicts Shipped to American Colonies," *American Historical Review*, II (1896), 18; G. Ives, *A History of Penal Methods* (London, 1914), pp. 113–19.
29. Furniss, *op. cit.*, pp. 54 and 56.
30. J. Cary, *An Essay towards Regulating the Trade and Employing the Poor of This Kingdom* (2d ed.; London, 1719), pp. 47–48.
31. The letter is quoted in Butler, *op. cit.*, p. 16.
32. The act is quoted in E. O'Brien, *The Foundation of Australia* (London, 1937), p. 122.
33. *Ibid.*, p. 123.
34. *Loc. cit.* The same juxtaposition of reform motives and "useful service" is to be found in the writings of Wm. Petty, whose whole approach to the problem of prisoners is determined by considerations of their usefulness; see his *Economic Writings*, ed. by C. H. Hull (Cambridge, 1899), I, 68.
35. A. E. Smith, "Transportation of Convicts to America," *American Historical Review*, XXXIX (1933–34), 238–41.

36. O'Brien, *op. cit.*, pp. 124–25.
37. *Ibid.*, p. 125.
38. Butler, *op. cit.*, p. 25.
39. C. Goodrich, "Indenture," *Encyclopaedia of the Social Sciences*, VII (New York, 1932), 645–46.
40. Ives, *op. cit.*, p. 119.
41. *Ibid.*, pp. 113 and 120.
42. C. Phillipson, *Three Criminal Law Reformers: Beccaria, Bentham, Romilly* (London, 1923), p. 175, quoting Bentham.
43. See, for example, the New Jersey act of July 8, 1730, quoted in H. E. Barnes, *A History of the Penal, Reformatory and Correctional Institutions of the State of New Jersey* (Trenton, N.J., 1918), p. 36.
44. Francis Bacon, *The Essayes or Counsels Civill and Morall* (London, 1914), p. 104.
45. F. von Holtzendorff, *Die Deportation als Strafmittel in alter und neuer Zeit und die Verbrecherkolonien der Engländer und Franzosen* (Leipzig, 1859), p. 662.
46. Justinian, *Digest*, 48.19.8.
47. For France, see R. Anchel, *Crimes et châtiments au XVIIIe siècle* (2d ed.; Paris, 1933), pp. 90–93; for the Netherlands, Stroobant, *op. cit.*, pp. 76–102. A. Crew, *London Prisons of Today and Yesterday* (London, 1933), p. 50, says that the jailer's desire to exploit as large a crew as possible went so far as to induce him to pay annuities to judges in return for a promise to deliver all their prisoners to his establishment. Sir Francis Mitchell, for example, a Middlesex justice, received a salary of £40 from the jailer of Newgate in 1638.
48. See the remarks in Stroobant, *op. cit.*, p. 89. On the development of the congregations, see Lallemand, *op. cit.*, IV, 31–52.
49. Bohne's attempt to prove, by reference to the Italian towns, that imprisonment was widely used as a punishment at a comparatively early date is unsuccessful. At any rate, the modern prison system did not arise from this source, and imprisonment at this time resembled corporal punishment as a means of torturing the body of the criminal; see Doleisch von Dolsperg, *op. cit.*, p. 47; and above, p. 10.
50. Holdsworth, *op. cit.*, IV, 397.
51. S. and B. Webb, *English Prisons under Local Government* (London, 1922), p. 18.
52. T. Mommsen, *Römisches Strafrecht* (Leipzig, 1899), p. 949; von Bar, *op. cit.*, p. 238. The *Karrenstrafe* was a favorite form of *opus publicum* in Germany; see Ebeling, *op. cit.*, pp. 3–13.
53. The quotation is found in Hippel, "Beiträge," p. 440.
54. *Ibid.*, p. 444.
55. *Ibid.*, p. 442.
56. *Ibid.*, p. 614. In Bern, vagrants, beggars, spendthrifts, idlers, and malefactors were thrown together; see Hafner and Zürcher, *op. cit.*, p. 8. For Lüneburg, see A. Ludolph, *Das Werk und Zuchthaus und die Kettenstrafanstalt zu Lüneburg* (Göttingen, 1930), p. 10.
57. Hippel, "Beiträge," pp. 629–30. On the refusal of the provisors of the Hamburg *Zuchthaus* to accept criminals, see Ebeling, *op. cit.*, p. 53. The regulations of March 8, 1622, quoted there, pp. 77–103, do not provide a final answer to the question; see especially p. 85, where it is debatable whether the regulation refers to the possible dangers in allowing the idle to remain at large or to convictions for actual misdemeanor. For a tentative differentiation between poorhouses, houses of correction, and prisons, see John Macfarlan, *Inquiries concerning the Poor* (Edinburgh, 1782), Book III, Chap. 6.

58. Hippel, "Beiträge," p. 640.
59. *Ibid.*, p. 647.
60. Gothein, *op. cit.*, p. 699.
61. Hippel, *Deutsches Strafrecht*, I, 248n.
62. Weissenrieder, *op. cit.*, p. 47. As late as 1805, the Weimar house of correction had the following composition: 37 sentenced criminals, 9 persons of bad moral conduct, 2 drunkards, 5 lunatics, and 5 other non-sentenced persons; see Lucht, *op. cit.*, p. 51.
63. E. Schmidt, *Entwicklung*, p. 18. The same is true of the French *Hôpitaux généraux* where the period of detention was so defined by law as to leave a great deal of freedom to the authorities of the houses, especially with regard to vagrants; on the first offense the vagrants and beggars could be set free as soon as they found employment, and a minimum of three months (but no maximum) was provided for the second offense; see F. Muyart de Vouglans, *Institutes au droit criminel* (Paris, 1757), p. 690.
64. Joussé, *op. cit.*, I, 48.
65. For the French practice of sending males into an *Hôpital* or into a *Maison de Force*, see *ibid.*, I, 82, where Joussé speaks of special grounds on which galley slavery could be replaced by these forms of punishment. See also the correspondence relating to the commutation of a galley sentence for a French nobleman, in *Correspondance administrative*, II, 941. It is interesting to note that the only basis for pardon was noble lineage. On the Italian practice of saving the nobility from galley servitude and corporal punishment, see P. Farinacius, *De poenis temperandis. Praxis et theoria criminalis*, Part III, 2 (Frankfurt, 1611), Nos. 98, 99, 102.
66. The case is cited in Hippel, "Beiträge," p. 610n.
67. See B. S. Carpzov, *Practicae novae imperialis Saxonicae rerum criminalium* (Frankfurt and Wittenberg, 1658), Quaestio XXV/1, where it is stated that at present all judgments are extraordinary.
68. See A. Hegler, *Die praktische Tätigkeit der Juristenfakultät des 17. und 18. Jahrhunderts* (Freiburg i.B., 1899), p. 88. The author uses the shortage of labor resulting from war casualties to explain this practice. See also Gwinner, *op. cit.*, pp. 265–66.
69. See the account of Hommel's theory in E. Landsberg, *Geschichte der deutschen Rechtswissenschaft*, III, 1 (München and Berlin, 1898), p. 391.
70. Banishment had already been abolished in Brandenburg under Frederick William I. The dates of the decrees are found in N. H. Kriegsmann, *Ein führung in die Gefängniskunde* (Heidelberg, 1912), p. 10.
71. Riedel, *op. cit.*, p. 82.
72. Knapp, *Bauernbefreiung*, I, 68.
73. See the remarks of J. Ch. Edler von Quistorp, *Grundsätze des deutschen peinlichen Rechts* (5th ed.; Rostock und Leipzig, 1794), I, 104. As late as 1861, an official Hungarian commission (the so-called Judexcurial conference) declined to abolish whipping for offenses against the rural police regulations, because imprisonment would have restricted the available labor power considerably; see P. Szende, "Nationales Recht und Klassenrecht," *Festschrift für Carl Grünberg* (Leipzig, 1932), pp. 472–73.
74. This is more true in Germany than in France where until 1788 the royal prerogative of mercy was severely restricted by the power of the courts to have sentences executed immediately.
75. Note the restriction which Cocceji, minister of Frederick II, held to be necessary in the application of the new ruling abolishing torture; see *Acta Borussica*, VI, 2 (1901), No. 7.

76. W. Dilthey, "Das allgemeine Landrecht," *Gesammelte Schriften*, XII (Leipzig and Berlin, 1936), 187; see also E. Schmidt, *Staat und Recht*, p. 33n.; Willen-bücher, *op. cit.*, p. 56. For Austria, see W. E. Wahlberg, *Gesammelte kleine Bruchstücke über Strafrecht, Strafprozess, Gefängniskunde und Literatur und Dogmengeschichte der Rechtslehre in Österreich*, III (Wien, 1882), 3.

77. Hippel, *Deutsches Strafrecht*, I, 273. For England, see Phillipson, *op. cit.*, p. 169.

78. R. Schmidt, *Strafrechtsreform*, p. 186.

79. Henelius, *op. cit.*, pp. 323–24.

80. *Ibid.*, p. 326.

81. J. F. Stephen, *A History of the Criminal Law of England* (London, 1883), II, 92.

82. When Hippel, *Deutsches Strafrecht*, I, 249, speaks of a retrogression from the penal institution of the earlier Amsterdam type to the German establishments after the Thirty Years' War, and complains that the reformatory purpose of the houses had become a dead letter, the reason for his view is probably to be found in the assumption that reform was the central idea in the Amsterdam establishment. The contradiction between reformatory and profit motives seems very questionable. High productivity of labor and improvement of character were indissolubly linked for contemporaries. We have seen that the productive purpose was considered before the question of improvement when the two were in direct conflict and always when the house was run by a lessee, so that the physical and moral health of the inmates suffered in the interest of productivity. The opinion of the Austrian criminologist, Wahlberg, *op. cit.*, II, 203, seems much more balanced; "The death penalty and mutilation appear as the saviors of society until the force of the frightful consequences compelled the state, in its deterrent types of punishment, to turn from this barbarous, savage, and useless system, so harmful to the country, to an effective and generally useful system of imprisonment and forced labor, to civilize criminal justice, to use the prisoners' labor power in a manner useful to society, to find more humane punishments, to restore his rights to the criminal, and to make his existence economically possible."

83. These figures are given by L. Bouchard, *Système financier de l'ancienne monarchie* (Paris, 1891), pp. 287–89.

84. S. Pufendorf, *Le Droit de la nature et des gens*, ed. by H. Berbeyrac, II (Amsterdam, 1706), Book VIII, Chap. III, for example, insisted on the idea that punishment should have general utility, and on the necessity of appropriateness as well as deterrence. A coherent discussion of the methods of punishments is lacking in Pufendorf's work, however, as in Grotius, whom he follows rather closely in this connection.

85. *Ouvrages posthumes de D. Jean Mabillon et de Thierri Ruinard, Bénédictines de la congrégation de St. Maur*, ed. by D. Vincent Thuillier (Paris, 1724), II, 321–35, "Réflexions sur les prisons des ordres religieux." See Th. Sellin, "Dom. Jean Mabillon—a Prison Reformer of the Seventeenth Century," *Journal of the American Institute of Criminal Law and Criminology*, XVII (1926–27), 581–602.

86. F. Kober, "Die Gefängnishaft gegen Kleriker und Mönche," *Theologische Quartalsschrift*, LIX (1877), 554; see also the interesting remarks of Goebel, *op. cit.*, p. 225n., on monetary redemption in ecclesiastical practice.

87. The same identification of life imprisonment and death occurs in Petty, *op. cit.*, I, 68.

88. Mabillon, *op. cit.*, p. 330.

89. *Ibid.*, p. 326.

90. *Ibid.*, pp. 333–35.

CHAPTER V

1. Phillipson, *op. cit.*, p. 31, quoting Necker.
2. K. Krohne, *Lehrbuch der Gefängniskunde unter Berücksichtigung der Kriminalstatistik und Kriminalpolitik* (Stuttgart, 1889), p. 20.
3. All references are to C. B. Beccaria, *An Essay on Crimes and Punishments with a Commentary by M. de Voltaire*, tr. from the French (new ed.; Edinburgh, 1788).
4. Hobbes, *Leviathan*, reprinted from the edition of 1651 (Oxford, 1909), p. 224.
5. *Ibid.*, p. 226.
6. Beccaria, *op. cit.*, p. 212.
7. See Section 8 of the publication order of Feb. 5, 1794, and Section 14 of the Introduction to the *Allgemeines Landrecht*.
8. See the valuable study of E. Carcassonne, *Montesquieu et le problème de la constitution française au XVIIIe siècle* (Paris, 1927), which discusses the different influences that found expression in his work, as well as the frequently contradictory interpretations of later eighteenth-century writers and politicians. Carcassonne rightly stresses the more conservative elements in the formation of Montesquieu's work. Today many scholars correctly hold that Montesquieu's doctrine of the separation of powers was, in its political implications, a defense of the anachronistic power of the parlements in eighteenth-century French society.
9. Beccaria, *op. cit.*, p. 25.
10. *Ibid.*, p. 33.
11. Bentham, *An Introduction to the Principles of Morals and Legislation* (Oxford, 1907), p. 70.
12. Montesquieu, *De l'esprit des lois,* especially Book XII, Chap. IV.
13. Beccaria, *op. cit.*, p. 86.
14. Quoted in Gwinner, *op. cit.*, p. 216. A similar rule is to be found as late as the Prussian prison regulations of Dec. 21, 1898, paragraph 18; see *Vorschriften über den Strafvollzug in den preussischen Justizgefängnissen*, ed. by A. Klein (Berlin, 1910), p. 40.
15. *Ibid.*, p. 87. Voltaire, "Prix de la justice et de l'humanité," *Œuvres*, L (Paris, 1834), 259–60.
16. Beccaria, *op. cit.*, p. 87.
17. See the description given by Voltaire, *op. cit.*, p. 257; cf. the remarks of Anchel, *op. cit.*, p. 230.
18. Beccaria, *op. cit.*, p. 110; cf. Voltaire, *op. cit.*, p. 258.
19. On Beccaria's pronounced class position, see also Radbruch, "Stand und Strafrecht," p. 30. In Boucher d'Argis's article upon theft in Diderot's *Encyclopedia*, XVII, 450, the possibility of the profitable employment of the prisoner's labor power is prominent among the arguments against retention of the death penalty for theft: "Thieves who do not kill, do not deserve death, because there is no calculable relation between the objects stolen—perhaps of a very small value—and the life which it is proposed to destroy. Employ the convicts in useful labor; to deprive them of their liberty will be sufficient punishment for their offense, and will provide sufficient guarantee of public order, and will profit the state. You will in this way avoid the reproach of injustice and inhumanity." But, continues the author in a melancholy vein, "it has pleased mankind to regard thieves as being beyond pardon, no doubt for the simple reason that money is the god of this world, and that after life itself nothing is more treasured than interest."
20. The letter is quoted in Willenbücher, *op. cit.*, p. 39.
21. *Loc. cit.*

22. J. P. Marat, *Plan de législation criminelle* (Paris, 1790), pp. 24 and 35.

23. Beccaria, *op. cit.*, pp. 167–69.

24. The bribing of judges was very common in the eighteenth century, despite the absolute integrity of some. We may be quite certain that in general every imaginable kind of deal was arranged, including agreements between judges and thieves, says Anchel, *op. cit.*, p. 10, in his evaluation of the French judiciary in the eighteenth century. Lucht, *op. cit.*, p. 63, hints at a similar situation in Germany in speaking of the absence of a sense of duty among the officials. The case is put more clearly by von Bar, *op. cit.*, pp. 232–33.

25. A. Desjardins, *Les Cahiers des États généraux en 1789 et la législation criminelle* (Paris, 1883), shows clearly that the main interest lay in questions of procedure.

26. Weber, *Wirtschaft und Gesellschaft*, I, 471.

27. Stephen, *op. cit.*, I, 286–92.

28. Weber, *loc. cit.*

29. Blackstone, *Commentaries on the Law of England* (2d ed.; Oxford, 1766), I, 354.

30. J. L. and Barbara Hammond, *The Town Labourer, 1760–1832* (London, 1917), pp. 60–63; cf. O'Brien, *op. cit.*, pp. 79–82.

31. O'Brien, *op. cit.*, pp. 99–100.

32. R. Holtzmann, *Französische Verfassungsgeschichte* (Berlin, 1910), p. 344.

33. Marat, *op. cit.*, p. 33.

34. The report of Lepeletier St. Fargeau is to be found in the *Moniteur universel* (1791), I, 622–23.

35. *Ibid.*, p. 644.

36. Köstlin, *op. cit.*, p. 242; cf. Hippel, *Deutsches Strafrecht*, p. 257; Dilthey, *op. cit.*, p. 186.

37. *Anmerkungen für das Strafgesetzbuch für das Königreich Bayern nach den Protokollen des königlichen geheimen Rats* (München, 1813), I, 7.

38. Willenbücher, *op. cit.*, p. 46, quoting the orders of May 23 and 26, 1771.

39. *Allgemeines Landrecht*, Part II, Title 20, paragraph 85, bluntly states that poor people of the lower classes should not be fined. According to Part II, Title 20, paragraph 1128, on the other hand, an heir defrauding part of the undivided community is to be imprisoned only if he is unable to pay a fine.

CHAPTER VI

1. Howard, *op. cit.*, p. 67.

2. *Ibid.*, pp. 145–46.

3. The report of May 4, 1779, is cited by Lucht, *op. cit.*, p. 53.

4. E. Rosenfeld, *Zweihundert Jahre Fürsorge der preussischen Staatsregierung für die entlassenen Gefangenen* (Berlin, 1905), p. 11; see also Hippel, "Beiträge," p. 658. Saam, *op. cit.*, pp. 38–39, 58–59, tried to save the reputation of the German houses of correction, where conditions never became so deplorable as in England and other countries. The German houses had always been animated by a definite idea, a positive conception of the state and religious principles. There is only one reason why Saam's defense must not be considered a failure, and that is because he is wrong in believing that he has actually made such an attempt at all. He mistakenly takes excerpts of a great many rules of houses of correction to be an actual analysis of the social structure of the houses. His discussion of the fundamental question of the organization of work, for instance, is limited to about two pages.

5. Hippel, "Beiträge," pp. 656–57.

6. *Ibid.*, pp. 658–59.

7. Kulischer, *op. cit.*, II, 6 and 464.
8. Levasseur, *Population française*, I, 202 and 211.
9. Mantoux, *op. cit.*, p. 188. The situation in England was aggravated by the influx of the "terribly hungry reserve of the poor Irish"; see J. H. Clapham, *An Economic History of Modern Britain* (2d ed.; Cambridge, 1930), I, 557.
10. Kulischer, *op. cit.*, II, 421. The condition of the labor market brought about fundamental changes in the agrarian policy of Germany as well, especially in East Prussia (*ibid.*, II, 436). As the labor market in the towns began to contract, the influx of workers from the country was checked and the landowners were able to abandon their opposition to the emancipation of the serfs.
11. P. Mombert, *Bevölkerungslehre* (Jena, 1929), p. 96.
12. A. Marshall, *Principles of Economics* (8th ed.; London, 1930), p. 177. In his first edition, Clapham characterizes as a legend the view that everything was getting worse for the working man down to some unspecified date between the drafting of the People's Charter and the great Exhibition. In the second edition, *op. cit.*, I, vii, however, he attenuates this statement considerably by remarking that he did not mean that everything was getting better, but only that recent historians have too often stressed the decline. He even admits (I, 557) that there is an element of truth in the Marxian doctrine of the reserve army of labor used by employers to beat down the pay of the regular troops. See also J. L. Hammond, "The Industrial Revolution and Discontent," *Economic History Review*, II (1930), 215–18.
13. F. J. Neumann, "Zur Lehre von den Lohngesetzen," *Jahrbücher für National-ökonomie und Statistik*, LIX (1892), 366–97.
14. Holdsworth, *op. cit.*, VI, 348.
15. See the characteristic attitude of A. F. Lueder, *Kritik der Statistik und Politik* (Göttingen, 1812), p. 74.
16. E. M. Burns, *Wages and the State* (London, 1926), p. 4.
17. Pike, *op. cit.*, II, 294.
18. Burns, *op. cit.*, p. 6.
19. Quoted in Sée, *op. cit.*, I, 361n.
20. Lueder, *Kritik*, p. 255.
21. Frohneberg, *op. cit.*, p. 54.
22. Lueder, *Kritik*, p. 253. Of course, moral arguments for the new policy were not lacking. Lueder, *ibid.*, pp. 235–36, writes: "Where is the man worthy of the name who would take a wife because a married man is better off than a bachelor according to the law? Who is going to marry and bring a crowd of children into the world merely for the sake of prices and pensions? And what sort of children would they be who had not been brought into the world by the mutual attraction of their parents? And what sort of breed that owes its existence to bribes for procreation?" Cf. *ibid.*, p. 244.
23. A. Menger, *Das bürgerliche Recht und die besitzlosen Volksklassen* (5th ed.; Tübingen, 1927), pp. 76–79.
24. M. Planiol and G. Ripert, *Traité pratique de droit civil français*, IV (Paris, 1928), 116–17.
25. The speech is quoted in M. Loiseau, *Traité des enfants naturels adultérins, incestueux et abandonnés* (Paris, 1811), p. 165; see also the recent publication of C. C. Brinton, *French Revolutionary Legislation on Illegitimacy 1789–1804* (Cambridge, Mass., and London, 1936).
26. Schmoller, *op. cit.*, II, 53; L. C. A. Knowles, *The Industrial and Commercial Revolutions in Great Britain during the Nineteenth Century* (London, 1926), pp. 128–29.

27. Schmoller, *op. cit.*, II, 295; see also H. Stein, "Pauperismus und Assoziation," *International Review for Social History*, I (1936), 39–43.

28. The report is quoted in B. Laum, "Geschichte der öffentlichen Armenpflege," *Handwörterbuch der Staatswissenschaften*, I (4th ed.; Jena, 1923), 951.

29. Schmoller, *op. cit.*, II, 386.

30. The statement appears in Mirabeau, *Rapport au nom du Comité des Lettres de Cachet publié pour la premièe fois avec une introduction et des notes par le Vicomte Henri Bégouin* (Paris, 1888), p. 13. O'Brien, *op. cit.*, p. 105, shows that Mirabeau merely took over the judgment of Romilly.

31. *Procès verbaux et rapports du Comité de Mendicité de la Constituante, 1790–1791*, ed. by C. Bloch and A. Tuetey (Paris, 1911), p. 344.

32. Justi, *Grundfesten*, II, 410 and 418.

33. Petty, *op. cit.*, II, 353–54.

34. Mirabeau, *L'Ami des hommes ou traité de la population* (Paris, 1883), pp. 349–50.

35. Paultre, *op. cit.*, p. 556.

36. *Ibid.*, p. 559.

37. *Allgemeines Landrecht*, Part II, Introduction, Paragraph 1.

38. Lallemand, *op. cit.*, IV, 2, 401; Sée, *op. cit.*, II, 93.

39. P. Colquhoun, *A Treatise on the Police of the Metropolis* (6th ed.; London, 1800), p. 313.

40. Malthus, *Parallel Chapters from the First and Second Edition of an Essay on the Principle of Population* (New York and London, 1895), pp. 34–38.

41. Clapham, *op. cit.*, I, 580.

42. Webb, *Poor Law*, I, 420.

43. Pike, *op. cit.*, II, 360–61; A. Redford, *The Economic History of England (1760–1860)* (London, 1931), p. 105.

44. Quoted in Redford, *op. cit.*, p. 106.

45. Sée, *op. cit.*, II, 272.

46. G. P. O. D'Haussonville, *Les Etablissements pénitentiaires en France et aux Colonies* (Paris, 1875), p. 243.

47. Schmoller, *op. cit.*, II, 534; Sée, *op. cit.*, II, 258.

48. See the remarks of Phillipson, *op. cit.*, p. 163.

49. Engels, *The Condition of the Working-class in England in 1844*, tr. by F. K. Wischnewetzky (London, 1892), p. 115.

50. All French figures are quoted from the *Compte général de l'administration de la justice criminelle;* the first published volume covers the year 1825. The figures in the text include only the convictions by the *Tribunal correctionnel* and do not include the convictions for *délits forestiers*. An unmistakable increase in crime can be observed in Germany, too; see Lucht, *op. cit.*, p. 90n.

51. Pike, *op. cit.*, II, 678–79.

52. Krohne, *op. cit.*, p. 148.

53. Wagnitz, *op. cit.*, II, 146–48.

54. Quoted by Hafner and Zürcher, *op. cit.*, p. 15.

55. *Ibid.*, p. 16.

56. See M. Marion, *Le Brigandage pendant la Révolution* (Paris, 1934), especially Chap. V, which, however, looks at the repression through the eyes of the ruling classes, as the title itself indicates.

57. "Exposé des motifs du livre Ier du Code des Délits et des Peines par Treilhard, conseiller d'État," in *Recueil général des lois et des arrêts* (Sirey), X (Paris, 1810), 568.

58. Garraud, *op. cit.*, I, 136. The punishments of the Code of 1810 were considered barbaric even in the first part of the nineteenth century, but this

aspect seemed less important than its distinct progress in legal techniques; see A. Chauveau and F. Hélie, *Théorie du code pénal* (Paris, 1837), I, 21.

59. Nagler, *op. cit.*, pp. 423–33; R. Schmidt, *Aufgaben*, p. 265.

60. E. Spangenberg, *Über die sittliche und bürgerliche Besserung der Verbrecher vermittelst des Pönitentiarsystems* . . . . (Landshut, 1821), p. 72; K. G. Geib, *Lehrbuch des deutschen Strafrechts* (Leipzig, 1861–62), p. 427.

61. The famous German criminologist Mittermaier remarked in his edition of P. J. A. Feuerbach's *Lehrbuch des gemeinen in Deutschland geltenden peinlichen Rechts* (13th ed.; Giessen, 1840), p. 16, that Feuerbach's theory led to an effort to avoid the danger of arbitrary justice, but that its insistence on fixed punishments together with their severity led to such harshness in the application of the code that frequent pardon became necessary. See also von Bar, *op. cit.*, p. 330.

62. O. Mittelstädt, *Gegen die Freiheitsstrafe* (Leipzig, 1879), p. 19.

63. H. Krausse, *Die Prügelstrafe. Eine kriminalistische Studie* (Berlin, 1899), p. 105; von Bar, *op. cit.*, p. 348.

64. The whole Prussian development is well described by Hippel, *Deutsches Strafrecht*, I, 316.

65. Krausse, *op. cit.*, p. 59.

66. Wahlberg, *op. cit.*, III, 16.

67. Feuerbach, *Kritik des natürlichen Rechts* (Altona, 1796), pp. 115–16.

68. The development of liberal principles in criminal law is fairly well treated by H. Drost, *Das Ermessen des Strafrichters* (Berlin, 1930). The social and political implications, however, are much more clearly emphasized by R. Schmidt, *Strafrechtsreform*, pp. 205–12.

69. Feuerbach, *Kritik des Kleinschrodischen Entwurfs zu einem peinlichen Gesetzbuch für die Kurpfälzisch bayrischen Staaten*, Part III (Giessen, 1804), pp. 10, 18, 33, and 34. See also Landsberg, *op. cit.*, III, 2, 129, where Feuerbach is praised for having abolished criminal punishment for mere vices.

70. O. Despatys, *Magistrats et criminels, 1795–1844* (Paris, 1913), p. 295.

71. See F. Exner, *Gerechtigkeit und Richteramt* (Leipzig, 1922), p. 23.

72. The rise of this ideology is accurately described by Nagler, *op. cit.*, p. 343, who says: "Considering it from a dogmatic point of view, it was nothing but the resurrection of the retribution principle which had disappeared in the eighteenth century as a result of the trend of thought characteristic of the police state (as, for instance, in France) and which now put in a reappearance through the back door of expediency . . . . but whereas in medieval times these retributory principles had been unconsciously applied as being self-evident, without any recognition of their full value, they were now perceived in their true light as important and full of blessing in their efficiency, and they were hailed as great political achievements."

73. Kant, *Metaphysische Anfangsgründe der Rechtslehre* (Königsberg, 1797), p. 199.

74. Hegel, *Philosophy of Right*, tr. by S. W. Dyde (London, 1896), paragraph 100, Note, pp. 97–98. For further discussion of these questions see J. Michael and M. J. Adler, *Crime, Law and Social Science* (New York and London, 1933), pp. 346–52.

75. This was the practical effect of idealistic philosophy in the sphere of criminal law; different theoretical interpretations were possible, of course. See R. Schmidt, *Strafrechtsreform*, pp. 189 ff.; G. Radbruch, *Rechtsphilosophie* (3d ed.; Leipzig, 1932), pp. 160–61.

76. See, for example, the following characteristic passage from Feuerbach, *Revision der Grundsätze und Grundbegriffe des positiven peinlichen Rechts* (Erfurt and Chemnitz, 1799–1800), I, 27; "It may well be advantageous to the

state to pardon a certain criminal. He may have been led to crime by chance circumstances, and, if he were censured and warned, he might be made into a good citizen again, whereas if he came into the clutches of the law it might mean that a useful member of society would be lost forever. But it is more important to the state that justice should show itself to be inflexible, that it should not be swayed by opportunistic considerations and thereby undermine the authority of the law and turn its threats into a child's plaything. In this way judges may prevent many useful citizens from being lost to the state, but at the same time they are only encouraging new infringements of the law, and, out of pity for the prisoner, they neglect their duty to the state and violate the rights of its citizens."

77. See H. Dannenberg, *Liberalismus und Strafrecht im 19. Jahrhundert* (Berlin and Leipzig, 1925), p. 6, whose conclusion that political liberalism cannot go beyond the formal notion of culpability seems quite correct.

78. See Landsberg, *op. cit.*, III, 2, 121, and R. Schmidt, *Aufgaben*, p. 28, both of whom insist on Feuerbach's intermediate position between rationalistic and idealistic conceptions. See also Dannenberg, *op. cit.*, p. 13; J. Hall, "Nulla poena sine lege," *Yale Law Journal*, XLVII (1938), 170.

79. Feuerbach, *Revision*, I, 9.

80. M. P. Rossi, *Traité de droit pénal* (Bruxelles, 1835), p. 40, for instance, bluntly admits the class function of criminal law.

81. It must be noted, however, that the total number of persons actually transported was far greater than the number sentenced to transportation, because most of the death sentences were commuted to transportation; see W. D. Forsyth, *Governor Arthur's Convict System, Van Diemen's Land 1824-36* (London and New York, 1935), p. 101.

82. *Loc. cit.*

83. The Bavarian Criminal Code of 1813, for instance, introduces a varied system of deprivations of liberty, ranging from *Festungsstrafe* and *Kettenstrafe* down to imprisonment in a house of correction or in a workhouse.

84. *Anmerkungen für das Strafgesetzbuch*, p. 192.

85. Beccaria, *op. cit.*, pp. 85–86.

86. Gwinner, *op. cit.*, p. 224.

87. Krohne, "Die Gefängnisbaukunst," *Handbuch des Gefängniswesens*, ed. by F. von Holtzendorff and E. von Jagemann, I (Hamburg, 1888), 485.

88. For Thuringia, see Lucht, *op. cit.*, pp. 55 and 64. The legislatures were opposed to such expenditures in other German countries too, as well as in Belgium and France.

89. Quoted from E. Bertrand, *Leçons pénitentiaires* (Louvain, 1934), p. 59.

90. *Ibid.*, p. 68.

91. The petition of C. P. Corneille addressed to the Emperor Napoleon on November 19, 1809, is reprinted under the title "Les Prisons sous le Premier Empire" in *Revue pénitentiaire*, XXX (1906), 246–63.

92. The expenditure on French prisons, which amounted to 3,640,000 francs in 1821, had decreased to 3,450,000 in 1827 in spite of a startling increase in the prison population from 1825 to 1827. C. Lucas, *Du système pénitentiaire en Europe et aux États-Unis* (Paris, 1828), I, pp. VII–VIII, quoting these figures from Dupin, severely criticized this development; he considers it inconceivable, at least as long as the administration did not reveal the methods by which it had obtained such results.

93. Webb, *English Prisons*, p. 111n, quotes the Report of the Select Committee on Secondary Punishments: "The number of persons charged with criminal offenses and committed to the different gaols of England and Wales for trial . . . . was, in [the] seven years ending December 31st, 1817, 56,308;

ditto, 1824, 92,848; ditto, 1831, 121,518. . . . . These numbers do not comprise offenders of every description who passed through the prisons, being exclusive of summary conviction before magistrates, vagrants, prisoners for re-examination and debtors."

94. T. M. Osborne, *Society and Prisons* (New Haven, 1916), pp. 86–87.

95. A. Jorns, *The Quakers as Pioneers in Social Work,* tr. by T. K. Crown (New York, 1931), p. 187; cf. F. von Liszt, "Das ausserdeutsche Gefängniswesen in Europa seit 1830," in Holtzendorff-Jagemann, *op. cit.,* I, 258.

96. Quoted in Webb, *English Prisons,* p. 111n, quoting Parker.

97. Peel's Gaol Act of 1823 marked the turning point in England, for instance; see Webb, *English Prisons,* pp. 73–75.

98. C. Lucas, *De la réforme des prisons ou de la théorie de l'emprisonnement* (Paris, 1838), II, 48, pointed out that virtually all crimes against property were committed by the lower classes, for they were most remote from a life of comfort and protection against want and lacked the education which prevents the abuse of wealth.

99. *Warum werden so wenig Sträflinge im Zuchthaus gebessert?* (Leipzig, 1802; reprinted Berlin, 1925), p. 37.

100. *Ibid.,* p. 61.

101. *Ibid.,* p. 35.

102. M. Béranger, *Des moyens propres à généraliser en France le système pénitentiaire* (Paris, 1836), p. 53.

103. Lucas, *Système,* II, 407.

104. J. Füsslin, *Die Einzelhaft nach fremden und sechsjährigen eigenen Erfahrungen im neuen Männerzuchthaus in Bruchsal* (Heidelberg, 1855), p. 350.

105. The report is reprinted in Lucas, *Système,* II, 370–81.

106. Lucas, *Réforme des prisons,* II, 48, consoles himself about the injustice inherent in the disproportionate effort necessary for the lower classes to comply with the requirements of the law by explaining that this constitutes a sort of selective process. F. C. Hepp, *Über die Gerechtigkeits- und Nutzungs-Theorien des Auslandes und den Werth der Philosophie des Strafrechts für die Strafgesetzgebungswissenschaft überhaupt* (Heidelberg, 1834), p. 45, quotes Bauer to the effect that it is unfortunately impossible to treat every prisoner individually with the care and discernment of a psychologist and thus to turn him into a moral being.

107. See p. 376 of the report quoted above in note 105.

108. Marx, "Ökonomisch-philosophische Manuskripte aus dem Jahre 1844," *Marx-Engels Gesamtausgabe,* ed. by V. Adoratskij, Abt. I, Vol. III (Berlin, 1932), 97–98.

109. *Loc. cit.*

110. Lucas, *Système,* II, 408.

111. *Report on the Discipline and Management of Convict Prisons of July 29, 1850,* by Lieutenant Colonel Jebb, Surveyor General of Prisons (London, 1851), p. 21.

112. Ives, *op. cit.,* p. 209.

113. C. von Voit, "Die Ernährung der Gefangenen," in Holtzendorff-Jagemann, *op. cit.,* II, 165–66.

114. Kriegsmann, *op. cit.,* p. 22.

115. Füsslin, *Einzelhaft,* pp. 251–52. The authorities attributed the prevalence of the disease and its rapid course to excessive masturbation.

116. All quoted in A. Bär, "Morbidität und Mortalität in den Gefängnissen," in Holtzendorff-Jagemann, *op. cit.,* II, 456.

117. *Ibid.,* p. 457.

118. Webb, *English Prisons*, p. 89.
119. Quoted in Webb, *loc. cit.*
120. *Ibid.*, p. 89n; Lipson, *op. cit.*, III, 475.
121. Lucas, *Réforme des prisons*, III, 304.
122. Krohne, *Lehrbuch*, p. 157.
123. Krohne, *ibid.*, p. 158, praises this system, which combines Prussian discipline with great economies, when he writes: "A great deal of fuss has been raised over militarism in the Prussian prisons, but one should not forget that it was this form of government that succeeded in instilling order and discipline into the undisciplined bands which were brought to the prison in large numbers, and in making the management run like clockwork without any elaborate preparations, all this at unbelievably small expense." As retired army officers had performed this task so well, it became the rule, and later the law, that only men who had been in the army could become governors of prisons (*ibid.*, p. 159).
124. The remarks of Wagnitz, *op. cit.*, II, 84, are not without interest in this connection: "When goods manufactured in houses of correction are freed from burdens that they otherwise would have to bear, I wish that care would be taken that the favored industry should not sell its goods at a cheaper rate, at the expense of similar industries and private factories, thereby forming a monopoly which is all the more unfair because it easily brings about the impoverishment of many citizens whom it thus incites to crime instead of deterring them."
125. G. de Beaumont and A. de Tocqueville, *On the Penitentiary System in the United States and Its Application in France,* tr. by Francis Lieber (Philadelphia, 1833), p. 157.
126. *Ibid.*, pp. 156–57.
127. Riedel, *op. cit.*, pp. 78–79.
128. The characteristic passages of Pearson's program run as follows (quoted from Webb, *English Prisons*, pp. 160–61): "I contemplate . . . . a restriction to seven hours sleep. There is nothing that a criminal so much covets as that dreamy, drowsy, lazy, idle, yawning, imaginative state, between sleeping and waking, when he is living, as it were, in an imaginative world. There is nothing which is calculated so to rivet upon a man his evil passions and feelings, as the habit which is fostered in our gaols of permitting, if not compelling, a man to be in a warm bed for 10 hours, such as we have heard of, between the sheets in a warm hammock, in a warm room at Reading. To tame the fiercest animals we resort to the privation of sleep, and there is no criminal who would not feel the utmost repugnance to that monotony of life which stinted him to a small measure of sleep, and required him to observe strictly the hours prescribed. I propose . . . . that instead of a soft hammock he shall be on a hard bed. . . . . I propose that he shall be fed with the zero diet of the gaol, water and coarse bread. . . . . I propose that he shall wear a coarse parti-coloured prison dress I have no sympathy for the humanity that spares the nice feelings of a criminal by rejecting a prison dress; it is necessary for security; it is necessary for distinction; and, in my judgment, it is one of the exigencies of a sound system of prison discipline that convicted prisoners should be all clothed in a prison dress."
129. Webb, *ibid.*, p. 85, quoting Holford.
130. C. Koch, "Der soziale Gedanke im Strafvollzug," in E. Bummke, *Deutsches Gefängniswesen* (Berlin, 1928), p. 389.
131. Webb, *English Prisons*, p. 97.
132. *Ibid.*, pp. 98–99.

133. Webb (*ibid.*, p. 149) describes the different methods used by prisoners to escape the treadwheel. The administration employed flogging as a remedy for self-inflicted maladies; cf. Ives, *op. cit.*, p. 208.

134. Webb, *ibid.*, pp. 98–99 and 147.

135. *Ibid.*, pp. 149–50. On the methods applied in colonial penitentiaries, see Forsyth, *op. cit.*, p. 74n.

136. Rosshirt, *op. cit.*, III, 226.

137. Mittelstädt, *op. cit.*, pp. 36–37.

138. *Ibid.*, pp. 9–10.

CHAPTER VII

1. See above, p. 61.

2. O'Brien, *op. cit.*, p. 129.

3. *Ibid.*, pp. 132–34.

4. Howard, *op. cit.*, p. 465.

5. O'Brien, *op. cit.*, pp. 161–62.

6. *Ibid.*, p. 165.

7. M. Madan, *Thoughts on Executive Justice* (London, 1785); W. Paley, *The Principles of Moral and Political Philosophy* (London, 1785). See Phillipson, *op. cit.*, p. 245; J. A. Farrer, *Crimes and Punishments* (London, 1880).

8. O'Brien, *op. cit.*, pp. 178–79.

9. *Ibid.*, p. 248.

10. *Ibid.*, p. 253.

11. *Ibid.*, p. 261.

12. *Ibid.*, pp. 294–300.

13. Of the 7,035 convicts who arrived between 1787 and 1800, only 1,440 were women; see *ibid.*, p. 384, and Forsyth, *op. cit.*, p. 105.

14. O'Brien, *op. cit.*, p. 328. He quotes other testimonies of the same kind.

15. *Ibid.*, p. 336.

16. See Holtzendorff, *Deportation*, p. 276. See also Ives, *op. cit.*, pp. 146–47, who believes that transportation was to some extent the wisest method of dealing with major criminals. It gave an army of more than a hundred thousand prisoners a fresh start with real possibilities of rehabilitation. Instead of being responsible only for the erection of prisons and workhouses, they established new states and developed a continent.

17. The figures are taken from the *Cambridge History of the British Empire*, VII, 1 (Cambridge, 1933), 115.

18. *Ibid.*, p. 198.

19. *Ibid.*, p. 169.

20. Ives, *op. cit.*, pp. 140–42. Governor Macquarie did everything he could to suppress this tendency because he wished to protect the convicts from any social stigma in order to help them make good, and he considered this feeling of degradation to be a greater humiliation than the forced labor during the term of sentence. But he met with the resistance of the other officials and received only moderate aid from the committee of the House of Commons which enquired into the system of transportation in 1812.

21. R. C. Mills, *The Colonization of Australia (1829–42)* (London, 1915), Chap. VII; *Cambridge History*, pp. 213–18. Note the trenchant criticism of Wakefield in Marx, *Capital*, tr. rev. by E. Untermann (Chicago, 1906), I, Chap. XXV.

22. Holtzendorff, *Deportation*, p. 293.

23. The parliamentary debates reveal all the points which in the eyes of the English and colonial ruling classes required a fundamental change in the transportation policy. The arguments are summed up in the speeches of

Molesworth and Lord John Russell before the House of Commons on May 5, 1840 (Hansard, LIII, 1235–79 and 1279–91 respectively).

24. Of the 160,663 convicts shipped to Australia between 1787 and 1868, 83,290 were sent to New South Wales, 67,655 to Van Diemen's Land, and 9,718 to West Australia; Forsyth, *op. cit.*, p. 99.

25. *Ibid.*, p. 110.

26. See p. 31 of the report of Colonel Jebb, quoted above, Chap. VII, note 67.

27. In 1835, for example, there were 3,130 applications for convict labor and 2,740 were assigned; Forsyth, *op. cit.*, p. 105.

28. *Ibid.*, p. 126.

29. *Ibid.*, p. 127. In the first quarter of 1836 the colonial expenditure of New South Wales on immigration was £5,676, of Van Diemen's Land only £739. For 1835, the figures were £10,400 and £5,561 respectively. See *Ibid.*, p. 121; Mills, *op. cit.*, pp. 196–97.

30. Forsyth, *op. cit.*, p. 138.

31. Note the emphasis placed on the inequality between the conditions of the free workers and those of the transported population by the Archbishop of Dublin in the House of Lords debate on May 19, 1840 (Hansard, LIV, 253–54). Holtzendorff, writing in 1859, made express reference to this difference between the lower classes in the colonies and at home. His somewhat exaggerated conclusion was that all in all the deportee was better off than a free worker in England. The deportee had better food, better clothing, a shorter working day, and economic security (*Deportation*, pp. 599–600).

32. Forsyth, *op. cit.*, pp. 134–35, quotes some passages from these instructions. It was stated that since transportation was to be an adequate penalty for the most heinous crimes, it must be made a severe punishment and an object of real terror to all classes of the community in order to achieve the great end of punishment, the prevention of crime by deterrence. That transportation was not having this deterrent effect was shown by the fact that numerous applications came from people sentenced to imprisonment for slighter transgressions who wished to participate in transportation. This state of affairs must cease, the instructions insisted.

33. *Ibid.*, p. 135.

34. *Ibid.*, p. 150. To a large extent, Arthur himself accepted the opinion expressed in the report of the commission, as can be seen from his correspondence and from his evidence before the committee (*ibid.*, p. 137). Beaumont and de Tocqueville (*op. cit.*, pp. 242–43) were also of the opinion that the punishment of transportation intimidated nobody, that sometimes its effect was to make useful and respected colonial citizens out of individuals rejected by the mother country, but that more often men whom severe punishment would have constrained to lead a regular life in England broke the law because transportation pleased rather than frightened them, and that for many transportation meant nothing but emigration to Australia at government expense.

35. See the speech cited above, note 23; this quotation appears on p. 1285; see also Forsyth, *op. cit.*, p. 161.

36. See *ibid.*, pp. 152–53.

37. *Ibid.*, pp. 162 and 165.

38. See the description of this system in Jebb, *op. cit.*, p. 48, and L. W. Fox, *The Modern English Prison* (London, 1936), pp. 13–14.

39. Forsyth, *op. cit.*, p. 103.

40. *Ibid.*, p. 129.

41. *Ibid.*, p. 167.

42. A petition presented to Colonial Secretary Grey says, "that your petitioners

are at present suffering great inconveniences and loss from the want of labour, and as they see little or no prospect of a sufficient number of emigrants being sent to this portion of the colony, respectfully begg that the exiles holders of ticket of leave may be sent to Moreton Bay." It is quoted in Jebb, *op. cit.*, pp. 38–39; similar documents will be found, *ibid.*, pp. 42–44. The statistics appear in Forsyth, *op. cit.*, p. 99.

43. E. H. Michaud, *La Question des peines* (2d ed.; Paris, 1875), pp. 8–9. Michaud was following the remarks of Lord Mahon in the House of Commons debate of May 5, 1840 (Hansard, LIII, 1295).

44. Paultre, *op. cit.*, p. 319.

45. Decree of July 5, 1722, quoted *ibid.*, p. 324.

46. Duvival *jeune*, "Galérien," p. 445. See also G. Vidal and J. Magnol, *Cours de droit criminel et de science pénitentiaire* (8th ed.; Paris, 1935), p. 569.

47. Holtzendorff, *Deportation*, p. 560. On French opinion, see, for instance, the discussion in the *Société générale des prisons* in 1924, summarized in *Revue pénitentiarie*, XLVIII (1924), 441–63.

48. Vidal and Magnol, *op. cit.*, pp. 580–81.

49. A. Mossé, "Chronique pénitentiaire," *Revue de science criminelle et de droit pénal comparé*, II (1937), 311–14. In spite of 700 to 800 new arrivals every year, the number of convicts remained fairly stationary at 4,000 to 5,000 because of excessive death rates and escapes. Mossé adds that repatriations were extremely rare, because the liberated convicts never succeeded in saving enough money to pay for their passage home.

50. D'Haussonville, *op. cit.*, p. 490.

51. The more recent developments are discussed in H. Donnedieu de Vabres, *Traité élémentaire de droit criminel et de législation pénale comparée* (Paris, 1937), pp. 320–21.

52. Vidal and Magnol, *op. cit.*, p. 581.

53. Some of the contracts with the societies appear in M. Pain, *Colonisation pénale* (Paris, 1898), pp. 113 ff. See also L. Moncelon, *Le Bagne et la colonisation pénale en Nouvelle Calédonie* (Paris, 1886), especially pp. 182 ff., where the whole administration is severely criticized from the standpoint of the free settlers, whose interests Moncelon represented in Paris.

54. Wagnitz (*op. cit.*, II, 150–51) described the lamentable conditions of the Hamburg houses of correction, where there was often not enough space to accommodate all the candidates. In such cases, the authorities were only too glad to donate a portion of this human ballast to foreign powers to help them found new colonies. Wagnitz did not wish to see this means of emptying houses of correction and spinning houses employed too frequently.

55. For Prussia, see A. Stölzel, *Brandenburg-Preussens Rechtsverwaltung und Rechtsverfassung*, II (Berlin, 1888), 352–57. For Hamburg, see Holtzendorff, *Deportation*, pp. 708–10, who refers to a cabinet order of Feb. 28, 1801, by which deportation was provisionally introduced in Prussia as a means of dealing with "incorrigible rogues" and as a police measure against criminals who had to be removed from the country because they had become a danger to public safety, or had attempted to escape with violence, or had been such a bad example to other prisoners that the attempts to reform them were rendered useless. On the unsuccessful inquiries of Sachsen-Weimar in 1826, see Lucht, *op. cit.*, p. 111.

CHAPTER VIII

1. A New Jersey statute of Dec. 1, 1802, for example, provided that inspectors of state prisons should not allow any prisoner to be discharged until he had

paid for the whole cost of prosecution and maintenance by his labor; see Barnes, *New Jersey*, p. 63.

2. Barnes, *The Repression of Crime* (New York, 1926), p. 29.
3. E. M. Foltin, *Amerikanisches Gefängniswesen* (Reichenberg, 1930), p. 15.
4. Füsslin, *Einzelhaft*, p. 345.
5. See William Roscoe's observations on penal jurisprudence (1823) quoted in O. F. Lewis, *The Development of American Prisons and Prison Customs 1776–1845* (Albany, 1922), p. 41.
6. Barnes, *New Jersey*, p. 453.
7. F. H. Wines, *Punishment and Reformation* (new ed.; New York, 1923), p. 159.
8. A. F. Lueder, *Über Nationalindustrie und Staatwirtschaft* (Berlin, 1800–1802), I, 105, wrote that England did not pay as high a wage to her workers as did the much poorer United States.
9. Beaumont and Tocqueville, *op. cit.* (French ed.), p. 312.
10. Adam Smith, *op. cit.*, p. 359. Lueder, *Nationalindustrie*, I, 105, wrote that the demand for working hands was so great that a young widow was doubly rewarded in having four or five children, for because of them she would be quite sure of finding a second husband.
11. B. W. Bond, *The Civilization of the Old Northwest* (New York, 1934), p. 506.
12. Quoted from Beaumont and Tocqueville, *op. cit.*, p. 108.
13. *Ibid.*, p. 103.
14. *Warum werden so wenig Sträflinge . . . .* , p. 7. In this connection, it is worth quoting J. M. Baernreither, a German writer at the beginning of the twentieth century, whose remarks in his *Jugendfürsorge und Strafrecht in den vereinigten Staaten von Amerika* (Leipzig, 1905), pp. 113–14, epitomize the difference in approach between American and Continental criminologists. He wrote: "One cannot deny that the inmates of the American prisons, and especially of the reformatory prisons and of the reform schools, are better off than they would be in the corresponding institutions of our country. It would be false, however, to ascribe this fact to the sentimentality of Americans towards offenders against the law, although I will not deny that an optimistic trait in the American character does make them more disposed to leniency and that the influence of women makes itself felt in the matter. But life inside a prison must never be judged without comparison with conditions outside. Thus, when a German writer recently called it carrying humanity to absurd extremes to fit the workrooms of the reformatory prison in Huntington (Pennsylvania) with electric fans, he forgets that these fans are merely intended to enable the prisoners to continue working in the tropical heat of the American summer and that such fans are part of the standard fittings in offices, workrooms, living rooms, etc., in those American states which suffer particularly from the heat. In the matter of food, too, people in those parts of Europe where the prime necessities of life are subject to so many indirect taxes in the form of customs and excise duties and where the standard of living of the working classes suffers accordingly, are apt to forget that the whole level of nourishment in the United States, where there are no such taxes, is quite different, and that meat, vegetables, fish, and fruit form part of the regular diet of the masses, that the adequate and healthy nourishment of the people is one of the particular cares of the governmental health policy, and it is therefore natural that, if a person is in prison, but is nevertheless expected to be given his freedom again and to have to earn his living through his own efforts, he cannot have his nourishment reduced below the usual level."
15. Barnes, *New Jersey*, p. 96.
16. Barnes, *Repression*, p. 165.

17. *Ibid.*, pp. 268–69.
18. *Ibid.*, pp. 164–65.
19. E. von Jagemann, "Vereinigte Staaten von Nordamerika," in Holtzendorff-Jagemann, *op. cit.*, I, 351.
20. Barnes, *Repression*, pp. 272–73.
21. Beaumont and Tocqueville, *op. cit.*, pp. 79, 279, and 281; see also B. McCalvey, *American Prisons* (Chicago, 1936), p. 13; Lewis, *op. cit.*, p. 131.
22. See the remarks of P. Pollitz, *Strafe und Verbrechen: Geschichte und Organisation des Gefängniswesens* (Leipzig, 1910), p. 30; cf. G. Aschaffenburg, *Crime and Its Repression*, tr. by A. Albrecht (Boston, 1913), p. 284.
23. On the history of American commutation practices, see T. Sellin, "Commutation of Sentence," *Encyclopaedia of the Social Sciences*, IV, 108–9.
24. Barnes, *Repression*, pp. 273–76. Illustrations of the campaign against prison labor by industrial interests will be found in E. H. Sutherland, *Principles of Criminology* (Chicago and Philadelphia, 1934), pp. 438–42.
25. S. and E. T. Glueck, *500 Criminal Careers* (New York, 1930), pp. 20–21.
26. Ives, *op. cit.*, p. 380.
27. Beaumont and Tocqueville, *op. cit.*, p. 15.
28. "All experience in prisons goes to prove that solitary confinement is one of the severest and most efficient forms of punishment and that it satisfies the most important requirement of criminal policy in that it is felt as a real punishment," wrote Pollitz, a German prison director at the beginning of the twentieth century, *op. cit.*, p. 58. See also Wagnitz, *op. cit.*, I, 190–91.
29. Jorns, *op. cit.*, p. 194.
30. F. Lieber, *A Popular Essay on Subjects of Penal Law* . . . . (Philadelphia, 1838), p. 7.
31. Füsslin, *Einzelhaft*, pp. 346–48.
32. *Ibid.*, p. 416. Ives, *op. cit.*, p. 185, justly remarks that even John Howard, to whom many cruelties as well as reforms were undoubtedly due, had all the hardness and strength of Puritan character and that Howard seemed more shocked at the flagrant irregularities which he discovered behind prison walls than at the actual human misery which they entailed.
33. Wines, *op. cit.*, p. 162. See also the official report of 1909 on the Prussian house of correction at Rawitsch, which noted that discipline can be easily maintained in solitary confinement without the help of additional punishment; quoted in A. Starke, "Disziplin und Hausstrafen," in L. Frede and H. Grünhut, *op. cit.*, p. 171n; cf. Pollitz, *op. cit.*, p. 60.
34. Quoted from Ives, *op. cit.*, p. 195; cf. Mittelstädt, *op. cit.*, pp. 12 and 17.
35. M. Liepmann, Preface to his edition of G. M. Obermaier, *Anleitung zur vollkommenen Besserung der Verbrecher in den Strafanstalten* (Hamburg, 1925), p. 7.
36. Wagnitz, *op. cit.*, I, 306.
37. J. H. Wichern, *Zur Gefängnisreform, Gesammelte Schriften*, IV (Hamburg, 1905), 263.
38. Beaumont and Tocqueville, *op. cit.*, p. 40.
39. Quoted from Webb, *English Prisons*, p. 131. In northern Europe, the work of Oscar, Prince de Suède, *Des peines et des prisons* (Paris, 1842), paved the way for the introduction of solitary confinement. In Belgium, as in other European countries, the cellular system was voted by parliament but its introduction was delayed by financial considerations until the last third of the century; see Bertrand, *op. cit.*, pp. 86 ff.
40. Webb, *ibid.*, p. 189, quoting Ruggles-Brise.
41. Ives, *op. cit.*, p. 181.
42. Michaud, *op. cit.*, p. 7, passes the following judgment on the treadmill:

"Véritable torture qui fait de l'homme le moteur, inutile d'une machine absente, un cheval en manège sans manège, système inventé pour concilier les exigences de la répression avec les prétendus intérêts de l'industrie libre, atrocité sortie d'une grosse bêtise économique et qui ait des effets aussi déplorables que le système cellulaire le plus rigoureux."

43. Webb, *English Prisons*, p. 151.
44. The report is found in *Application du régime d'emprisonnement individuelle* (Paris, 1888), p. 101. J. Jaeger, *Rechtsbruch und Rechtsausgleich in der Strafjustiz* (Leipzig, 1907), p. 201, cites the report of a prison chaplain about the impure air in the cells, which the inmates could clear only by giving up the already insufficient amount of heat. A report of July 29, 1850, printed with Jebb, *op. cit.*, p. 22, ruled that no more heat should be provided than was absolutely necessary for health.
45. Füsslin, *Einzelhaft*, pp. 237–38.
46. Webb, *English Prisons*, p. 184n.
47. Beaumont and Tocqueville, *op. cit.*, p. 40.
48. Dickens, *American Notes* (Scribner's ed.; New York, 1926), pp. 305–6; cf. pp. 316–17. His protest was a powerful argument in the hands of the opponents of the Pennsylvania system and provoked a heated discussion; see J. Adshead, *Prisons and Prisoners* (London, 1845), p. 119; Sutherland, *op. cit.*, p. 384.
49. See Mittelstädt, *op. cit.*, pp. 30–31, who partially acknowledges the real state of affairs. Whether complete isolation for a long period of time has a good or a harmful effect, he wrote, depends on the psychology of the person who is thrown completely on his own. Where mind and spirit take a certain measure of intelligence, feeling, and ethical culture into solitude with them, however much they may have been crowded out and choked by vice and crime, the individual has all that is needed to take himself in hand and a sufficient reason for meditation. Where these are lacking, however, the individual is faced with a barren void.

CHAPTER IX

1. See the remarks of Kulischer, *op. cit.*, II, 426.
2. Clapham, *op. cit.*, II, 285, 461, and 464.
3. Sée, *op. cit.*, II, 508.
4. Pike, *op. cit.*, II, 387.
5. E. Worms, *Les Rapports du droit pénal avec l'économie politique* (Paris, 1870), p. 19.
6. Exner, *op. cit.*, p. 24. It must be remembered that the second quarter of the nineteenth century was the flourishing period of so-called *Kathedersozialismus*, and the period when social insurance legislation was first introduced.
7. E. Ferri, *Criminal Sociology*, tr. by J. I. Kelly and John Lisle (Boston, 1917), pp. 566–69.
8. A. Prins, *Criminalité et repression* (Brussels, 1886), pp. 86–87.
9. F. von Liszt, *Strafrechtliche Aufsätze und Vorträge*, II (Berlin, 1905), 3.
10. Prins, *op. cit.*, p. 113.
11. Hall, *op. cit.*, pp. 184 and 192.
12. A brilliant sketch of this struggle and its economic background is to be found in E. Kehr, "Genesis der preussischen Bürokratie und des Rechtsstaats," *Die Gesellschaft*, IX (1932), 101–19. The detailed exposition in A. Wagner, *Der Kampf der Justiz gegen die Verwaltung in Preussen* (Hamburg, 1936), completely misrepresents the underlying principles of this struggle. In reviewing the book in the *Zeitschrift für die gesamte Staatswissenschaft*, XCVII (1937),

p. 370, E. R. Huber says: "Administrative justice is an institution which supports the integrity of administrative practice. By its very nature it has nothing to do with the protection of the subjective rights of individuals against the state." This approach is sociologically and historically false, for "nature" has no meaning in this context.

13. Most of the existing rules make free legal aid accessible only in special cases, such as aggravated cases of recidivism and cases coming under the jurisdiction of jury courts. In the vast majority of cases, no legal aid is available to poor defendants and therefore no effective defense. For Germany, see the restrictive terms of paragraph 140 of the Code of Criminal Procedure. For France, see R. Garraud, *Traité d'instruction criminelle*, VI (Paris, 1929), 131.

   Conditions in England are quite similar despite the Poor Prisoner's Defense Act which theoretically renders free defense possible to some extent; see the remarks of Solicitor, *English Justice* (London, 1935), p. 214, and his criticism based on 1935 statistics in *The New Statesman and Nation*, XIV (1937), 828–29. According to the *Criminal Statistics, England and Wales 1934*, p. 150, a total of 237 legal aid certificates were granted in courts of summary jurisdiction in 1934, that is, in 1.1 percent of all cases where indictable offenses were involved.

14. In England the consumption of the state of martial law as a purely factual situation makes the creation of special courts by means of special laws or emergency decrees unnecessary; see E. C. S. Wade and C. G. Phillips, *Constitutional Law* (rev. ed.; London and New York, 1933), pp. 335–39.

15. R. Schmidt, *Aufgaben*, p. 265.

16. See, for example, J. Vargha, *Die Abschaffung der Strafknechtschaft*, II (Graz, 1897), especially pp. 460 and 572.

17. Liszt, *Aufsätze*, II, 171.

18. This is the point on which T. Herbette, Inspector General of the French Prison Administration, insists in the *Bulletin de l'administration pénitentiaire* (Mélun, 1886), p. 16.

19. Prins, *op. cit.*, p. 43.

20. S. Glueck, *Crime and Justice* (Boston, 1936), p. 226; Hentig, *op. cit.*, p. 238.

21. R. Schmidt, *Strafrechtsreform*, pp. 205–12; cf. Dannenberg, *op. cit.*, pp. 5–6. Radbruch later gave up this position in the 1932 edition of his *Rechtsphilosophie*, p. 161n. It is characteristic that one of the chief National Socialist attacks against the social-liberal school of Liszt is directed against the principle that the arbitrary discretion of the judge in the selection of preventive measures goes hand in hand with the strict adherence of the judge to the law in ascertaining guilt; see H. Henkel, *Strafrecht und Gesetz im neuen Staat* (Hamburg, 1934), p. 32. On the connection between the positivist reform school and recent German penal theory, see Hall, *op. cit.*, p. 189.

22. Cf. F. Exner, *Studien über die Strafzumessungspraxis deutscher Gerichte* (Leipzig, 1931), pp. 23–27.

23. R. Rabl, *Strafzumessungspraxis und Kriminalitätsbewegung* (Leipzig, 1936), *passim*.

24. Compiled on the basis of the terms of imprisonment and fines inflicted by the *pretori tribunali* and *corti d'assise* (exclusive of arrest and *ammenda*). The statistics in the *Statistica della criminalità* cannot be used because the terms of imprisonment are not differentiated according to length, but according to the type of institution to which the prisoner is sent, and secondly, because the last volume, which appeared in 1935, refers to 1928.

25. We have chosen the figures for larcenies reported to the police rather than the number of convictions because the amnesty policy of the last few years renders the latter figures useless for our purpose.

26. Webb, *English Prisons*, pp. 208–10.

27. Hölscher, for example, wrote in *Strafvollzug in Preussen*, ed. by Preussischen Justizministerium (Berlin, 1928), p. 1: "The prisoner is convicted, the judge has sentenced him to prison, the accused will be placed behind locked doors. What will be attained there? We can accept but one answer to this question: education and reform. The first and foremost guiding principle is not that the infringed right shall be expiated, not that vengeance shall be exacted, but that reform and a change of spirit shall be attained. This reform shall be brought about, not by intimidation and iron discipline that breaks the spirit, but by education."

28. *Protokoll über die Verhandlungen des Parteitages der sozialdemokratischen Partei Deutschlands, abgehalten zu Mannheim vom 23. bis 29. September 1906* (Berlin, 1906), p. 376.

29. Ferri, *op. cit.*, p. 241. See also G. Boimeron, *Les Prisons de Paris* (Paris, 1898), p. 52, whose investigation of Paris prison conditions in 1891 led him to the same conclusion. The fact that his formulation of the problem coincides with Béranger's (1836) shows that the problem has remained the same despite the somewhat changed social conditions.

30. This is particularly clear for France, where the rate of crime among foreigners is double the rate among the native population even when we exclude such offenses as passport violations and violations of expulsion orders; see O. Kirchheimer, "Remarques sur la statistique criminelle de la France d'après guerre," *Revue de science criminelle et de droit pénal comparé*, I (1936), 377–78; E. Hacker, "Statistique comparée de la criminalité," *Revue internationale de droit pénal*, XIII (1936), 305–49, especially the table on p. 329. It is well known that the presence of a large number of aliens, a population without reserves and with uncertain opportunities of finding employment, is a factor in increasing crime; see L. Belym, "Un Projet de réforme pénitentiaire," *Revue de droit pénal et de criminologie*, XVII (1937), 249.

31. Fox, *Modern English Prison*, p. 89.

32. Polenz, "Gefängnisarbeit," *Strafvollzug*, p. 218; cf. the special chapter on this subject in A. Mossé, *Variétés pénitentiaires* (Melun, 1932).

33. The question was raised in the Reichstag in June, 1925: "What does the government of the Reich intend to do to protect trade and industry from the unfair competition of prison labor?" Lubert in *Strafvollzug*, p. 230; see also A. Starke, "Die Behandlung der Gefangenen," in Bumke, *op. cit.*, p. 160; Fox, *op. cit.*, p. 90.

34. Note the enthusiastic account of prison farm labor by Wutzdorff in the official Prussian work, *Strafvollzug*, pp. 239–40: "It is impossible not to give the prisoners more freedom of movement outside than within a prison. There will always be a carefully chosen group of prisoners who are sent to do work outside, especially when one takes into consideration that to be allowed to work outside is itself a concession within the system of punishments, so that the greater number, if not all the prisoners, who are working outside belong to the second or third stage. Consequently, they can be regarded as reliable, and it can be assumed that they will think twice before they run the risk of being put back into the first stage, that is to say, into the very strictest confinement for having run away or for having attempted to do so."

35. Fox, *op. cit.*, p. 91, on recent developments.

36. Mossé, *Les Prisons* (2d ed.; Paris, 1929), p. 140; D'Haussonville, *op. cit.*, p. 315. But even where the convicts are largely dependent upon the official food supply, as in England, the maxim is retained that the food is not de-

signed to do more than maintain the prisoner in health. English prison descriptions show that much food which is intended for the prisoners fails to reach them because of one manipulation or another; see Fox, *op. cit.*, p. 114, and the unofficial but much more vivid description in W. F. R. Macartney, *Walls Have Mouths* (London, 1936), pp. 122–37. H. Fischer, a German medical observer, writing in an official report which naturally seeks to emphasize the better side of the prison system, comments on the monotonous character of prison fare and on the disproportion between quantity and quality; "Gesundheitsfürsorge in den Gefangenenanstalten," in Bumke, *op. cit.*, pp. 220–23.

37. See W. Gentz, "Das Sexualproblem im Strafvollzug," *Zeitschrift für die gesamte Strafrechtswissenschaft*, L (1930), 406–27, especially p. 408, where the principle is laid down that penal institutions must always conform to the mores accepted by the society in which they are established and for which they exist. On the treatment of the sex problem in Soviet prisons, see Lenka von Koerber, *Soviet Russia Fights Crime* (New York, 1935), pp. 154–55, 180–81. On the consequences of enforced abstinence and on the sex practices current in prisons, see the instructive chapter in Macartney, *op. cit.*, pp. 418–26.

38. Hygienic conditions in the cells are often poor today despite all the new and remodeled prisons, especially insofar as the possibilities of moving around, air, and sunshine are concerned; see Gentz, "Die praktische Ausgestaltung des Strafvollzuges," in Frede and Grünhut, *op. cit.*, p. 70; Fischer, *op. cit.*, pp. 205, 224–31.

39. In smaller prisons, the problem is partly an organizational one, because they frequently hire outside doctors for a small fee. This is a most unsatisfactory method from the standpoint of adequacy of treatment and of time available. Even where the prison has a staff doctor, however, an extensive medical system is faced with great difficulties. Suspicion of malingering is ever present. See the discussion of the whole problem by F. Brucks, "Die innere Organisation der Gefangenenanstalten in Deutschland," in Bumke, *op. cit.*, pp. 113–15; Gehrman and Kuttner, "Parlament und Strafvollzug," *Strafvollzug*, pp. 34–35.

40. See the characteristic comment of R. Gutfleisch, *Strafvollzug und Erziehung* (Freiburg, 1926), p. 53: "Games should not be allowed in the exercise-yard of a prison as they are incompatible with the seriousness of the prison regime and with the position of the prisoners as unfree agents. It is possible that such arrangements might have the effect of arousing healthy ambition and of being sources of enjoyment which would spur the prisoner on to training and self-denial, and the prisoner should be content with .the enjoyment that every bodily and mental effort gives him."

Athletics are not allowed in French prisons, and occasional fire drills are seriously proposed as an adequate substitute; see Mossé, *Prisons*, p. 317. In England, prison exercise is modeled after the system used in the army; see Fox, *op. cit.*, pp. 113–14, who hastens to add that "organised games form no part of the system at the ordinary local or convict prison." Ferri, the dean of the modern reform school, rejected athletics because they were practice sessions for future attempts to escape; see his report on the London congress in *Revue internationale de droit pénal*, III (1926), 60–61.

41. Ferri, *Criminal Sociology*, pp. 540–42, for example, condemned solitary confinement as one of the greatest mistakes of the nineteenth century; cf. Ives, *op. cit.*, p. 181. For an intermediate position, see the recent treatise of Donnedieu de Vabres, *op. cit.*, pp. 357–61.

42. A noteworthy system prevails in France. The law of June 5, 1875, gave con-

victs free choice of solitary confinement, whereby they could reduce their terms by one-quarter. An exception was made in the case of prisoners condemned for anarchistic activities. Mossé, *Prisons*, p. 215, considers this automatic remission system to be an "élement solide de comfort moral." Most states today have only a compulsory period of solitary confinement at the beginning of the sentence.

43. L. Belym, "L'État actuel du système pénitentiaire dans l'Europe," *Revue de droit pénal et de criminologie*, XIII (1936), 1085.

44. Fox, *op. cit.*, p. 78.

45. See the *Actes du congrès pénal et pénitentiaire international*, Vol. Ib (Berne, 1936), 85–86. The resolutions of the Congress consider the fundamental difference between punishment and measures of security to lie in the "diversity of conception" rather than in the "difference of application." "On close study," says the official commentary, "it is found difficult to make a definite and clear theoretical distinction. But it is still more difficult to establish in practice, that is to say, during the period of execution, the proper characteristics for differentiating between the two forms of detention." The differences proposed are limited to minor favors like differences in dress and reading matter, additional monetary wage, use of tobacco, etc.

46. Macartney, *op. cit.*, p. 73.

47. A comparison of the French and English statistics on prison discipline shows that a technically well-developed stage system helps maintain adequate discipline. In England, with its system of automatic reductions of sentence, 15.3 percent of the males in convict prisons were subjected to disciplinary measures in 1932. In France, however, 94 percent of all male convicts were disciplined in 1932, and this can be easily understood in the light of the fact that only 6.87 percent received pardons or remissions of sentence. See the *Report of the Commissioners of Prisons and the Directors of Convict Prisons for the year 1935* (London, 1937), p. 30, and *Statistique pénitentiaire pour l'année 1932* (Melun, 1934), p. 24.

48. The official German reform literature of the post-war years is filled with eulogies of the warden, revealing a complete failure to understand the character of bureaucratic administrators; see, for example, Brucks, *op. cit.*, pp. 103–5. Fox, *op. cit.*, p. 54, shows greater clarity in his more or less official account of the English system. He emphasizes the "decisive role of the governor" and speaks of a "combination of administrative, educational, and social qualifications."

49. Pollitz, *op. cit.*, p. 54, says: "His duty does not go beyond maintaining order and discipline and seeing that the prisoners do their work, and this he must do in a tactful, earnest, and cultured way according to the regulations. Enough men of the right type can be found for this limited task among former noncommissioned officers. It is not to be expected that guards, most of whom are not particularly well educated, will have an educational, reformatory, or religious influence, nor is this to be desired."

50. Schulze, "Der Strafanstaltsbeamte," *Strafvollzug*, p. 153: "With the greatest zeal and consciousness of their calling, prison officials now put up a battle for the soul of the prisoner."

51. T. Sellin, "Penal Institutions," *Encyclopaedia of the Social Sciences*, XII (New York, 1934), 63.

52. See the discussion in G. F. Falchi, *Diritto penale esecutivo*, II (Padua, 1935), 41–52; cf. F. Wolff, *Strafvollzug und Rechtsstaat* (Breslau-Neukirch, 1933), p. 16.

53. See the interesting correspondence of the prison commissioners with Fenner Brockway and Stephen Hobhouse over the refusal of the former to provide a

copy of their standing orders; published in Hobhouse and Brockway, *English Prisons Today* (London, 1922), pp. VI–VIII.

54. Fox, *op. cit.*, p. 121.
55. Fox, *ibid.*, p. 122, is incomplete, to put it mildly, when he neglects to mention the possibility of punishment for complaints. See the more complete picture in Macartney, *op. cit.*, p. 180, further supported by the anonymous author of the very recent *Five Years for Fraud* (London, n.d.), p. 19. See also Gentz in Frede and Grünhut, *op. cit.*, pp. 94–95.
56. The story of the ex-convict is brilliantly told in Hans Fallada's novel, *Wer einmal aus dem Blechnapf ass*, tr. by Eric Sutton as *The World Outside* (New York, 1934).
57. Muntau, "Entlassenenfürsorge," *Strafvollzug*, p. 279.
58. See C. Rollmann, "Keep Your Convicts," *The Forum*, XCVII (1937), 102–5.
59. Bertrand, *op. cit.*, p. 635.
60. The questionnaire published by J. A. Roux under the title, "La Crise de la libération," in *Revue internationale de droit pénal et de criminologie*, VII/VIII (1930), 15–125, does not fully bring out the inadequacy of the work of prison societies. The following table, compiled from the French *Statistique pénitentiaire* for the years 1922 and 1932, gives a much truer picture.

Plans of Convicts at Time of Release

	1922		1932	
PROSPECT	MALE	FEMALE	MALE	FEMALE
Seem to have funds	110	86	140	9
Have jobs	777	66	320	73
Without jobs	555	272	991	100
Unable to work	25	3	18	6
Turned over to an aid society	*49*	*8*	*89*	—
Deported (aliens)	368	10	335	17
Enlisted in the army	1121	—	333	—
Sent to hospitals	117	—	12	3

These figures immediately reveal the crying disproportion between the number of ex-convicts without prospects for the future and the number taken over by the prison societies. The army was far more important, even after the law of April 3, 1928, which limited the opportunity for ex-convicts to enlist. It should also be noted that ex-convicts who chose the army were put into a special battalion in Algeria, obviously not a desirable environment for them. See in general P. Mercier, "L'Initiative privée, le patronage des condamnés et des mineurs délinquants dans ses rapports avec la législation pénale," *Bulletin de la société générale des prisons*, LVI (1932), 576–98.

Italian official sources boast of the fact that the *cassa di ammenda* spent 606,900 lire in 1935–36 for the support of 13,000 families of prisoners and 11,500 ex-convicts, but these woefully inadequate sums are really nothing to boast about. See the report of Carapelle in the chamber of deputies, reprinted under the title, "Il bilancio del Ministero di Grazia e Giustizia per l'esercizio 1937/38," *Rivista di diritto penitenziario* (1937), 502.

61. G. H. Dession, "Psychiatry and Criminal Justice," *Yale Law Journal*, XLVII (1938), 339; see also the conclusions of F. Tannenbaum, *Crime and the Community* (New York, 1937), p. 475.
62. F. Exner, *Krieg und Kriminalität in Oesterreich* (Wien, 1927); M. Liepmann, *Krieg und Kriminalität in Deutschland* (Berlin, 1930); see also the

bibliography in *Statistik des deutschen Reiches,* CDLXXVIII, *Kriminalstatistik für das Jahr 1933* (Berlin, 1936), 383–84.
63. A similar development took place in England; see *Criminal Statistics, England and Wales 1918,* p. 7.
64. See F. von Liszt, "Strafrechtliche Vorgänge," *Zeitschrift für die gesamte Strafrechtswissenschaft,* XXXVIII (1916), 343–57.
65. Figures taken from the annual *Statistique pénitentiaire.*
66. *Report of the Prison Commissioners . . . . 1919,* p. 24.
67. Quoted by Braune in the *Zeitschrift für die gesamte Strafrechtswissenschaft,* XXXVIII (1916), 168.
68. Figures taken from the *Concise Statistical Year Book of Poland 1936* and from the *Informations statistiques 1932,* Vol. IV, *Statistique judiciaire, pénitentiaire et criminelle.*
69. Figures taken from the *Annuaire statistique hongrois.*
70. Figures taken from the *Annuaire statistique du Royaume de Bulgarie* and from the *Statistique criminelle.*
71. See the condemnation of French prison conditions by the conservative Bertrand, *op. cit.,* pp. 172–73. As for the reformatories, the best picture of the methods still being pursued today is not to be found in the scattered newspaper and periodical articles, but in the second volume of Roger Martin du Gard's *Les Thibaults,* entitled *Le Pénitencier,* tr. by S. H. Guest as *The Reformatory* (London, 1933).
72. See below, p. 170.
73. *Concise Statistical Year Book of Poland 1936.*
74. The best available information on the actual prison conditions in Eastern Europe will be found in the travel report, "Howard League Expedition to Eastern Europe," *Howard Journal,* V (1938), 8–47. This report covers Hungary, Bulgaria, Yugoslavia, Rumania, and Greece. It would have been still more impressive if the authors had had the opportunity to devote more time to a study of typical prisons and less time to the more advanced institutions.

CHAPTER X

1. Statistics on the use of fines for specific crimes in England, France, and Italy are given below, pp. 172 and 193–205.
2. Beccaria, *op. cit.,* p. 87.
3. Petty, *op. cit.,* I, 68–69, was careful enough to restrict its application to "solvent" criminals.
4. Bentham, *op. cit.,* pp. 194 and 191.
5. Montesquieu, *Esprit des lois,* Book VI, Chap. XVIII.
6. *Allgemeines Landrecht,* Part II, Title 20, paragraph 85: "Fines shall not be levied against impoverished persons of the lower classes, and where they are provided by law, they shall be commuted into a comparable term in prison." Paragraph 88: "A 5 Thaler fine will ordinarily be considered equal to 8 days in prison." Paragraph 89: "The judge may, however, according to the special economic condition of the delinquent, raise it to 10–40 Thaler for 8 days in prison."
7. See the criticism of the revolutionary legislation in Chauveau and Hélie, *op. cit.,* I, 240–42; see also W. Seagle, "Fines," *Encyclopaedia of the Social Sciences,* VI (New York, 1931), 250.
8. E. Henke, *Handbuch des Criminalrechts und der Criminalpolitik* (Berlin and Stettin, 1823–38), I, 482–88.

9. M. A. Bonneville, *Des pénalités pécuniaires au double point de vue de la répression des méfaits et du soulagement des classes indigentes* (Versailles, 1847), pp. 8 and 15.

10. Ihering, *op. cit.*, I, 375–76.

11. See, for example, the characteristic argument of Michaud, *op. cit.*, pp. 182 and 224.

12. Fox, *Modern English Prison*, p. 199.

13. One of the most recent criminal codes, the Italian of 1930, which is allegedly not a product of the capitalist spirit, retains in Article 136 the notion of reconversion in all its nakedness when referring to the fortunate finder of cash: "The condemned man can always end the substitute punishment of imprisonment if he pays the fine; a deduction will be made corresponding to the length of the term already served."

14. Bonneville, *op. cit.*, pp. 13–14, considers it to be one of the most positive achievements of the system of *contrainte de corps* that it is only a matter of imprisonment for debt, and has nothing whatsoever to do with penal imprisonment either in theory or practice.

15. Most recently E. Neymark, "La Peine d'amende," *Revue de droit pénal et de criminologie* (1928), 1070–71.

16. See the instructive debate in *Recueil général des lois et arrêts* (Sirey), LXVII (Paris, 1867), 169n.

17. This official commentary on the statute will be found in M. Heuman's report on Sweden in the *Zeitschrift für die gesamte Strafrechtswissenschaft*, LVII (1938), 549–51. See also Article 49, 3, of the new Swiss penal code of December 21, 1937 (to go into effect on January 1, 1942), which is conceived along the same lines as the Swedish statute. It provides, at least in theory, that there shall be no commutation if the offender proves that "he is unable to pay the fine through no fault of his own."

18. *Report of the Commissioners of Prisons . . . . 1935*, p. 8. The tendency to reduce the number of imprisonments in default of fines goes back to the Criminal Justice Administration Act of 1914 (4 & 5 Geo. 5, c. 58).

YEAR	NUMBER OF IMPRISONMENTS IN DEFAULT OF FINES
Average, 1909–13	83,187
Average, 1928–30	13,433
1931	11,543
1932	11,244
1933	11,615
1934	11,128
1935	10,542

Source: *Report of the Commissioners of Prisons . . . . 1935*, p. 9.

A similar tendency is noticeable in France in the declining percentage of of fines for which *contrainte de corps* was applied:

YEAR	PERCENT	YEAR	PERCENT
1900	6.5	1924	1.5
1905	5.0	1927	1.8
1912	4.8	1930	1.8
1913	3.7	1931	1.5
1921	1.8	1932	1.5

Source: Compiled from the *Compte général. . . .*

19. A similar relationship between imprisonment in default of fines and market conditions cannot be established for France and England because the present tendency in both countries is to keep such commutations to a minimum.

20. *Criminal Statistics, England and Wales 1928*, p. 66; *1934*, p. 66.

21. *Kriminalstatistik für das Jahr 1933*, p. 182. Under the National Socialist regime, conditions have become still worse. A report of the *Gewerbeaufsichtsamt*, cited in *Soziale Praxis* (1938), p. 241, notes the widespread practice of evading legal prosecution for violations of labor laws by voluntary contributions to charity organizations.

22. Marx, *Capital*, I, 267.

23. Figures taken from the *Statistique criminelle*.

24. *Criminal Statistics, England and Wales 1928*, pp. 67 and 68; *1934*, p. 66. On the infliction of fines upon prostitutes in England, see I. Jennings, "The Criminal Statistics 1935," *Howard Journal*, V (1938), 11–12.

25. For this reason, fines are rarely levied against prostitutes in American cities; see Sutherland, *op. cit.*, p. 536. The tendency against fines is stronger in France, too, where regulation of prostitution is strictly an administrative affair (apart from Alsace-Lorraine).

26. Hentig, *op. cit.*, pp. 224–25, has recently taken a stand against considering the fine as a "purely fiscal receipt," and he has advocated its use as a compensation for damages. That would lead far beyond the process of commercialization, however, and would make the state a free collection agency to a much greater degree than at present, when it performs this function largely through the threat of punishment inherent in the legal system.

27. See the remarks of Solicitor, *English Justice*, p. 222.

28. See, for example, Article 28, b, 1, of the *Reichsstrafgesetzbuch*, and, most recently, Article 49, 1, of the new Swiss code already mentioned.

CHAPTER XI

1. *Criminal Statistics, England and Wales 1928* (London, 1930), p. LXII.

2. W. Dziembowski, "Rückblick—Ausblick am Jahresanfang 1932," *Der Strafvollzug*, XXII (1932), 3–4.

3. H. Finke, *Der Rechtsbrecher im Lichte der Erziehung* (Weimar, 1931), p. 49. Cf. Eberhard Schmidt, *Strafrechtsreform und Kulturkrise* (Tübingen, 1931), p. 19: "Many of the postulates of German reform policy are in grave danger of sinking to the level of cheap and hackneyed slogans, the true meaning of which is lost. The reformer's ideals, which should be the foundation of all the preventive measures of the stage system, stand in such peril. It has correctly been pointed out that, whereas frequent use is made of educational terminology in laws and regulations as well as in newspaper articles and literary works, no actual educational or reformative penal administration is created in this manner."

4. Although such complaints were less frequent before 1933, we have expressions like the following from W. Sauer, *Kriminalsoziologie* (Berlin and Leipzig, 1933), p. 169: "When the people continually hear with regard to the modern penal system that a professional felon, a confidence man, a usurer, a gambler, a fence, a dishonest trustee, a blackmailer, is well fed, entertained with music and radio, receives free vocational training, is made happy with health baths, summer vacations, and free dental service, then the worse elements of the population are stimulated to crime while the better elements lose whatever faith they have left in the state, whatever hope they have left in a just and comprehensive administration of justice—until finally they, too, become enervated and fall victim to the first criminal breeze." After the political change

in 1933, the "Weimar prison paradise" became one of the favorite items in the new ideology, endlessly repeated in books, periodicals, and newspapers.

5. See E. R. Huber, *Verfassung* (Hamburg, 1937), pp. 253–56.

6. For a further discussion of this whole problem, see F. Neumann, "Der Funktionswandel des Gesetzes im Recht der bürgerlichen Gesellschaft," *Zeitschrift für Sozialforschung*, VI (1937), 542–96. On the breakdown of the separation between law and morality, see the characteristic statement of R. Freisler, "Gedanken zur Technik des werdenden Strafrechts," *Zeitschrift für die gesamte Strafrechtswissenschaft*, LV (1936), 510: "The replacement of the previous formalistic principle of justice by the principle of material justice rests on a recognition of the fact that law is rooted in morality and cannot exist apart from this root, and that the administration of criminal law must not only retain this connection, but must strengthen it. This new principle is protected by creating the possibility of deriving law immediately from the racial conscience (*Volksgewissen*) . . . ."

7. Article 2 of the German penal code now reads: "Punishment is meted out if an act is committed which the law declares to be punishable, or which deserves punishment according to the basic idea of a penal statute or according to the healthy national sentiment." Article 266, 2, now reads: "Imprisonment is replaced by *Zuchthaus* up to ten years in particularly severe cases. A case is particularly severe especially if the act damages the welfare of the people . . . ."

8. Freisler, "Zur Stellung des Verteidigers im neuen Strafverfahren," *Deutsches Strafrecht*, IV (1937), 125.

9. This is the formulation of Carl Schmitt, *Über die drei Arten des rechtswissenschaftlichen Denkens* (Hamburg, 1934), p. 60.

10. The phenomenological approach has been taken over in order to get away from too precise a conceptual formulation. That is supposed to permit one to get at the essence of a criminal act, not identical with statutory definitions; see G. Dahm and F. Schaffstein, *Methode und System des neuen Strafrechts* (Berlin, 1937). There has been violent opposition to this complete decomposition of criminal law, however; see, for example, E. Schwinge and L. Zimmerl, *Wesensschau und konkretes Ordnungsdenken im Strafrecht* (Bonn, 1937); and the article of E. Mezger in *Zeitschrift der Akademie für deutsches Recht*, IV (1937), 417–21, with the same title. Regardless of their methodologies, however, both camps lay the same emphasis on material justice at the expense of legal security, the wish-dream of the political philosophies of monopoly capitalism; see Schwinge and Zimmerl, *op. cit.*, p. 58; Dahm and Schaffstein, *op. cit.*, p. 281.

11. Hall, *op. cit.*, pp. 186–87.

12. See F. Antolisei, "Per un' indirizzo realistico nella scienza del diritto penale," *Rivista italiana di diritto penale*, IX (1937), 164.

13. *Ibid.*, pp. 135 and 163.

14. G. Bettiol, "La regola in dubio pro reo nel diritto e nel processo penale," *Rivista italiana di diritto penale*, IX (1937), 243.

15. Rietzsch, "Abnahme der Strafen—Zunahme der Verbrechen," *Deutsche Justiz*, XCV (1933), 397.

16. Horkheimer, *op. cit.*, pp. 222–24.

17. See, for example, G. Dahm and F. Schaffstein, *Liberales oder autoritäres Strafrecht* (Hamburg, 1933): "The state uses punishment to show its power to all the world. The dignity of the state is symbolically revealed in punishment; the death penalty in particular shows in a most impressive way that the individual may be sacrificed for the welfare of the state." E. Kempermann,

"Grundzüge eines ständischen Strafrechts," *Zeitschrift für die gesamte Straf-rechtswissenschaft*, LVI (1937), 10, says even more characteristically: "We are conscious of the fact that nothing much can be accomplished with human purposes in criminal law, and that the furthering of the main purpose of punishment, the eradication of crime, only occurs, as if of itself, when we are true to the irrational, metaphysical meaning of punishment."

18. K. Daluege, "Verbrecherbekämpfung gestern und heute," *Hakenkreuzbanner Mannheim* for November 5, 1936.

19. E. Siefert, *Neupreussischer Strafvollzug: Politisierung und Verfall* (Halle, 1933), pp. 10–17, gives a vivid picture of the new attitude: "The contract con-cluded between the criminal classes and the state, guarantee of mutual good behavior, is Marxist. The disregard for the principles of command and dis-obedience is also Marxist; also the pacifist, defeatist attitude towards the offender, who is considered as the victim of a general social guilt; the exag-gerated humanitarianism towards him; the ice-cold indifference towards his wretched victims, robbed, shamed, murdered, their claim for retaliation mocked and denounced as a moral anomaly; the godlessness and hatred of natural, simple sentiment; the barren emphasis on the intellectual and ma-terial, which finds its primitive, unmistakable expression in the cunningly at-tractive bait of the stage system. All this is Marxist without exception. . . . . Today, happily, the greater part of the prisoners follow their ordered discipline without making any obvious difficulties, and only a few are so reckless as to abuse every weakness in the system. . . . . This semi-anarchic state of affairs can find no cure from within. Instead, it is necessary to turn back the whole wheel of development. . . . . Respect, order, and discipline above all must be restored." See, in the same sense, H. Frank, "Der Sinn der Strafe," *Blätter für Gefängniskunde*, LXVI (1935), 191–92: "The National Socialist state, as an authoritarian leader state, is determined with all its power to maintain the state of war, which the criminal world seeks to force upon the upright and moral portion of a people, until the criminal world has been extirpated."

20. Capital punishment was reintroduced into Italy by the penal code of 1930, but it has been used much more sparingly than in Germany. According to the *Annuario statistico*, 10 people were executed in 1933, 9 in 1934, and 18 in 1935.

21. E. Wolf, "Das künftige Strafsystem und die Zumessungsgründe," *Zeitschrift für die gesamte Strafrechtswissenschaft*, LIV (1935), 546–47.

22. E. Wolf, *op. cit.*, p. 553. Kempermann, *op. cit.*, p. 10, considers beggary, vaga-bondage, and evasion of compulsory labor service to be significant violations leading to the destruction of a specifically estate (*ständische*) disposition. They are estate felonies. "They reveal a lack of estate ethos, a lack of a sense of honor, so that they must be considered as a departure from the idea of estate tasks, as treason against the idea of the estate office, and therefore, as treason against the idea and reality of estate in general." This mental operation is in such striking contradiction to the unchanged repressive function of punishment in existing society, however, that it cannot be carried through even in theory; see the warning of Freisler against excessive application of the concept of felony, "Der Treuegedanke im deutschen Strafrecht," *Deutsches Strafrecht*, III (1936), 193–209.

23. On the *Gerichtshilfe* before 1933, see F. Hartung, "Sociale Gerichtshilfe," *Zeit-schrift für die gesamte Strafrechtswissenschaft*, L (1930), 208–30; W. Gentz, "Aufgaben und Aufbau der Gerichtshilfe," *ibid.*, 235–47.

24. The Committee's conclusions were published in *Gerichtssaal*, CIX (1937), 191.

25. See the discussion in *Ermittlungshilfe und Straffälligenbetreuung*, ed. by R. Freisler (Berlin, 1937), and especially the article by Freisler, "Sinn und

Wesen einer Ermittlungshilfe für Staatsanwalt und Gericht," pp. 9–22, whose ideas were closely followed in the decree of October 7, 1937. The text of the decree was published in *Deutsche Justiz*, XCIX (1937), 1564–69.

26. See E. Mezger, *Kriminalpolitik* (München, 1934), p. 174.

27. K. Siegert, "Der Einfluss der Strafzwecke auf Schuld und Strafmass," *Zeitschrift für die gesamte Strafrechtswissenschaft*, LIV (1935), 431, repeated in his *Grundzüge des Strafrechts im neuen Staate* (Tübingen, 1934), 48–49. F. Schaffstein speaks of the "questionable average standard" in his *Politische Strafrechtswissenschaft* (Hamburg, 1934), p. 21. Older hands are more conservative in this respect and cling to the tested "notions of the average type of citizen"; see E. Schaefer in *Das kommende deutsche Strafrecht*, Allgemeiner Teil, *Bericht über die Arbeit der amtlichen Strafrechtskommission*, ed. by F. Gürtner (2d ed.; Berlin, 1935), p. 50.

28. Siegert, "Einfluss der Strafzwecke," p. 431.

29. In his review of Rabl's *Strafzumessungspraxis* in the *Monatschrift für Kriminalpsychologie*, XXVIII (1937), 253–54, K. Lehmann naïvely admits that it is not ideology but the social conditions which are responsible for the avoidance of too close an examination into the social basis of crime.

30. In Italy, amnesties were proclaimed by royal decrees No. 1403, November 5, 1932, and No. 77, February 15, 1937. Paragraph 1 of the 1932 decree orders full amnesty for all first offenders sentenced to less than five years in prison, and paragraph 2 orders a corresponding reduction of more severe sentences. The second decree provides for full amnesty under three years. On its application, see F. P. Frisoli, "Considerazioni sulla recente amnestia," *Rivista italiana di diritto penale*, IX (1937), 29–50. The motive for these decrees is not to be sought in the extraordinary strength of the *Italia di Vittorio Veneto*, as the preamble to the 1932 decree states, but in the hopelessness of any real struggle against mass criminality in a period of crisis.

In Germany, besides the pre-Hitler amnesty law of December 20, 1932 (*RG. Bl.* I, 559), there are the following laws, which are apparently becoming a regularly recurrent affair: March 21, 1933 (*RG. Bl.* I, 134), August 7, 1934 (*RG. Bl.* I, 769), April 23, 1936 (*RG. Bl.* I, 368), May 1, 1938 (*RG. Bl.* I, 433). This batch differs from the Weimar law in that the decrees not only release en bloc all prisoners within certain categories of punishments (one to three months, or an equivalent fine) and file away pending cases, but also apply to adherents of the regime who have been sentenced to longer terms if their crimes committed "in the struggle for the National Socialist idea." The effect on the criminal statistics is discussed below, pp. 203–4.

The difference between a totalitarian amnesty and a parliamentary "compromise-amnesty" becomes quite clear in the French amnesty law of July 12, 1937 (*Journal officiel*, pp. 7914–15), which was the outcome of long parliamentary discussion. This law is not very generous in its general provisions, but it contains numerous special provisions in the interest of adherents to the most varied social groups who had come into conflict with the ever-increasing maze of regulations which are more administrative than penal in character.

31. It is made quite clear to the judges that it is advisable to inflict the punishment suggested by the prosecution. It is pointed out that with similar training, experience, and—what is most interesting for the problem of the independence of the judiciary—attitude to crime, the determination of punishment by both arms of the state must necessarily coincide. The average length of prison terms has been increased by about one-third as a result of this new penal policy, and the tendency towards applying the more severe types of imprisonment has progressed in the same degree; see W. Brinkmann, "Die

Ungleichheit der Strafzumessung," *Deutsche Justiz*, XCVIII (1936), 1653–57.

32. Rietzsch, "Strafensystem," *Das kommende deutsche Strafrecht*, pp. 100–101.

33. R. Freisler, "Strafensystem," *Denkschrift des Zentralausschusses der Strafrechtsabteilung der Akademie für deutsches Recht über die Grundzüge eines allgemeinen deutschen Strafrechts* (Berlin, 1934), p. 111.

34. *Loc. cit.*, and A. Schoetensack, R. Christians, and H. Eichler, *Grundzüge eines deutschen Strafvollstreckungsrechts* (Berlin, 1934), pp. 33–34.

35. Freisler, *ibid.*, p. 109.

36. Schoetensack *et al.*, *Ergänzungen zu den Grundzügen eines deutschen Strafvollstreckungsrechts* (Berlin, 1936), p. 25, speak about the sparing application of this severe punishment, but they are only referring to the confiscations carried out for treason within the framework of the penal code. That gives a false picture, for in addition to confiscations against those who threaten the monopoly of political power, we must also consider confiscations against outsiders for the protection of economic monopolies, as provided in a whole series of special laws. The extent of the latter is well described in Goering's speech, "Zur Durchführung des Vierjahresplans," delivered on October 10, 1936, published in *Deutsche Justiz*, XCVIII (1936), p. 1629.

37. Freisler in *Denkschrift . . . . allgemeinen deutschen Strafrechts*, pp. 104–7; Schoetensack *et al.*, *Grundzüge*, pp. 57–61.

38. Rietzsch in *Das kommende deutsche Strafrecht*, p. 131; Schoetensack *et al.*, *Grundzüge*, p. 75.

39. "Was bedeutet Strafverbüssung?" *Westdeutscher Beobachter* for July 17, 1935.

40. Schoetensack *et al.*, *Grundzüge*, pp. 96–97.

41. *Ibid.*, p. 97.

42. See the conclusions in the report of O. Weissenrieder, *Actes du congrès pénal . . . . 1935*, III, 205. It is worth noting that throughout the discussion on prison standards during times of depression, pp. 121–218, the representatives of so-called poorer nations, like Greece, Germany, and Italy, spoke up for a policy of keeping the standard of living within the prisons below that of the poorest classes, while spokesmen from the wealthier countries cautiously avoided a clear statement of principles by pointing to the impossibility of comparing the two.

43. No statistics are available for the German prison population. The approximate total of 113,000 (excluding those in concentration camps and other forms of administrative detention) recently given by Freisler in *Deutsche Justiz*, C (1938), a ratio of 136 per 100,000 population, should be compared with the French ratio of 59 (deportation included) for 1932, the British ratio of 29.9 for 1935, and the Italian ratio of 131.9 (excluding administrative detention) for 1935.

44. D. de Castro, "L'andamento della criminalità in Italia negli ultimi anni," *La Scuola positiva*, XVI (1936), 245.

45. See *Blätter für Gefängniskunde*, LXVIII (1937), 135–37.

46. See T. d'Arienzo, "La vita penitenziaria attraverso le statistiche dal 1928 al 1933," *Rivista di diritto penitenziario* (1936), 307–43, especially 324–25. He seeks to conceal the conditions by speaking of an "occasional overpopulation," but he must admit that isolation at night cannot be universally enforced. See the critical survey of Italian prison conditions by L. Belym, "La Statistique pénitentiaire d'Italie et la crise du régime cellulaire," *Revue de droit pénal et de criminologie* (1932), 547–67, who speaks of the "clearly repressive character of the Italian prison system."

47. See O. Weissenrieder, "Überbelegung trotz Sinken der Kriminalität," *Blätter für Gefängniskunde*, LXVII (1936), 316–19. He carefully avoids giving any concrete figures for the present prison overpopulation, but he openly admits

the fact, and, what is even more interesting, the poor prospects for change in view of the present criminal and penal policy. Cf. the Polish figures, above, p. 165.

48. See, for example, the relevant chapter in Mossé, *Variétés pénitentiaires.*

49. In Poland in 1930, only 124 out of 346 prisons had workshops, and in these, there were only 2,217 workdays out of a total of 10,190 prison days; see *Statistique judiciaire, pénitentiaire et criminelle.*

50. D'Arienzo, *op. cit.,* p. 333, states that unemployment from lack of work decreased 3.5 percent in 1934 and 1.5 percent in 1935.

51. *Loc. cit.*

52. Freisler, "Strafensystem," p. 106. The theory for such forced labor had already been laid down in 1932 by Sauer, *op. cit.,* p. 159, who considered the intensification of labor to be an adequate punishment when accompanied by a diet planned according to the calorie requirements of a reducing cure.

53. Rule 10 of the regulations laid down by the International Penal and Penitentiary Commission in 1929 and recommended by the Assembly of the League of Nations in 1934 as a minimum program; *Series of League of Nations Publications* IV. Social 1934. IV. 11, *Penal and Penitentiary Questions,* p. 5.

54. See for example, Heider, "Eine zeitgemässe und wirtschaftlich wertvolle Gefangenenarbeit, die keine Konkurrenz sein kann," *Blätter für Gefängniskunde,* LXVIII (1937), 124–30; Langenhan, "Der Vierjahresplan und die Gefangenenarbeit," *ibid.,* 294–96; Dubbers, "Vierjahresplan und Aussenarbiet der Gefangenen," *ibid.,* 365–69; R. Freisler, "Arbeitseinsatz des Strafvollzugs im Dienste des Vierjahresplans," *Deutsche Justiz,* C (1938), 584–86.

55. See the significant statement of G. Novelli, "L'autonomia del diritto penitenziario," *Rivista di diritto penitenziario* (1933), 21: "The whole history of penal execution expresses itself in the progressive effort to limit the sphere of administrative discretion so as to bring it under the domination of the statute." Cf. Novelli, "L'intervento del giudice nell' esecuzione penale," *ibid.* (1936), 1059–79. See also Falchi, *op. cit.,* whose efforts have been primarily devoted to developing the legal position of the relations between the administration and the convicts.

56. The reports on prison administration in the Italian parliament are merely official documents, revealing no critical appraisal; see, for example, the report published in the *Rivista di diritto penitenziario* (1937), 509–14, under the title, "Il bilancio del Ministero di Grazia e Giustizia per l'esercizio 1937/8." A more realistic appraisal will be found in E. D. Monachesi, "The Italian Surveillance Judge," *Journal of the American Institute of Criminal Law and Criminology,* XXVI (1935–36), 819–20.

57. *Actes du congrès pénal . . . . 1935,* II, 1–9.

58. H. Eichler, "Vor einer Neuordnung des deutschen Strafvollzugs," *Blätter für Gefängniskunde,* LXVIII (1937), 7, wrote: "It shall be guaranteed by statutory means that whatever is desired as the content of punishment shall actually be inflicted upon the prisoner. The danger of slipping into a lenity that does not conform with the aims of punishment shall be prevented. That is precisely the opposite of Magna Carta, for the sake of which liberalism called upon statutory regulation."

59. See the principles laid down in Schoetensack *et al., Grundzüge,* pp. 109–11.

60. Eichler, "Strafvollzug: II. Rechtsweg," *Handwörterbuch der Kriminologie,* II (Berlin, 1936), 703.

61. Paragraph 4 of the *Ausführungsverordnung des Reichsjustizministeriums* of January 22, 1937, published in *Deutsche Justiz,* XCIX (1937), 97. See Otto Kirchheimer, "Recent Trends in German Treatment of Juvenile Delinquency,"

Journal of the American Institute of Criminal Law and Criminology, XXIX (1938), 362–70.

62. On the discussion, see K. Peters, "Die Behandlung der Halberwachsenen im kommenden Strafrecht," *Zeitschrift für die gesamte Strafrechtswissenschaft*, LVI (1937), 495–522; W. Gallas, "Strafe und Erziehung im Jugendstrafrecht," *ibid.*, 635–41; E. Kohlrausch, "Für das Jugendgericht," *ibid.*, 459–84.

CHAPTER XII

1. *Criminal Statistics, England and Wales 1928*, p. xxx.
2. T. Sellin, *Research Memorandum on Crime in the Depression*, Bulletin 27 of the Social Science Research Council (New York, 1937), pp. 71–84.
3. *Criminal Statistics, England and Wales 1928*, pp. ix–x.
4. Sellin, *op. cit.*, p. 74.
5. *Criminal Statistics, England and Wales 1934*, p. 101.
6. Figures are taken from the *Annuario statistico*.
7. Rabl, *op. cit.*, pp. 37–48.
8. The figures for suspended sentences in 1910 were 25 percent, in 1931 they were 10.2 percent, and in 1935, 13.9 percent; see the *Annuario Statistico*.
9. These figures are taken from the official report, "Zahlenmässige Auswirkung des Straffreiheitsgesetzes vom 23.4 1936," *Deutsche Justiz*, XCVIII (1936), 1441.
10. Ferri, *Criminal Sociology*, pp. 220–25.
11. F. Schaffstein, "Der Erziehungsgedanke im deutschen Strafvollzug," *Zeitschrift für die gesamte Strafrechtswissenschaft*, LV (1936), 281–82, tacitly accepts this position when he says that the effects of a mild penal policy are not to be found in a rise in the crime rate, but in its influence on later decades. His thesis is thus reduced to the commonplace that a given type of social or cultural procedure is a causal factor in later developments. See also the completely agnostic stand of Michael and Adler, *op. cit.*, p. 175; their conclusions are based on very scattered materials (pp. 180–82).
12. G. Tarde, *Penal Philosophy*, tr. by R. Howell (Boston, 1912), p. 476. The examples which he chose in order to illustrate his thesis are poorly selected.

INDEX

INDEX

INDEX

Immigrants, welcomed by mercantilists, 31

Imprisonment, responsibility of profit motive, 68; in monasteries, 70; solitary confinement, 70, 127, 129, 132-37, 154; as chief punishment, 103; forms and gradations, 103; development of punishment by, during period of reform school and prosperity, 145-60; fines substituted for, 167 ff.; fines commuted into, 168, 169 ff.; under Fascism, 185 ff.; *see also* Prisons

"Impulse of acquisition," 37

Inama-Sternegg, K. T., 25

Indecency and sexual offenses, 196, 198, 199, 202, 203

Indentured servants, 60, 61

Individual, Fascist conception of superior, 185

Individual liberty, measures restricting, 26 ff.

Industrial Revolution, social and penal consequences, 86-113; end of mercantilist social policy, 87-95; increase in crime and its effects on the theory and practice of punishment, 95-102; new aims and methods of prison administration, 102-9; new attitude toward prison labor, 109-13

Industry during mercantilist period, 30 ff.

Installment system of fines, 170

Italy, trend toward severity, 148, 201; prison conditions, 149; larcenies, 150; fines, 172; penal policy under Fascism, 180, 189, 191, 192; prison population, 188, 189; criminal statistics illustrating relation to penal policy, 196, 201-5

Jagemann, E. von, 130

Jailer, office of, 62

Jesuits, establishment of *Hôpitaux généraux*, 43, 51

Jews, persecution of, 21

Joret, C., 51

Jorns, A., 105

Joussé, D., *Traité de la justice criminelle . . .*, 54

Judges, supervisory, 191

Judicial administration, 73, 79, 80

Judicial independence, 78, 142, 143; under Fascism, 179, 180

Justi, I. H. G. von, 31, 91, 92

Justices Procedure Act, 170

Juvenile delinquency, 192

Kamptz, von, Minister of Justice, 100

Kant, Immanuel, 101, 102

Kantonreglement (1733), 29

Kidnaping of children for colonies, 58

Knapp, F. G., 67

Knights, social conditions, 13

Kraus, J. B., 37

Krohne, K., 72, 104, 110

Kulischer, J., 51

Küstrin contract of 1750, 43

Labor, serfs, 8, 12, 67; medieval struggles, 14; wages, 14, 25, 31, 35, 88, 138, 153; shortage during mercantilist period, 25; distribution, 26; government policy, 30, 35; regulation, 31; emigration, 31; child labor, 32, 58; working hours, 32; factory regulations, 32; forced, 33, 67; oversupply and its results, 35, 86; medieval and mercantilist doctrines, 35; shortage caused by mendicancy, 41; poor laws, 41; houses of correction as source of supply, 42 ff.; galley servitude, 53-58; convict labor in colonies, 58 ff., 115 ff., 124, 125; money value, 60; Negro slaves, 61; evolution of methods of exploiting, 63; punishments for, 67; during laissez faire period, 87; impoverishment, 88; rise of modern proletariat, 88; recognized as part of social system, 92; fight for the right to work, 94, 95; effects of shortage in America, 128; *see also* Prison labor

Labor laws, violation by employers, 173, 175

Laissez faire, period of, 87 ff.

Landowning society, relationships, 8, 12; criminal law in favor of, 9, 67, 80

Larceny, 77; relation to social order based on property, 76; statistics, 96 ff., 139, 150, 166, 177, 194-203 *passim; see also* Property, offenses against

Legal aid, free, 142

Legal protection, prisoner's right to, 157, 191

Levasseur, E., 31, 35

Liberalism, *see* Reform school